The Full Circle for Mick

The Full Circle for Mick

Michael G Kramer OMIEAust.

ISBN = 978-1-7640-275-0-2

Copyright © 2025

This book may not be copied in whole or in part or reproduced in any way, without the written permission of the author. This is a work of historical fiction, and the author/publisher disclaims any liability for any damages arising from the contents of this story. Other than what is historical fact, as is made clear by the use of the Havard System of written quotes, the story is fictional and is not about any person, living or dead. Although this historical fiction, it is as close to the facts as possible.

All rights reserved.

Synopsis of *The Full Circle for Mick*

In very early January of 1904 Fritz Kramer arrived at Tsingtao in northern China. He was working for F.H Schmidt, a German engineering company which specialised in the building of railways, steel bridges, jetties, and canal work. He knew that it was critical for his Chinese workforce to have the Buddhist religion preached to them in order to have harmonious relationships among the workers. So, he hired a Vietnamese Buddhist Monk to offer spiritual guidance for his Chinese workforce. At the completion of the railway in early January in of 1907 and after receiving a promotion from his employer, he was sent to Namibia.

After WW2 ended, his son, Friedrich (Fritz) Kramer the younger and his family migrated to Australia. In 1967, the grandson of engineer Fritz Kramer the elder lied about his age in order to serve with the Australian infantry forces in Vietnam. While in the field with the First Battalion Royal Australian Regiment (1RAR), he met an old Buddhist monk who was the son of Hao An Dung, the Buddhist Monk who worked for his grandfather. Mick Kramer had served with 1RAR and returned to Australia. After time, he qualified as an engineer before returning to Vietnam and putting right his karma.

Table of Contents

Subject	Page
Synopsis	2
Table of Contents	3
Forward	8
Parts of Vietnam Taken over by France	8
Fall of Saigon & Three Eastern Provinces	10
Royal Court at Hue in Disarray	26
French Adventurers & Mercenaries	29
French Army Takes Hanoi	40
French Violation of 1874 Treaty	42
Establishment of French Colonial Gov.	47
Organisation of Education and Culture	49
Using Education as a Means of Control	50
Taxes	52
Economic Movement & Beginning of National Revolution	54
Rise of a National Leader & Hero	55
Political Views Because of Education in France	61
Bringer of Light	65
Destroyer of Enemy Forces is Born	67
Exile and WW2 for Giap	75

Japanese Troops Enter from China	76
Vietnam During WW2	80
The Insurrection of 23rd of Nov. 1940	84
Living Under Two Foreign Yokes	91
Birth of the Viet Minh	95
1945 - the Turning Point	104
The August Revolution	106
"O" Group 5th of March 1945	111
Coup d'état Against the French by Japan	112
Battle of Lang Son	113
Japanese find the Viet Minh Hard to Fight	117
Independence?	118
Aftermath of Coup d'état of 1945	122
Viet Minh Take-over	123
Vietnamese Opposition to Chiang Kai Shek	124
Founding of the Democratic Republic	126
Establishment of a National Democratic Peoples' State	127
Allied Take-over	129
Fist Indochina War	133
Battle at Hanoi & Lo River	134
Operation Condor	137

1st of March 1947	139
Operation Vulture	145
Operation Vulture - the Plan	148
Interference in Indochina from 1950	153
The Navarre Plan	156
Repression and War	157
Migration Agreement with Australian Gov.	157
Operation Boa Dai	160
Heyfield	161
Strengthening of the Resistance	163
Actions Against the People by S Vietnam Gov.	166
Tiger Cages	167
Attitudes of American People & Politicians	169
Border Campaign Strategies –	
New Franco-American	170
New Gains by the Resistance	180
Dien Bien Phu	181
First Phase: destroy the Northern Sector	189
2nd Phase – Occupy the Hills in the East.	191
3rd Phase: Annihilation of the French Enemy	196
Talks at the Geneva Conference	198
2nd Indochina War – Enter USA & Allies	204

Australian Involvement in Indochina	209
Australian Advisors Arrive	212
First Battalion Sent to Vietnam	214
Choice of Mick's Nationality	220
Australians Set-up at Nui Dat	221
1st Australian Task Force	225
Northern Territory	226
Australian Army	231
Infantry Corps Training	233
AN/PRC 25 Radio	234
M72 LAW	235
M79 Grenade Launcher	236
GPMG M60	236
A Posting to 1RAR?	238
The Mortarman's Course	239
Telling the Story from the Other Side	240
Areas of Responsibility for D445 & D440	241
Establishing the D440 Battalion	241
The Tet Mau Than Offensive 1968	247
1RAR Goes to Vietnam on its 2nd Tour	258
Operation Pegasus	261
Operation Blaxland	262

Operation Toan Thang One	262
1st Battle of Coral	263
2nd Battle of Coral	272
Operation Elwood /The Buddhist Monk	275
Operation Platypus	278
Operation Nowra	280
Operation Windsor	280
Operation Capital	281
Operation Goodwood One	282
Operation Goodwood Two	286
Mick Sent to D&E Platoon	289
2nd Indochina War – People's Attitudes	290
Richard Nison's War	295
Expansion of Nixon's War	298
Coming Home	301
Back in Australia	307
Transfer of Bank Account to Bank of NSW	310
Marriage of Carolyn and Mick	310
In Australia, the 1st signs of PTSD	315
Diagnosis of PTSD	319
Studying Engineering Honours and Graduation	325
Bibliography	329

Forward

This novel is classed as Historical Fiction and should be read as such. Although the over-all story is factual and much of it is a matter of historical record, some of the characters were invented. So, some of their stories did not happen. It is a matter of record that I was diagnosed as suffering from PTSD and that resulted in my medical discharge from the Australian Army. It is also a matter of record that I qualified as an Engineer after using study to manage my PTSD. So, because this novel contains fiction, I disclaim any possible legal action by any person because of the small fictional content of this novel.

Parts of Vietnam are Taken Over by France.

The government of France in the year 1858, was that of Napoleon III and that administration lasted from 1852 to 1870. At his palace in Versailles, the French ruler Napoleon III was in conference with his advisors and generals.

He suddenly said to them, *"Gentlemen, it is high time for France to take over in most of the South East Asian nations, including Vietnam! This has been made easy for us by the greed and double dealing of the Bishop of Adran, called Pigneau de Be'haine who has weakened the administration of the Nguyen rulers considerably by his greed and double-dealings.*

King Louis XVI did in fact want to send a naval task force to take over Vietnam, but this has not happened yet due to the internal difficulties faced by French citizens! I now want some suggestions from you generals and naval commanders as to how best to proceed with the annexation of Vietnam into French territory! Well, do not just stand or sit there, produce suggestions immediately or lose your positions!"

He was answered by a general and two of French naval officers, with a naval officer saying to him, *"Your Majesty, in Vietnam we are simply facing the decaying feudal monarchy of the Nguyen dynasty which took the throne after putting down a popular and large-scale uprising known as the "Tay Son Uprising." The Nguyen administration then proceeded to restore the previous feudal system, complete with all of its repressive institutions.*

The end result Is that the peasants are In constant revolt because the administration made up of mandarins are duplicated in the villages and have become the ruling class. The land is rented out to the peasants at exorbitant rental prices and the people are yet again being made poor in what should be a wealthy country. It is apparent that this territory which stretches for over two thousand kilometres from North to South is on a major trade route and there are reserves of tin, gold and silver which would be very beneficial to France.

All France has to do is to go to Vietnam and other South East Asian countries and take them over, making most of South East Asia French colonies! I strongly urge you to send my naval squadron taskforce to attack the Vietnamese city of Da Nang immediately.

I would like that to happen by 31st of August 1858, thereby launching the French take-over. That will in due course result in the total annexation of Vietnam and most other South East Asian nations!" Faced with the French invasion, the Vietnamese organised themselves into two opposing groups, one saying, *"It is best for us to* compromise, so we would not have to face the French weapons such as artillery which has proven to be effective against all of our traditional weapons. They have exploding rounds for their artillery which makes it very deadly.

Also, their rifles have such a long range that they can be at so great a distance from our soldiers that our men cannot inflict casualties upon the French, but they can do so to us. Anyway, the French have come from far away and they think less about conquering Vietnam than obtaining trade concessions!"

And so because the Nguyen monarchy was constantly suppressing revolts it could not oppose foreign aggression. This ensured that the king and his officials implemented a policy of appeasement by granting more and more concessions. However, not so inclined were the people of Vietnam who put up a tough resistance.

The Fall of Saigon and Three Eastern Provinces.

The French invaders were talking to each other, and their naval commander was saying, *"Gentlemen, our French soldiers have taken Da Nang and also, they set fire to and destroyed the town. The problem facing us is that our forces are not strong enough to threaten the capital city or to make the Hue Court provide France with more concessions!*

This is an impossible state of affairs for France, and I am at my wits end how to make things better for France. Therefore, gentlemen, I am turning this problem over to you so that we can have some of your more positive suggestions! Please let me have your suggestions on how we can force these Vietnamese heathens to obey France!" He had barely finished speaking when he was answered by Bishop Pellerin who proposed, *"Sir, if you were to attack the Red River Delta in the north of Vietnam, I am sure that you could count on support for France from the four hundred thousand Catholics who are there!"*

This was answered with, *"That may well be, Bishop, but we must ensure that France gets riches from these ventures into South East Asia and does not become bogged down into a very costly war of attrition which we cannot win! For those reasons, we shall concentrate on taking over the countryside around Da-Nang and Saigon. It is those two areas which are of high importance at the moment because of the flourishing trade in rice and other commodities that France enjoys because of our business set-ups in the Saigon area. We shall protect the business interests of France in this Asian zone at all costs! The northern part of Vietnam can wait until later on."* And so, the French chose to attack southwards and keep the area around Saigon under their control.

The siege of Saigon started in the morning of 17 February 1859 A.D... The organisers of the defence of the city had arranged for the Royal Vietnamese Soldiers to leave Saigon while at the same time reinforcements arrived from neighbouring areas, resulting in five thousand eight hundred volunteers being available to the commanders at Saigon. Nguyen Van Thieu, an officer with a rank equivalent to that of a major in western armies, was discussing the situation with junior officers. He said, *"Gentlemen, we have the soldiers necessary to encircle Saigon and then kill these French invaders! We should also send word of our deeds to the Royal Court in Hue and get them to approve massive counter-attacks upon the French forces!"*

That was agreed to by all present and so, the French were in fact encircled and placed into a very bad position.

Instead of using this advantage to get rid of French forces, the Hue Court stalled and made no decisions and refused to order a counterattack against the French forces. Of course, the French took full advantage of this indecision by the Vietnamese to stall for time to implement their plans to annex Vietnam. It was now the year of 1860, and after a victorious offensive against China by European countries, and the USA, France was able to concentrate all of its naval forces in the Far East and send them to Saigon in order to break the siege.

In 1861 A.D., they conquered the three eastern provinces of Cochinchina. While the French were bringing in their naval forces and bombarding Saigon, Nguyen Anh Dung was saying to those nearest to him, *"We will now set up a revolution against these French invaders everywhere in our country! There will be centres of resistance everywhere, sub-divided into almost as many military units as there are Vietnamese people! This way, by giving the French no rest and no support from our people, we will wear the enemy down!"*

The popular resistance against the French resulted in different tactics being used. The Royal Vietnamese soldiers operated in close-knit formations, which made them vulnerable to the long-range rifles and artillery used by the French. On the other hand, the peoples' forces used either guerrilla warfare or surprise attacks, often engaging in close quarter combat. Nguyen Trung Truc was determined to take the fighting directly to the French sailors and soldiers.

So, he said to his subordinates, *"Men, we are taking the fight directly to the French! We will get in very close to the invaders and attack them! That way, the long range of their rifles and artillery will be useless against us. For now,* our target is the French warship the 'Esperance.' She is one of the last timber built and wind powered ships afloat! So, Nguyen Phuc Quang, I want you and your nine men to go to the foreshore where the Esperance is anchored and to observe the French on that ship. In particular, I need to know how often the French crew rotate the duties of the various watches of that ship."

He then spoke to Khac Nhat Trang saying, *"You Khac are to take your nine men and record everything that goes to the ship or comes out from it. In particular, make a note of how many guns it has, which is something that you should be able to see from the number of gun ports in the sides and stern of the ship, it may even have deck mounted guns. Once we have all of the information from both units, we will silently move our men onto the ship and just kill every French person on it. After that, we shall burn the ship which is now a symbol of the French occupation of Vietnam."*

Nguyen Trung Truc now said to his men, *"We shall meet here again in two days from now. I want your comprehensive reports of approximate timing of supply, re-supply and re-inforcements of the warship, its crew, and the French soldiers we see around us. It is critical that we know almost exactly when the French enemy is about to do things and also what they are likely to be doing.*

The only way that we can take on and beat the French is close quarter fighting and for that we must first get into position very close to the enemy so that we can in fact grab them by their own belts! I think that it will also help us a lot if we stage false divergence attacks in places so that the French will send some of their soldiers to other places where our forces can close with and engage them in close quarter combat. This is the only way that we can eliminate the threat coming from the long range of French artillery and rifles! So, men, for now and until we meet again here in two days, gather what intelligence you can and make sure that you also rest and are ready for action when I demand it! Dismiss!"

While his men were getting the information about the French warship, its crew and its supplies, Nguyen Trung Truc was given information about the French garrison at Nhat Tao. He thought it best to consult with his advisors about this, because he was thinking that an attack upon the French there could also have the result of the French using some of the troops available and have the result of scattering the French forces, resulting in fewer of them being available to defend the ship!

Having called his advisors and officers into a conference with him he said, *"I want an all-out attack upon the French at Nhat Tao to take place as quickly as possible. I want the French there to be overrun and killed. Once that is achieved, I want the French messengers to be allowed to reach the French commander here. That should cause the French commanders in this area to send some of the soldiers and sailors guarding the Esperance to re-take Nhat Tao. We will have combat units in ambush positions along the way between here and Nhat Tao.*

Our task is simple, we shall kill all the French we encounter as long as we can close in on them by being very close to them in the first place. Once the French have sent their forces to Nhat Tao, we shall silently board the Esperance and burn her down to the waterline, thus inflicting a double-edged defeat upon the French!"

It was now that he ordered, *"Attack the French in Nhat Tao now and also get my infantry into ambush positions on* the way between Nhat Tao and here. Remember to instruct all of our men to only attack when they are in very close proximity to the French. In this way, we will rob them of their advantage of having long range artillery and rifles which we cannot match but remember to allow French messengers through!" That was done and when the French occupiers of Nhat Tao saw the Vietnamese rebel force, they sent messengers asking for urgent re-inforcements.

The two days of observing the French ship and French forces had passed. During that time news had reached him that the objective of Nhat Tao had been taken by the Vietnamese at the cost of many French lives. Many of those who died were relief soldiers from the Esperance. He now also had all necessary information prior to launching an attack upon the Esperance.

He now ordered, *"Gentlemen, gather your small combat units and their sub-units and have them ready. I want two infantry sections to begin burning down the church in town and also to burn down the French rice stores near the wharf. While that is happening, Danh Tho Trung will lead the units in silence onto the Esperance."*

Danh Tho Trung led his small forces, and they boarded boats which were silently rowed toward the French warship. After they had attached their boats to the side of it, they silently climbed up ropes which had been thrown down to them from their comrades on the deck of the warship above them. These men had boarded the French warship by simply walking onto it up the gang plank from the ship to the wharf where it was tethered.

The Vietnamese had made themselves less visible in the moonlight by the wearing of black clothing and the rubbing of soot onto the skin of their faces and the back of their hands. Suddenly, there was a commotion coming from the direction of the French rice store and the church, both of which were under attack and in the process of getting burned down. This caused the weakened French garrison and the crew of the Esperance to now rush out and try to rectify the situation that they now found themselves in. At the disadvantage of being surprised at night, and of having many of their usual strength sent to Nhat Tao to help there, the French were now closed with and killed. Soon afterward, the Esperance was set on fire and burned to the waterline.

The Royal Court at Hue in fact helped the French to get out of the tight situation by the proposing of negotiations. On the 5th of June 1862, Phan Than Gian negotiated with the French Admiral Bonnard a treaty involving the three eastern provinces of Cochin-China, agreeing to pay twenty million Francs, and opening the three ports in Annam and Tonkin. That was followed by the Royal Court at Hue ordering that the peoples' forces be withdrawn from all conceded provinces. However that order was not obeyed.

The French historian F. Vial wrote: *"While the Admiral thought he had happily ended the war, he came across one perhaps more active, more redoubtable than a serious war against the king's regular troops!"*

Leading the protests was Truong Dihn who was managing an agricultural estate when the French attacked Saigon. When Saigon fell into French hands, he left in order to go to Go Cong province. Upon arrival there, he began speaking to people informing them that Saigon had fallen to the French. Typically, he said to all Vietnamese people that he came across, *"The French invaders have taken Saigon after they bombarded it using their ship mounted artillery.*

They also have horse drawn artillery of long range for use on land and their rifles are accurate over very long distances!

This means that in order to successfully engage the French in combat, we must get very close to them and then attack them suddenly so that we will have surprise aiding our just cause! I am recruiting volunteers to oust the French from our country. Join me in ending this French occupation of our Fatherland! Join me in the liberation of Saigon and help to get rid of these foreign invaders from our country!"

Soon afterward, word of the fact that that he was indeed liberating southern Vietnam reached the ears of the Royal Court in Hue. The king said to the members of his court, *"Send messengers to this Truong Dinh and tell him that he has been appointed the Deputy Commander of Vietnamese Forces!"*

Meanwhile, the newly appointed deputy commander moved his volunteers who now numbered six thousand, into various positions around Saigon and retook that city from the French. Following the Treaty of 1862, the king ordered him to retreat towards An Giang Province and to stop all resistance. This caused Truong Dinh to hesitate for some time because although a strong patriot first and foremost, he did not want to give up the fight for his country. However, his Confucian training was also strong, and this would not allow him to disobey an order from his king.

He was about to carry out this order when delegates from the peoples' forces and the people streamed into his camp, asking him to remain at his post as commander of the patriotic movement and hailed him as *"Commander,*

Conqueror of the French" He bowed to the will of his people and again, took command of the uprising.

The guerrilla tactics used by the Vietnamese resistance proved to be very wearying for the French occupiers. Pallu de la Barriere wrote: *"No sight is more miserable, more monotonous, more tiring than that of the French on land and water. One enemy is constantly in sight, but the other is hiding. From the way that the enemy continually gets away, it seems that we are beating the air.[1]"*

The people of Vietnam now also organised civilian resistance in various forms. The majority of senior figures of Vietnamese society and mandarins refused to collaborate with the French. The order of the Royal Court at Hue to stop all resistance to the French invaders planted doubt into the minds of the people. So, the Royal Court at Hue sent a diplomatic mission led by Phan Thanh Gian to France to negotiate the return of the lost provinces.

On the 20th of August 1864, Truong Dinh was leading an attack upon a French outpost near Saigon. He said to his followers, *"Gentlemen, we must make war upon these foreign invaders who are taking over our country and raping our women, while also killing our men! We will wipe out the enemy here and everywhere else in Vietnam! The enemy is before you. They are only French men and as long as we quietly move forward while it is still night, we must be able to get into an advantageous position very near to the enemy well before the morning twilight! We will then attack all the French soldiers and mercenaries anywhere within our reach!"*

---

[1] Vien, 2009.

The Full Circle for Mick

Having said this, he went on with, *"Move your units forward and make sure that all units and their sub-units are in position within two hours before the morning twilight."* That was done and as soon as the twilight was beginning, the attack began.

Seeing the attack coming, a French artillery officer who had managed to get two cannons set up on high ground overlooking the battlefield ordered his guns, *"Ranging shot at eight hundred metres, bearing at three hundred and fifty-five degrees, one round, fire!"*

This resulted in the overshooting of the target area by approximately twenty-five metres and so the artillery officer commanded, *"Stay on the bearing of three hundred and fifty-five degrees, adjust range by lowering by twenty-five metres! And report the fall of shot!"*

The new range with the same bearing was quickly taken up by the gun crews and the next ranging shot was fired. It was reported as, *"An undershoot! Raise elevation by ten metres!"* That was done and the next ranging shot was reported as, *"On target, three rounds, fire for effect!"* That was being done when Truong Dinh was leading his men into attacking the French outpost. An artillery shell exploded near the top of a tree, making the blast apply in a downwards arc as well as sideways directions. That wounded the Vietnamese leader.

He called his officers to his side and said to them, *"Gentlemen, I have suffered some bad wounds from today's actions. I want you all to follow my son, Truong Quyen, from now on, because I cannot continue. I am badly wounded, and I can no longer take part in battles. In order to make sure that the French cannot use me to obtain information about*

Vietnam's fight for freedom, I shall be taking my own life. Be sure to follow my son and keep the resistance going so that I do not die in vain!"

Having said this, Truong Dinh took a sharp knife and cut the arteries in his wrists. He was satisfied that he had done the best he could for his people and just watched as his blood and life drained away. No matter what others may think about him, he safe – guarded the revolution against the French by his unselfish act of courage in taking his own life so that the French enemy could not obtain information from him with which to help put an end to the revolution.

In 1836 A.D., France forced the king of Cambodia into a treaty which proclaimed his country as a French protectorate. Cambodian people, their patriots being led by Bronze Pokumbo, contacted, and joined the Vietnamese insurgents in opposing the French colonialists. This was the first step in an alliance which bought the people of Cambodia and Vietnam together in their joint struggle against the forces of European imperialism.

In 1867 A.D., France had been victorious in the military actions against the rebels in Mexico found that it now had sufficient troops and naval ships to begin a campaign against the people of Vietnam in earnest. Launching a new offensive, the French soldiers marched into the three eastern provinces of Cochinchina. The Vietnamese governor of the three provinces was Phan Thanh Gian and he tried to oppose the French forces coming into his provinces.

With this being the situation, he called a "Council of War" with his senior commanders saying, *"Gentlemen, I am being bombarded with bad news about the French enemy* taking over more and more of our country! The weapons that my soldiers have on hand are the old traditional weapons of long ago and these are useless in all situations against the French where distances of greater than thirty metres are involved. The only modern French weapons that are in Vietnamese hands are those which were used by the Hue Court and their mercenaries.

The Hue Court is now but a puppet of the French and the court even issued orders for Vietnamese not to fight the French. I want to hear some good news for a change and most of all, I want constructive suggestions for the defence of these three provinces of Vietnam from French aggression."

There was total silence for a long time before anyone spoke, with the silence only being broken when a sergeant of the Governor's Guard said, "Sir, I have heard that units of Vietnamese patriots have managed to take over a French warship which was bombarding Saigon and burn it to the water line.

Also, and I think that the important thing for us here to learn, is the fact that some patriot units have closed with and killed off the French even though the French had superior weapons and numbers. This was done by closely observing the French and never offering resistance or attacking them unless the French were in compromising situations or where the Vietnamese units could get very close to them and then overwhelm them. That must mean that their lines of communication are very long and therefore a protracted guerrilla war against the French is the only option that we have. It will be to our advantage to contact and join up with the forces of Bronze Pokumbo"

Phan Thanh Gian considered what had been said by his guard sergeant and stated, *"Sergeant Nguyen Quan, I am most disturbed by what you say, but I can also see sense in it. You have my blessing to retrain my soldiers in all forms of combat and specialising on close quarter combat which it appears is the only way for us to win against the invaders! Also, send a small unit to find Bronze Pokumbo and join him in harassing the French. You will have full authority to do whatever needs to be done, I just hope that we are not too late in resisting the French invaders!"* For a short time, things were going well for the patriots, and they caused mayhem among the French.

Pokumbo was leading his patriots against the outpost of a French unit in Cambodia when he said to his men, *"Look over there near the tower on the western wall of my father's palace. There you should be able to see the unmistakable shape and colour of a French soldier. Also note how the jungle vegetation grows against the wall at that point! I want two men armed with crossbows to go to that point.*

At the sound of the trumpets, I want all crossbow units to kill all the sentries at the same time. After that has been done, the trumpets will sound for three short blasts. That will signal that the ground attack is to begin. I shall lead the attack upon the palace which has become a French outpost!"

Soon afterwards, the trumpets sounded three short blasts which resulted in Pokumbo yelling, *"Patriots of Cambodia and Vietnam, it is time to drive the arrogant French out of our countries! Follow me and wipe out the French in my father's palace! Stay close to me for Heaven has given me a vision that I cannot be harmed by the French weapons, so just follow me, and wipe out the French!"*

He then boldly rushed forward to attack the former palace of his father. He was running forward in front of his men using vegetation to hide the movements of himself and his followers when suddenly, a French artillery shell hit the top of a tree, and this resulted in shrapnel being spread into a fan-shaped downward projection. A large piece of shrapnel caught him in the chest and neck. This cut his carotid artery, and he died soon after this. As a direct result of his death, the resistance in Cambodia and the north-western parts of Chochinchina were scaled down.

Meanwhile, in the western area of the Mekong River Delta, two of Phan Thanh Gian's sons took the leadership of the peoples' movement while the son of the hero who had set the French Frigate Esperance on fire, was in command of operations against the French.

At an orders group with his men, which took place in the evening of 13th of June 1868 A.D., he stated, *"I want you all to rest while supplies and provisions are being taken to our next area of attack against the French. I have received reports that the French in the post of Kien Giang in Rach Gia Province are constantly taking rice and other goods from our people there as well as raping our women!*

Our people in that area are barely surviving and are hungry as a result of French soldiers taking their rice crops and other things from them! Although the French have their long-range weapons like rifles and artillery, we have already shown that if we get close to the French, we can beat them.

Starting tomorrow morning, we will ambush all roads and paths leading to and from Kien Giang. We will not take prisoners because that will slow us down and put us at a disadvantage against the French. You are to kill all the Frenchmen whom we encounter! By doing this, it will make the French fearful. We will attack the French garrison at twilight in the morning of 16th of June 1868 and we will kill all of them!"

So, early on the morning of 15th of June 1868 A.D., the ambushes were set around Kien Giang, and this resulted in the elimination of twenty French infantry soldiers. Happy with this result, he now said to his men, *"Even though we have only managed to kill twenty French soldiers, it is a good start because the death of every French soldier will be felt by the French who have to obtain their reinforcements from France. We attack as planned at twilight tomorrow morning!"* That was done and Kien Giang was taken by Nguyen Trung Truc and his men, while all French personnel were killed.

A few days later, a traitor from his army of patriots went to the French commander nearest to him and said, *"If you reward me well enough, I will deliver to you my leader, the son of Nguyen Trung Truc, the man who burned the Esperance down to the waterline and who was a thorn in the side of Frenchmen!"*

That was answered by the French major who said, *"Thank you for this service to France! You shall have riches from this!"* but he was thinking, *"You fucking gutless arsehole! There is nothing on earth that is worse than a traitor! All the same, I will use you to capture Nguyen Trung Truc and he will be given a show-trial and condemned to death by firing squad! That should result in a promotion for me. As for you, I am planning to have my men kill you on the false grounds that you escaped from lawful French custody!*

Your death at the hands of my men will serve you right, you low grade traitor!"

In order to make sure that he did capture the Vietnamese hero, the French major now said to the traitor, *"Make sure that you have the outlaw called Nguyen Trung Truc with you when you come here again tomorrow, and you will get your money as soon as I have him in custody!"* At 14:00 hours of the next day the two men approached the area where the French major and his men were waiting.

The French waited until the two men were close to them when they suddenly revealed themselves with the major yelling, *"Nguyen Trung Truc, you are under arrest for the crime of treason against France! Surrender now or die."*

That simply prompted the Vietnamese hero to draw his sword and kill the French soldier closest to him. Eventually he was overcome and found himself in chains and imprisoned. The French major went to where the hero was being held and said to him, *"In a few moments from now, you shall be taken to your court marshal and tried for the crime of treason against France!*

You will be given a fair French trial and when you are found to be guilty, you shall be taken to a place of execution and then you will go before a firing squad. Do you have anything to say?"

That was answered by Nguyen Trung Truc who said, *"You fucking arrogant French arsehole! It is you French who are the invaders and therefore your argument that I am a traitor is as false as is everything French! I am and proudly remain, a true patriot of Vietnam. Oh yes, you can kill me, but that is all you can do to me, you European low life!"*

This now resulted in him being taken to where the show-trial was conducted, and the French Court Martial quickly found him guilty of treason as charged. The French major now read out the sentence of death by firing squad. He said, *"Nguyen Trung Truc, you have been found guilty of treason and for that your sentence is death by firing squad. You shall immediately be taken to a place of execution and shot. Do you have anything to say?"* Nguyen Trung Truc answered with, *"Up you! You French arsehole, get on with it!"* and so, he was taken to a small clearing where he was tied to a tree.

The lieutenant walked up to him and offered him a blindfold which he refused to accept, because he wanted to look the French in the eye as they were shooting him. From where he was commanding the firing squad, the lieutenant now asked him, *"Any last words before the sentence is carried out?"* Nguyen then shouted, *"So long as grass still grows on the soil of this land, people will continue to resist the Invaders!*[2]*"* Very shortly after this, the Lieutenant could be heard ordering, *"Present, aim, fire"* and with that Nguyen Trung Truc died in a salvo of bullets. With the French now occupying all of Indochina, they quickly explored the length of the Mekong River to see if this could be used to transport goods between Saigon and southern China, but it was found to not be the case.

Royal Court in Hue in Disarray

The loss of Cochinchina was deeply resented in Vietnam. Patriots submitted many petitions to King Tu Duc which asked for reforms which would strengthen the country's defence capabilities.

---

[2] Vien, 2009

Nguyen Truong To was granted an audience with King Tu Duc was ushered in to see him at his throne in Hue. Upon arriving before the king, he bowed, lowered his eyes, and said, *"Your Majesty, I, Nguyen Truong To hereby appeal to your wisdom and fairness that the people of Vietnam modernise all of our ways and reform everything.*

It is critical that we reorganise the army along European lines. If we do not, then we will end up becoming slaves and vassals of European powers within our own country! The only way for us to deal with these people is to be able to compete with them at their own games using their equipment and tactics!

I beg you my Lord King, reform the country and the Vietnamese army along the lines which have already been presented to you. As well as those reforms, I have with me a petition from many people asking for the opening up of Vietnam to international commerce, to renew handicrafts, to develop industry and trade, and we must change the educational system and send our students to learning centres aboard. We must in particular reorganise the army along European lines!"

King Tu Duc was silent for several moments before he answered with, *"Nguyen Truong To, I have considered what you have bought before me, and I hereby reject everything that you have asked for! I do not know of developments in other countries, and I do not care about them anyway! Everything in Vietnam shall stay the way that it currently is, and the teachings of Confucius shall remain as the guide. We do not have to change or modernise anything and we shall not do so!*

The Royal Army of Vietnam shall remain as it is, and our soldiers will continue to use the weapons that they currently have! With regards to the French aggressors of this country, we can reach a peaceful settlement with them through negotiation, thereby nullifying the need to fight them. Therefore, the cost of reorganising and re-equipping the Royal Army cannot be justified.

Also, the French will not dare to attack us because Vietnam has the support of the Qing dynasty which is ruling China. The foreign invaders will not dare to attack us because we have the backing of China!" He was unaware that the European powers and the USA had beaten the Chinese, and that the Chinese were now subject to these outside powers.

In 1862 near Hanoi, Cai Vang was upset by many wasteful practices of his county's government, and he spoke out against them. The re-imposed conservatism and weakness of government agencies came from the fact that the re-imposed Nguyen government had bought back the feudal systems in place before the Tay Son uprising and land reforms. Cai Vang was so upset by all of this, that he led the protest movement.

Meanwhile, the French missionaries took advantage of the instability. They typically, would at the Catholic Church Services held in the communities of the Red River Delta be heard saying to their congregations, *"Obedience to France is the will of God! Those of you who continue to pledge allegiance to the Vietnamese Court at Hue shall be excommunicated!"* These things combined and became an open rebellion, which was led by Le Bao Phung.

Meanwhile, there was an influx of from China of Taiping troops who had been driven out by the Ching forces. They had split into bands before taking refuge in the north of Tonkin. These bands which were identified as White, Yellow and Black Flags, proceeded to carve out territory for themselves. After that, they plundered them.

Accordingly, only the Black Flags being led by Liu Wing-fu had allegiance to the Hue Court. Due to the Catholic missionaries passing on information to the French Command, the French were fully informed about the situation. As it was not possible to reach southwestern China via the Mekong River, the French tried to seize the mouth of the Red River and the ports in Tonkin.

French Adventurers and Mercenaries

Doctor Alexandre Babineaux hurried to the home of Mrs. Dupuis on the 8th of December 1829 A.D., because he had been informed that she was experiencing difficulty in giving birth. He got to the home and was ushered in to where she was lying in her bed, and it was obvious to him that she was both uncomfortable and in pain.

In order to be better able to help her he asked, *"Out of a pain level of one to ten with one being slight and 10 being unbearable, what is your current pain level?"* She answered with, *"The pain is about level 8, it is bad! Can you do something about it for me?"* The doctor answered with, *"Try to do without drugs for the time being, as what I have on hand are opioids and they may make you an addict if used too often!"*

Next, he proceeded to take her temperature and then he put on clean rubber gloves and felt around her birth canal. He then calmly said, *"Mrs. Dupuis, I have felt around you* birth canal, and I have found that you have a son in there, but he is upside down and unless I can turn him around, this will be a breach birth."

She said, *"Doctor, do what you must, but how do you know that I have a son, can you somehow see in there?"* The doctor answered with, *"Mrs. Dupuis, no, I cannot see what is happening inside of you, but I can feel things with my hand and fingers! As I was feeling around to find out if your child is facing the correct way for a normal headfirst birth, I felt that your child is positioned for a feet-first delivery.*

Not only that, but I also felt his big balls, therefore I know that you are carrying a son! I will now attempt to turn your son over so that he is facing the correct way for a normal birth. If that cannot be done, then I simply must twist and turn him as he is being born. If that must happen, I need to make sure that the umbilical cord does not go around his neck and choke him!" He then proceeded to again insert his hands into the birth canal and after some time, he announced, *"I have been successful in turning your son around. At your next contractions, push and do what you must to get him out of there! I will be on hand if anything at all goes wrong, but all should be well, and I now expect that you will have both a normal and an easy birth!"*

After some more time had passed and the mother had experienced some more pain, the birth was complete and there was the sound of an infant crying. Alexandre now said, "Mrs. Dupuis, you have a fine and healthy son, do you have a name for him?"

She answered with, *"Jean, I want my son to be named as Jean! He will be educated locally, and I expect that he will end up being as adventurous as his father!"* After his childhood, Jean Dupuis went to Egypt in 1858, where he began his commercial career of supplying whatever was in demand to those who had the money to pay for it.

He was moderately successful in his business dealings and in 1860, he sailed to China. Upon arrival there, he set up his first business there in Shanghai and later in Hankow. He learned the Chinese language and established good relations with local officials while he was running a moderately successful business in the selling of arms and military equipment in general.

He was talking to one of his French aids and in 1864 said to him, *"Allard, we are in the capital of the Yunnan Province of China, and I would like for us to be able to find a permanent river route to Yunnan Province in general and right here in Hankow in particular. I think that we shall have to explore the Red River from Yunnan Province from here in Hankow and see where it leads us!"*

Allard said, *"Alright Jean, we can most certainly explore, but we had best make sure that we have both firearms with us as well as men who know how to use them, because we will be going into unknown areas and the reception of the people there may be a hostile one!"*

Jean answered with, *"Allard, you, me, and a party of ten French ex-infantry soldiers are leaving here in the morning and we will see if the Red River can be used for transport purposes or not. We may not be able to go all the way, but at least we can see how much of the Red River can be used to open-up southern China for French commerce. We will go as far as we can. If things get a bit too hostile for us, we can return here until such time as we can use a stronger force to help us impose my will."*

Accordingly, Jean Dupuis and his party began to explore the Red River, looking for a sustainable route into southern China. After two months they returned to Hankow, after some armed clashes along the way. Jean and his men kept on trading in military equipment and arms with moderate success. In 1868, an expedition led by Ernst Doudart de Lagree and Francis Garnier passed through Hankow and that resulted in those leaders conferring with Jean Dupuis.

Jean said to Ernst, *"Ernst, it is so very good to speak to another French man. Please tell me what you and your party are doing here and how I may be able to assist you!"* Ernst said to Jean, *"We are returning from assessing whether or not the Mekong River can be used as a means of shipping goods to and from China. We have decided that the Mekong route is not suitable for that purpose. However, it may interest you to know that we have also been along the entire length of the Red River, and we think that it is possible to ship goods between southern China and France using the entrance to the sea at the mouth of the Red River near Hanoi."*

Hearing this excited Jean Dupuis who excitedly exclaimed, *"That is very good news! Your report about the Red River having an exit to the sea near Hanoi in the north of Vietnam saves me the bother of further exploring of the river myself. That allows me to concentrate on making money through the supply and sale of French armaments to the highest bidders!"*

Back at his depot of arms and military equipment in Hankow, Jean Dupuis was speaking to Allard saying, *"It is now very late 1870 A.D., and I have to obtain many more French artillery pieces. As well as French rifles and French*

The Full Circle for Mick

army members or ex-army mercenaries. These can both fight for us and where necessary also instruct my customers in the use of French cannons, rifles, and use of bayonets.

By having a small mercenary force to protect and enforce our business interests, we will make a lot of money! So, in order to obtain these things and to get approval, whether overt or covert, to send an expedition to provide the Chinese General Ma Ju-Jung and his army in Kunming with French weapons and to train them in the use of the French weapons, I must again go to France to get the artillery, rifles, and soldiers/mercenaries and to bring them back here ready for use."

Arriving in Paris, he held discussions with French Government Officials he said to these senior public servants, "Great business opportunities abound for us in southern China and the north of Vietnam. There is a great deal of money to be made in supplying the Chinese and others with French artillery and also the training of their armies in the best use of the modern French weapons! General Ma Ju-Jung has already ordered and paid me very well for the French weapons that I have so far supplied him with. He has now ordered and paid for another one hundred and fifty French canons. The benefit to France of this deal is great and it will keep our industries going for some time. I do not have permission from the Vietnamese in the north of that country travel through it to deliver the canons to the general in Yunnan, but I can do so by having a small and well-armed mercenary unit. For this I need to have about one hundred men."

The senior French public Service Officials gave him the backing that he was seeking, not overtly, but covertly. They said to him, *"We completely sympathise with you, and* we will help you as much as we can. However, France cannot be seen to be directly involved, and we must be able to deny all knowledge of this if it becomes a major international diplomatic incident.

We will supply you with all the weapons and artillery pieces that you need, but it must be done covertly so as to officially keep France out of it. In that regard, you are being supplied with one hundred French army personal who have volunteered to serve under your command in Vietnam and China. These men are a mixture of infantry who can train the forces of your Chinese general in the use of French rifles and bayonets and artillery men who will train his forces in the use of French artillery."

In November of 1872 Jean Dupuis accompanied by a large shipment of arms and one hundred French mercenary soldiers set from Hong Kong to the Red River Delta. He and his men and cargo then proceeded to sail up the Red River even though he did not have the permission of the Vietnamese Government (Royal Court at Hue) to do so. He found himself approached by a greedy official of the Royal Court at Hue who was named as Thanh Duong.

Thanh was escorted to see him and said, "Sir, I can help you get the permission you need for your journey up the Red River to China. If you pay me four bars of gold, I will see to it that it is recorded in the records that Royal Approval has been granted for you to do so. That will work and allow you, your men, and your cargo safe passage through this country. No-one will find out until it is too late that the approval was not actually given, but by then you people will be safely in Hankow!"

That was considered by Jean Dupuis who now said, *"Very well, Thanh Duong, you shall have your four bars of gold, but remember this, I, and my men even though small in number, have sufficient military capability and fire power to completely wipe the citadel at Hue from the map and kill everyone in it.*

Also, I can call upon the French military units in southern Vietnam and in China for assistance if need be. So, do not even think of double-crossing me otherwise you will become enslaved, and the country of the northern Vietnam will also be annexed by France."

The court official from Hue said, *"Do not worry yourself, Jean Dupuis, things will be fine!"* In reality he was thinking, *"You are correct to not trust me completely. I will put it into the official records that you have been granted Royal permission to sail up the Red River by King Tu Duc, but he will not have knowledge of that! In order to maintain my position at the court, I will announce that I am doing an audit of the official records after word has reached me that your party has landed in Hankow.*

Once that happens, I will announce that I have found an illegal entry in the Royal Records and bring to the attention of the king that you and your men have travelled on the Red River without permission. Then we will see who has power over whom!"

So, it was that Jean Dupuis, and his men arrived at Hankow with the shipment of French arms including canons. Upon arrival, Jean went to General Ma Ju-Jung and said, *"General, your weapons including the most modern artillery from France and instructors to train your army in the use of these weapons have arrived here. The armaments and the*

French military advisors who shall train your army are present and awaiting your inspection if that is what you would now like to do."

The Chinese general said, *"Thank Jean my friend, I accept your kind offer to inspect the weapons and the instructors immediately."* And so, the pair went out to where the men and weapons were, and the inspection was concluded. This had so pleased the General that he said, *"Jean, I like what I have seen, is it possible for you to get more of these weapons and instructors? If so, I will pay you very well indeed!"*

Having delivered the cargo in Yunnan, Jean now returned to Hanoi to begin plans for the next shipment of arms to the Chinese General. Upon arrival in Hanoi, he found that his Vietnamese associates had been arrested and were in jail. He also found that his ships had armed Vietnamese guards upon them and that they were not permitted to sail up the Red River. He had become concerned about the welfare of his Vietnamese associates and so, he spoke of this with Allard.

He said, *"Allard, it is with regret that I must inform you that we have been double-crossed by the Court Official from the Royal Court at Hue! As a result of his actions, our Vietnamese friends associated with us are imprisoned and other than attacking the Vietnamese in Hanoi and later at Hue I do not know what to do. How do you think that we should handle this?"*

Allard answered his friend with, *"Jean, I think that you must now get out your pen and paper and write an urgent letter to the French governor of Cochinchina, who is Admiral Mari-Jules Dupre! I think that in your letter, you* should ask to be granted urgent talks with him which will be to the strategic advantage of France. This letter must be sealed with a wax seal to ensure any tampering with it becomes immediately obvious.

In it, you should also express your desire to have an immediate response from the Admiral and that the response is to be sent directly to you using the very same messenger who bought him your original letter in the first place. Only by doing that will you both have the security of what you are saying to the admiral and also an answer to your letter to him in a short time."

Jean Dupuis said, "Thank for that advice Allard, I shall now draft the letter to the admiral, and have you take it to the Admiral! There is no-one whom I trust more than you, so I would like you to be the messenger who takes my letter asking for an audience with Admiral which I want to take place as quickly as possible. When you get to see him, also tell him that I am on my way to Saigon to see him and hurry back to me so you can let me know of the developments!

Also, let him know that I still have my mercenary army armed with the most modern French arms possible and that I am willing and able to assist him and any forces that he may wish to send to take the Hanoi Citadel and other areas which will then allow complete French control of northern Vietnam, in particular once we have also directly taken over the Royal Vietnamese capital city of Hue. I shall now write the letter to Admiral Dupre. As soon as it is finished, I want you to travel to Saigon and give him my letter while you wait for him to write an answer to it.

Point out to him that I am on my way to Saigon and that I shall arrive there soon in order to discuss the new and potentially advantageous tactical situation for France by taking over the Red River Delta areas. I am travelling to Saigon via the imperial capital of Hue, where I hope to see King Tu Duc.

As soon as it is finished, I want you to travel to Saigon and give him my letter while you wait for him to write an answer to it. Point out to him that I am on my way to Saigon and that I shall arrive there soon in order to discuss the new and potentially advantageous tactical situation for France by taking over the Red River Delta areas." With that said, and the letter from Jean Dupuis in his possession, Allard departed from Saigon, while Jean Dupuis also left for Saigon later in the same day.

Arriving at the Royal Palace at Hue, Jean Dupuis attempted to be granted an audience with King Tu Duc, but this was refused, leaving Jean Dupuis upset and fuming that he had been treated as a mere ordinary foreigner by the Royal Court. Rather than waste time in trying to rectify a hopeless situation, he decided to resume his journey to Saigon for the all-important meeting with Admiral Dupre.

Meanwhile at the Saigon palace, which was housing Admiral Dupre, Allard had been given an audience with the admiral, and he was saying to him, *"Admiral Dupre, I am Allard, the right-hand man of Jean Dupuis, who has written a letter to you which I have with me. In the letter he is asking you for a direct audience with him so that the two of you can discuss advantageous tactical situations for France that are presenting themselves in the north of Vietnam. Jean is currently on his way here to plead his case before you so that* he can get help in rectifying the situation in northern Vietnam."

The admiral now answered with, *"Fine Allard, please give me the letter so that I can read what Jean Dupuis has to say!"* With that said, Allard handed the admiral the letter from Jean, and it was immediately read. Next the admiral said to Allard, *"Allard, I need you to go back to Jean and bring him here. We have much to discuss and I would like both him and you here when we hold these critical talks for the expansion of French power!"*

Allard immediately set about finding Jean Dupuis and finally found him. He said to Jean, *"Jean my friend, Admiral Dupre has stated that he will grant an audience involving the two of us at his palace near Saigon as soon as you can get there!"* That pleased Jean immensely and so he simply said to Allard, *"Very good Allard, that being the case, let's go immediately and let's not keep the Governor of Cochinchina waiting."* Upon arriving at the palace of the French governor of Cochinchina, the two men were ushered in to see the admiral who was seated at a large table with a French lieutenant.

As the two men approached the table, the admiral stood up, held out his right hand and said to them, *"Allard it is nice to see you again and I assume this is Jean Dupuis, whom I have heard so much about!"* Jean took the admiral's proffered hand and said, *"Sir, you do me a great honour in agreeing to have a conference in private with me. In my letter to you, I have outlined the strategic and commercial value of a permanent French garrison in Hanoi and other areas.*

By using the Red River, we can have a viable route for trade with southern China straight up to the Yunnan and Hankow in particular! So, sir, will you give approval for me to take over the Hanoi area of the Red River?" Admiral Dupre said, *"Jean Dupuis, you are ambitious and that it is good! I not only give you the approval to proceed, but also, I am providing you with the assistance of Lieutenant Francis Garnier and his men. Please allow me to introduce you to Lieutenant Garnier. Lieutenant Garnier, this is Jean Dupuis whom you have heard so much about.*

I shall now leave you two men to get to know each other. That is very important as you will now be working towards the same goal, that of French dominance of this part of the world. Both of you, make contact with Bishop Puginier who has gathered the defeated followers of the rebel Le Bao Phung."

French Army Takes Hanoi

So, it was that the French lieutenant Francis Garnier was sent to Hanoi with an armed escort, enabling him to make contact with Bishop Puginier. Francis Garnier, used his own initiative and stated, *"From now on, shipping shall be free on the Red River and customs duty shall be abolished!"* The Vietnamese authorities refused to go along with this edict from Garnier who was regarded as an invading French upstart of little to no knowledge of Vietnamese affairs.

Garnier on the other hand was impatient with the amount of time taken by Vietnamese authorities. So, on the 19th of November 1873, he said to his men, *"Move our artillery into positions overlooking the Vietnamese city of Hanoi! Opposing us is an old Vietnamese general called*

Nguyen Tri Phuong. We will send a delegation to see the general and to demand his surrender. If he chooses to fight on, we shall bombard the city of Hanoi and then take him prisoner!"

A short time passed and then the delegation to General Nguyen Tri Phuong returned and this caused Garnier to exclaim, *"Fucking hell! Does that fool not know when he is beaten? So, he wishes to make Hanoi the prize in a contest between my French forces and the Vietnamese rabble soldiers? Very well then, he shall have the contest!*

Using our artillery, conduct ranging shots upon selected targets of Hanoi including the citadel. Once the ranging shots have been carried out and you have the exact range between our canons and the Vietnamese positions recorded, begin the all-out assault shots of all selected targets. These artillery attacks shall be accompanied with infantry attacks, and they shall be successful!"

The artillery did as it was ordered and soon the French had the exact ranges of the Vietnamese positions recorded. As Garnier had said, the artillery attacks were followed by infantry attacks. All attacks upon the Hanoi area were successful and they were accompanied by French attacks upon Nam Dinh, Hai Duong, and other places in the Red River Delta.

All of these attacks were considerably aided by the complicity of the northern Vietnamese Catholic Communities which greatly assisted the invading French. As a result, Hanoi was taken, and General Nguyen Tri Phuong was captured. The French tried to get him to betray his country, but the old general instead chose to starve himself to death, thereby depriving the French of any advantage they may have had by his capture.

A Vietnamese patriot called Anh Dung Tuan was speaking to his superiors saying, *"Sir, I have just managed to shoot the French commander using a captured French rifle! That has come about as the result of the ambush that I was in command of, located just outside of Hanoi. As a result of the French leader being killed, the French are milling about the outskirts of Hanoi in total confusion, so now is the right time to counterattack the foreign forces!"*

That was considered by the leaders of the peoples' forces, and they went back to Anh saying, Anh you have done well, the name of the French leader whom you have killed in your ambush on 21 of November 1875, is Lieutenant Garnier and he has been a bad thorn in the side of the Vietnamese forces, so we thank you for this service to our country!

The Vietnamese forces counter-attacked and encircled Hanoi and also liberated some other areas of the Red River Delta from the French. France, which was still in disarray from its defeat at the hands of Prussia in 1871 no longer wanted to become very deeply involved in Vietnam.

Failing to exploit his now favourable military situation, King Tu Duc stuck to his policy of compromise and negotiated the treaty of 1874 under which France gave back the areas and towns it had seized but obtained permission to establish garrisons in Hanoi and Haiphong also to open up the Red River for French commerce.

The French Violation of the 1874 Treaty!

In the last twenty years of the 19th century, the major European powers rushed to other continents and proceeded to divide the world up between them. As a result, the colonial policy of France became tougher and more systematic, partly because of the British presence in Burma.

These things combined and France violated the treaty of 1874 A.D., resulting in the French sending new military units to Tonkin. They were commanded by Henry Riviere. He decided upon a conference with his senior and middle ranking officers to discuss the possible enforced take-over of northern Vietnam. He said to his officers, *"Gentlemen, we are faced with the problem of probable major resistance by the Vietnamese in the north, especially near Hanoi and the Red River Delta.*

I need you all to consider the best possible way for a complete French take-over there so that France will control the alternative trade routes to China up the Red River Delta! I am now turning this problem over to you for constructive suggestions as how best to completely conquer the Vietnamese people while at the same time having low French costs in terms of money, equipment, and the lives of French soldiers! Come on now speak up quickly and do not be shy, I need as much input from you all as possible and as quickly as possible!"

There was the sound of the French officers discussing the situation placed before them by their commander and then suddenly, a French major loudly said, *"Sir, if we send an ultimatum to the governor of Hanoi and in it say that France hereby demands both the complete demolition of all defensive works in the city and surrounding areas. As well as the instant removal of Vietnamese soldiers and naval forces from Hanoi and the Red River Delta, that may result* in the Vietnamese trying to fight us. We could then attack Hanoi on the grounds that France knows that its forces are threatened by the war-seeking preparations of the Vietnamese. We need to have an excuse like this in case we end up with a war against the British who are already In Burma, or worse still, another war with the Germans who have just beaten France."

Henry Riviere was happy with that response and said, *"Thank you major, I like the way you have said that we are being threatened by the war seeking preparations of the Vietnamese defenders of Hanoi. Such an argument should even be accepted by the British and German Governments! Scribe, immediately draft up documents demanding the complete demolition of all defensive works in and around Hanoi as well as the complete evacuation of all Vietnamese forces from the city and its surrounds!*

I want our infantry and artillery to take and occupy any high ground surrounding Hanoi. I want artillery deployed in all advantageous positions round Hanoi. I also want the ground cleared in front of the artillery positions as well as the ground measured and then marked with ranging pegs, which must clearly show the range from our guns to that point. By doing this, it will make it exceedingly difficult indeed for the defenders to launch a successful attack on our positions! Now hurry up and get things done! No more excuses!"

With this being ordered, the scribes prepared the ultimatum, while French infantry and artillery located their most favoured areas and moved into position. That was quickly followed by the French clearing away vegetation from view and then measuring distances. That was followed by the placing of ranging markers every twenty-five metres.

The ranging markers were long stakes driven deep into the ground and these had large discs on their tops with the range clearly marked upon them.

The ranges were easy to read using the field telescopes and binoculars of the French army. After six of these advantageous artillery positions had been set up and a battery of artillery placed at each one of these, the prepared ultimatum was taken to the governor of Hanoi called Hoang Dieu.

After reading the ultimatum, Hoang Dieu cried out loudly, *"The arrogant French have demanded that we, the Vietnamese people demolish all of our fortifications within and outside of our city and in our own country! This is intolerable! Mobilise our army and navy personal and take the fight to the arrogant invaders! Send them all to hell!"*

The French infantry was actively patrolling the areas near their artillery positions. It was a very sunny day when Lieutenant Louis Michaud was informed of Vietnamese infantry approaching a French gun position by corporal Beaumont he said, *"Very good corporal! I now want you and your infantry section to stay here under cover and observe what the Vietnamese are up to. I think they are here to find out what we are doing.*

If they see our artillery positions and report back to the Hanoi Governor, he may realise that the Vietnamese cannot win because of our artillery and that may make him surrender to us. So, if you see a reconnoitre party of five to ten men, let them go and take word back to their superiors in Hanoi.

On the other hand, if you happen to observe a much larger force coming toward us, then signal this using three short flashes of sunlight followed by three long flashes of sunlight which should then be followed by another three short flashes of sunlight. That system of communication is called "Morse Code" by the British. It means, SOS.

If you happen to see a large force, signal that to us on the high ground and quietly make you way back to the gun positions. In order to make the sunlight flashes, you will use the mirrors that I have issued you with. So corporal, do you completely understand what you are to do and how you and your section must do it?" The corporal answered with, *"I understand sir, there is no problem!"*

The corporal returned to where his section was hidden from view and was observing the area to the front of them. Soon, he was alerted by one of his section members that a large force of Vietnamese infantry was approaching. He now went to a small clear area and using his mirror, he signalled the gun positions above him that a large force was approaching.

Lieutenant Michaud went to see the officer commanding the artillery unit and said to him, *"I have intelligence that a large Vietnamese force is approaching. It is on course for this locality and should be here soon. This will prove to be a good test of the effectiveness of our having the ground range marked for up to two kilometres from here depending on the rises and fall of the ground. It will also be a good test of the combined effectiveness of both our infantry and artillery"*

With the Vietnamese force getting ever closer, Lieutenant Michaud said to the artillery commander, *"When those slant eyed soldiers get to the two hundred and fifty metres mark, do your ranging shots, and wipe the bastards out! It would be great if you could let a small number of them escape so that word of the power of French artillery and rifles is taken back to Hanoi!"*

That was done and the Vietnamese force, other than four men, was wiped out. The survivors took word of this defeat back to Hanoi and the news worried Hoang Dieu, who sent word of this to King Tu Duc in Hue. In the meantime, the Vietnamese king had died, so the French took advantage of the death of King Tu Duc and the fact that he did not have an heir, thereby causing in-fighting and confusion in the Royal Court at Hue. Soon, French rule of Vietnam was complete.

Establishment of the French Colonial Government

The main concern of the French conquerors was the setting up of a stable, efficient political and administrative system. In Cochinchina, which was annexed in 1862, the French encountered systematic non-cooperation by mandarins and scholars. The French historian Cultru wrote:

"If by some miracle the scholars had come over to the French and betrayed their sovereign, the administration of Cochinchina would have been perfectly straightforward. But the learned Annamite's, the elite faithful to the laws of their country, could not but consider us as enemies. The peasants, tied to their fields and their cattle, remained in the countryside in a state of outward obedience which in no way implied moral submission.[3]"

The French therefore resorted to direct administration using subaltern agents. Many of these were uneducated and without any real standing in their communities. The

---

[3] Vien, 2009

continuing rebellions defeated all inducements by the French colonial administration. In order to maintain French rule, the colonial government shamelessly used the violent and cruel means of government.

Using on one hand, cruelty and on the other, colluding with the most regressive and corrupt elements of the Vietnamese population. Many years later, the USA and its allies used neo-colonialism in Vietnam and even refined tactics such as these.

In a report for the Governor of Tonkin, the provincial governor Muslier wrote: *"Native mandarins hesitated to rally to our side or at least serve us without having afterthoughts, and abandoned their posts, preferring to retire, while others, fewer in number and more energetic, became effective political chiefs of the rebellions. In administration posts there were only a few ambitious mandarins who had more awareness of the future.[4]"*

The rest were made up of plotters, rascals, or people whom only events have bought to our side and on whom we have sometimes conferred a high rank, which they use to hold ransom the country without any scruples and make our presence hated. Worming their way up without merit and outside all the rules of hierarchy, they have no prestige whatsoever![5]"

Vietnam was divided into three so-called different countries, which were merely different administrative regions. They were Tonkin, Annam, and Cochinchina. Each of these so-called countries was put into "French Indochina," which also included Cambodia and Laos. They were ruled

---

[4] Vien, 2009
[5] Vien, 2009

by a French Governor-General. It is clear that the intention of France was aiming at destroying the Vietnamese nation in order to enslave it more easily.

Each of the five "countries" of Indochina (Tonkin, Annam, Cochinchina, Cambodia, and Laos) was governed by a French Governor. All-important services – security, finance, public works, posts, agriculture, health trade and so on were in the hands of the French. The colonial government was only able to exist because of continued military protection[6].

Organisation of Education and Culture

The French Governor-General called Doumer was speaking to his sub-ordinates and saying, *"We do not give a fuck about the standard of education of the Asian peoples! Educating those little brown monkeys is a waste of money! We shall set up and nurture a denationalised intelligentsia that will lose all contact with Vietnamese culture and therefore slow the desire for independence!*

I am determined to subjugate the population of all of Indochina and I think that we can use education as a means of obtaining total control." He then invited others who were there, to present their ideas of how this should be accomplished.

He even said, *"I am at my wit's end in trying to civilise and control these rebellious Vietnamese people, I am asking each of you to give me some ideas of how to control these seemingly unconquerable people! So, please speak up if you have any ideas, no matter how extreme or questionable you may think the idea to be!"*

---

[6] Vien, 2009.

He was quickly answered by an ambitious French army major, who said, *"Sir, we have here in Vietnam a strong force of both African troops and French Foreign Legionnaires. By using these as a nucleus of the imposition of French will, we could also set up a "Native Militia" which has French officers and these "Native Militaria" units could be set up at the provincial level, thus pacifying the Vietnamese insurgents!"*

That suggestion was agreed to, and the "Native Militia" units were indeed set up at provincial levels throughout Vietnam. However, none of these measures worked and often resulted in the members of the "Native Militia" units turning their guns upon their French officers and then defecting to the national liberation movements.

Using Education as a Means of Control

The French Governor-General of Indochina called Doumer, thought of using traditional education as a means of dominating the people. In Tonkin, he maintained the system of mandarin competitions until 1915, while in Annam, it was continued until 1916.

Because he was trying desperately to impose a system of full control, he was speaking to his sub-ordinates, saying to them, *"Our attempt to control the people in this country through the use of "Native Militia" units have failed, and it has simply resulted in the murder of the French officers concerned. We need to be able to somehow control the hearts and minds of these people! I would be grateful if someone here has some ideas about how France can make these little brown monkeys obey us! Well, do not just sit there or stand there, produce ideas, please somebody!"*

He was soon pleasantly surprised to hear a young lieutenant speak up. He said, *"Sir, France has the know-how and intellectual might to transcribe the entire Vietnamese language into the Latin script. By doing that and then enforcing laws which state that all people of Vietnamese origin must learn the Latin-based alphabet and only use it and nothing else for all written communication between all people and at all levels, we will be able to make them all learn that alphabet which we will call **quoc ngu** and make them use it.*

We must also forbid the use of the traditional Chinese characters that the people of Vietnam have been using until now and we should also decree that continued use by Vietnamese people of the Chinese characters that they have formerly used for writing, will be considered illegal and make it punishable by death! By doing that and making it compulsory for some subjects used in mandarin competitions have French used as the official language, we can ensure that French shall be the dominant language used by all in Indochina!

*By also making it compulsory for Vietnamese to include French language essays in their examinations, you will counter the feelings of Vietnamese national pride and possibly even strip away their national identity because more and more they will become French. This is of course dependent upon the successful implementation of **quoc ngu** and the doing away with the written Chinese characters!"*

As a result, the traditional writing/reading system was replaced over time by a *"Franco-Vietnamese"* system which was designed for the supply of workers and low-level supervisors for the colonial government. In 1901 the Medical College was set up to train auxiliary physicians who were simply health officers. Everything in the education system was *"Education for a little money as possible."*

French became the language used for instruction and the study of the national language and history of Vietnam was downgraded. At the University of Indochina, there was not either the studies of sciences or engineering available. A direct result of this was growing illiteracy and even though the population was rising, food production was either stagnated or falling[7].

The French Imposition onto the Vietnamese population of quoc ngu in order to replace the old Chinese ideographic script proceeded rapidly. This resulted in in newspapers and books being printed in quoc ngu and the Vietnamese national movement adopted it for use in spreading the ideas about independence and development.

Taxes

Doumer was speaking to his sub-ordinates saying, *"France has established a cumbersome colonial administration which is a huge burden for the people of Vietnam. The people here are paying for the cost of French officials, public servants and the presence of both French Foreign Legion and French African troops, politicians, and political parties. The cost of these are all exceedingly high and soon, the number of French officials in Indochina will almost equal the number of British officials in India.*

Our French presence in Indochina must be paid for and in order to do this, we shall substantially increase all taxes. The poll-tax shall therefore increase from 0.50 piasters to 2.50 piasters and land tax shall go from 1.00 to

---

[7] Vien, 2009.

1.50 piasters. As well, the overall budget shall increase because we are applying customs levies on all alcohol, salt, and opium.

The monopoly of the making and selling of alcohol has been given to the French company of Fontaine and soon, I will pass laws which state that the drinking of alcohol is compulsory! All villages shall have to consume a set quantity of alcohol each year in direct proportion to its population. All private production of alcohol is now banned and when offenders are found, they shall be severely punished using prison terms, confiscation of property and even deportation![8]"

The result of these measures was that the Fontaine company, which had a capital investment of 3.5 million francs, earned two to three million francs in operating profits per year. Alcohol which cost five to six cents per litre in 1902, was being sold at twenty-nine cents per litre in 1906[9].

Doumer was again speaking to his sub-ordinates, and he said, *"My administration has bought salt from small producers and resold it at greater profits each year. We made 0.05 piastres for everyone hundred kilograms in 1897 and that climbed to 2.50 piastres in 1907.*

This is an increase in the price of salt of five hundred percent over ten years. My administration has reserved for us only, a monopoly in the trading of opium. We are actively encouraging the use of this vile substance by the "Little Brown Monkey" populations of Indochina. The income from these three sources has gone from eight million piasters in

---

7 Vien, 2009
9 Vien, 2009.

1899 to ten point four million piasters in 1903 and to twelve million piasters in 1911[10]!"

Doumer went on to say, *"The Vietnamese people, whom I call 'Little Brown Monkeys" now must pay more than ninety million gold francs which is about three times as much as they were paying before! Also, the introduction of the customs excise shall from now on be accompanied by a system of repression of the 'Little Brown Monkeys' such that on the slightest denunciation, my customs officials will search and arrest anyone at all without having to worry about obtaining a warrant in order to do so!"*

Economic Movement & Beginnings of National Democratic Revolution

The ten years after World War One were used by the French colonialists to intensify their economic exploitation of Vietnam. This resulted in important modifications to Vietnamese society. Because of new social pressures the national movement took on new forms. These resulted in the laying of the foundations of the coming national and democratic revolutions.

Due to the very low wages paid to Vietnamese workers, the foreign owned companies operating in Vietnam made huge profits and they also paid very little in taxes and other charges. The main taxes were in fact paid by the Vietnamese workers, called proletariats by Communist Governments.

The French invested 490 million francs in Indochina between 1888 and 1918. Those investments rose to 8,000 million francs between 1919 and 1929. The investments did

---

[10] Vien, 2009.

not benefit the economy of Vietnam or the welfare of its people. They did, however, respond to the needs of the French capitalist investors at the expense of the people!

More than half of this capital was used in France for market and financial operations. The sending to France of profits and savings by French officials and payment of interest on credits caused a continuing financial deficit in Vietnam. The simple fact was that French investment was acting like a powerful suction pump which was sucking the Indochinese economy dry! The French in the meantime directed investments towards mining and rubber plantations. The operations of which resulted in large quantities of raw materials being taken out of Indochina[11].

The Rise of a National Leader and Hero

On 19th of May 1890, at Hoang Tru in Vietnam which was in Nghe An province located in central Vietnam, a woman was visiting her original hometown suddenly experienced labour. She was the wife of Nguyen Singh Huy, who was a Confucian scholar and a teacher.

A midwife was in attendance with her and after the elapse of more time and experiencing more discomfort and some pain, a baby boy was born. The midwife said to the new mother, *"My dear young woman, you have given birth to a healthy boy! What names shall you be calling him?"* The new mother answered with, *"I will name my son as Nguyen Singh Cung. I had a dream about him last night. In that dream, I saw him and another man who I think was called Giam, Siam or Giatt or something like that.*

---

[11] Vien, 2009.

Anyway, this other man together with my son was successful in driving the French invaders and other foreign oppressors out of our country and the land was given back to the peasants. Just like when the Tay Son Brothers gave the land back to the peasants after taking it off the corrupt Trinh officials and Nguyen Family in the south. So, I think that he and his companion, who-ever he really is, will liberate us all!"

Nguyen Singh Cung had a sister known as Thanh and a brother called Nguyen Singh Khiem. Some years later, their father, Nguyen Singh Huy spoke to his family saying, *"We are moving to the village known as Kim Lien."*

The family moved to Kim Lien and Cung was working well at his studies by studying with his father. His life was eventful and marked by the death of his new brother and mother when he was ten years old. His father came to see him shortly afterwards and said, *"Son, it is time for you to take on more formal studies and in order to help you towards this end, I have arranged for you to have classes with the scholar named as Vuong Thuc Do."*

A result of this was that the young Nguyen Singh Cung quickly mastered Chinese writing while also becoming expert in Vietnamese writing. In his private moments, he liked to fly kites and to go fishing. In time, he would become fluent in the languages of Chinese, French, Russian, English, and Thai as well as his native Vietnamese. Nguyen Sin Huy said to his son, *"Cung, you have done well in your studies, and you are now ten years old. That means it is time for me to follow the Confucian Tradition of giving you a new name. I therefore rename you as Nguyen Tat Thanh." ("Nguyen the Accomplished")*

He went on to say, *"Son, do not forget how the French invaders have impoverished and made slaves of the people of Vietnam. I want you to constantly look for ways of liberating our country! I shall introduce you to some revolutionaries who want you to act as a messenger for them, are you willing to do this?"* His son answered with, *"Of course Father, I think that is what all Vietnamese people must do! We must show our desire for independence from all foreign powers!"*

Sometime after this, his father made the announcement, *"I have been appointed as an Imperial Magistrate at Quin Nhon. I will be here as much as possible in order to further guide you and help to develop your many skills!"* So, it was that Nguyen Sinh Huy took up his position as Imperial Magistrate in Qui Nhon. Time passed uneventfully until an urgent case requiring his judgement of an influential man occurred. This influential person had been accused of stealing some property and rape of a young woman. Soon after the offender was bought before him, Huy had no option but to find the accused guilty as charged.

Nguyen Sinh Huy said, *"This court finds you guilty as charged! You shall be taken to the nearest prison where you shall receive one hundred strokes of the cane upon your bare back as your punishment! The sentence shall be carried out immediately! Do you have anything to say before the sentence is carried out?"*

The offender answered with, *"I am of the opinion that you have exceeded your authority by sentencing me to receive one hundred strokes of the cane upon my bare back! Be warned magistrate, that I have a lot of both power and influence, and this will go badly for you, so it will be best for you to simply let me go!"*

Before much longer, the sentence was carried out with the result that this influential offender died from receiving the one hundred strokes of the cane. Upon his death, his family took steps to obtain revenge. That in turn resulted in Nguyen Sin Huy being demoted for the abuse of power.

In deference to his father, Nguyen Tat Tanh received a French education, by attending the Lycee in Hue, which was also the school of his later disciples, Pham Van Dong, and Vo Nguyen Giap. He began to speak out against the French presence in Vietnam while he was studying at the National Academy in Hue and that resulted in the French dismissing him from the academy.

Resulting in Nguyen Tat Tanh speaking to some friends when he suddenly said, *"I have decided to leave here and go teach at Duc Thanh school in Phan Thiet! After I have had my fill of that, I intend to travel overseas and for that, I think the best way will be to take on a role as a cook on a French steamer so that I can travel the world for some time! On account of the fact that I have often spoken out in public against the French overlords, The French have dismissed me from this academy! When I go overseas as a crew-member of a French ship, my name shall be Ba or else I will take up and use the name of Nguyen Ai Quoc! (Nguyen the patriot) at the time it becomes advantageous to do so."*

So, while he was using the alias of Ba, he went to the northern Vietnamese port of Haiphong in 1911 and approached the master of a French freighter which was in the process of conveying cargos around the world. He approached the captain of the ship saying, *"Sir, I am Nguyen Ba, and I am a very good cook. I would very much like to join your crew!"* The French captain answered with, *"Glad* to see you Ba, my usual cook has fallen ill and so he cannot perform his duties as it may infect the crew members!

This ship will remain here in the Haiphong Port for the next four days while unloading present cargo and the loading of new cargo takes place. During that time, I am giving you the opportunity of being the cook of this ship on a trial basis. If your work is satisfactory, you shall be offered a permanent position on my ship."

That was answered by Nguyen Ba who said, *"Thank you sir! When shall I report to you for the commencement of my duties?"* The captain answered with, *"I want you to begin by preparing the evening meal for today! Please be ready to start cooking today, in time to serve the evening meal. If you have belongings to take with you, gather them now and make sure that you have your documentation available."* So, it was that he gathered his few belongings and boarded the French ship.

After again reporting to the captain, he was shown where his sleeping area was and shown around the ship. Upon getting to the galley, he was shown where the cooking utensils were kept and the larder which also had a refrigerated cool room.

The captain now said to Ba, *"You have some hours before you have to actively start cooking, so please draw up a proposed menu making sure that you make use of as many fresh vegetables as possible."* Ba answered with, *"Sir, you and the crew will find that I am expert in the making of delicious sauces and that by using them together with any fresh or frozen vegetables on hand as well as any fish, pork or beef that may be on board, I will make you tasty and satisfying meals. I like to call many of these combinations 'Stir Fry' meals."*

He then prepared the evening meal which was a pork/chicken and vegetable stir fry served up with Chinese noodles all of this was immersed with a sweet and sour sauce. The crew loved his cooking and praised his work. Next, Ba took his pen and paper and drew up proposed menus of one week of operations for presentation to the captain of the ship immediately after he had served the meals.

The captain of the ship sent for him and upon his entry to the captain's quarters, the French man said, *"I have spoken to the crew, and they all think that your cooking is bloody marvellous! I agree with what the crew is saying, and I am now offering you the job of permanent cook on this ship!"* So, it was that Ba became a seaman for over three years, visiting Africa, the USA, and other places.

While visiting the United States of America, he met with some Korean nationalists, and this began to develop his political outlook. While speaking to his Korean friends, Ba discovered the possibility of changing the views of some people by the use of petitions. That resulted in him submitting a petition to the US administration of President Woodrow Wilson, seeking the help of the USA in obtaining freedom and justice for the people of French Indochina (Cambodia, Laos & Vietnam).

Next, in 1913 he went to England and while there, he was at the Carlton Hotel in the Haymarket, Westminster where he met with the legendary French pastry master, Escoffier in a bar there.

Reverting to his original name of Nguyen Tat Thanh, he said to Escoffier, *"Good Day to you sir! My name is Nguyen Tat Thanh, and I have heard of your great work, and I would love to be able to train under your guidance and to work with you. May I buy you a beer?"*

Escoffier said, *"Yes, you most certainly may."* Nguyen bought both men a beer and then went on to say, *"I will be honoured if you could train me in the art of being a pastry chef of your standing! Your skills are the sort of things that I want to bring back to Vietnam when I am good enough to do so. Please help me to become as good as you are in this amazing field!"* Escoffier said, *"Very well, come here at 09:00 hours tomorrow and we shall get you started!"*

So, at 9:00 am of the following day, Nguyen was taken into the kitchen of the Carlton Hotel by his mentor, Escoffier and his training and new occupation began. After a week of this on a Friday afternoon the two men were discussing football.

Escoffier said to Nguyen, *"I am going to the football tomorrow to see Chelsea Football Club playing, would you like to come along? We could have some beer while we are there and perhaps, we may even get lucky and be able to fuck a woman!"* Nguyen answered with, *"Most certainly, I would love to see Chelsea play! I hear that they are considered to be a very good football team!"* And so, the two men watched the football game which resulted in Nguyen becoming a regular Chelsea Football Club supporter.

Political Views Because of Political Education in France

Between 1919 and 1923, Nguyen Tat Thanh was living in Paris. One evening in 1919, he was at a crowded bar when he heard Marcel Cachin speak. Marcel was saying to the people in the crowded bar, *"My friends and comrades, you have all been living under adverse conditions inflicted upon you by the capitalists of France! Not only are these poor excuses for humans exploiting the working man here, they are in particular doing so in the French colonies such as Algeria and Vietnam.*

I know this because I have seen what the capitalists are doing in both of those countries! In particular in Vietnam, France has impoverished the entire population of that country just so that the capitalists can have vast plantations there.

They are forcing the people there to have rubber plantations owned by Michelin on their agricultural land and they are forced by the capitalists to work in the rubber plantations for very little pay if they like it or not! The amount of money paid in wages by the capitalists to the Vietnamese workers is a mere pittance and the government of France should not allow it!

My friends, it is only the Socialist Cause that will grant you any justice anywhere at all. Friends and comrades, we must look towards the possibility of obtaining a socialist government if there is to be any justice for working people anywhere in the world, and here in France in particular!"

This attitude was most welcome to Nguyen Tat Thanh who now became very interested in what he was beginning to see as the only means of liberating his people in Vietnam.

He therefore said to Marcel, *"Thank you my friend for letting me know this. I think that by obtaining the backing of the British and the United States of America, we could be quickly successful in removing the French colonialists from my country! I have already gone to work and petitioned for* the recognition of civil rights for the Vietnamese people through the aid of the winners of World War One.

I have read the story of the armed struggle for independence by the American revolutionaries against the British and I have read about the spirit of the United States' Declaration of Independence! Because the Americans have already gone down this sort of a path themselves, they may support our struggle against foreign exploiters and invaders!

Accordingly, I have prepared and submitted a direct petition to President Woodrow Wilson of the United States of America for help to remove the French from Vietnam and to replace them with a new Vietnamese Nationalist Government and I will also petition the British Government to do the same things. Because of the fact that this will be reported in French newspapers available in Vietnam, I am now going to change my official name to "Nguyen Ai Quoc" (meaning Nguyen the Patriot).

By me having that name and it being reported in the French and Vietnamese newspapers back in Vietnam, it should make my new name of Nguyen Ai Quoc well known within and also outside of Vietnam and that should enable us to get help from places outside of Vietnam when we need it!"

Marcel was supportive of this, and he said to Nguyen Ai Quoc, *"My friend, you will need all of the help possible from all sources I therefore urge you to officially become the man that you are at heart! You will have great difficulty in obtaining help through the USA or Britain, because both of those nations are well known as capitalists who keep their workers down so they can further exploit them.*

It seems to me that at heart, you are in fact a communist and that shows itself in the way that you share things with others while at the same time respecting the person concerned! You may not like the idea, but I get the impression that it will be necessary for you to travel to both Moscow and China seeking help in what must become an armed struggle for your people.

I think that your idea of changing your name to Nguyen Ai Quoc is a stroke of genius and when it is reported in newspapers around the world that the capitalistic powers of USA and Britain have refused to help you on the grounds that they have alliances with the French capitalists, you will get overwhelming support, at least in Vietnam and Indochina in general!"

The answer from both the British and the USA was not long in coming! Nguyen was told, by both the Americans and the British, *"We have alliances with the French, and we shall be supporting the French masters of Vietnam and not you! We also have more in common with the French whom you are calling capitalists.*

That sort of talking makes you sound like a communist, even if you are not one of them. So, take yourself away and just acknowledge the fact that France rules your country, and it will continue to do so, with backing from us. Therefore, you cannot win, so just accept things for what they are and accept that French rule of Vietnam is here to stay!"

So, it was that in 1920, during the Congress of Tours, in France, that Nguyen Ai Quoc became a founding member of *"Parti Communiste Francais"* This was the French Communist Party also known as PCF. Meanwhile, due to newspaper articles about him throughout the world, Nguyen achieved the status of a national hero in his home country of Vietnam.

During May of 1922, he wrote articles in French magazines criticizing the use of English words mixed in among written French which was being carried out by French sports writers. He spent a lot of time in Moscow and became the Comintern's Asia Correspondent and the main theorist on colonial warfare. With so much work to do, he became very tired and one night he again decided to go to the bar where he had met Marcel Cachin. Upon arrival there, he saw and was most impressed by a woman.

He was Thinking to himself, *"What a lovely lady! I must introduce myself to her and form a relationship with her!"* He next went to where she was sitting at a table and he said, *"My name is Nguyen Ai Quoc, and I admire you greatly! So greatly that I would like to make amazing love to you! I am both intelligent and strong, as you will discover! Also, I just love to make a woman happy! I will not leave you and I shall always be there for you!"*

He was answered by Marie Briere, the dressmaker who said, *"All right then, let's go and fuck, my place is close by, so we can have a drink and get a bottle of wine to take with us, let's go!"* The couple left the bar and soon after arriving at the home of Marie, they made love.

The Bringer of Light

Nguyen left Paris for Moscow and became employed by the Comintern. While so doing, he also studied at the Communist University of the toilers of the East. He also took part in the Fifth Comintern in June 1924. Later, he arrived at Canton.

In 1925 he said to those around him, *"As of now, I am holding Youth Education Classes to which all are welcome! I am occasionally giving lectures about the revolutionary movement in Indochina at the Whampoa Military Academy. As some of you may know, I am living with a Chinese woman, her name being Tang Tuyet Minh and I shall marry her, no matter what you or anyone else thinks!"* They married and lived together at the residence of Mikhail Borodin.

So it was that Nguyen left Paris for Moscow and became employed by the Comintern. While so doing, he also studied at the Communist University of the toilers of the East. He also took part in the Fifth Comintern in June 1924.

In 1927, Chiang Kai-shek launched an anti-communist coup which set off a new round of wandering for Nguyen. Leaving Canton, he returned to Moscow. After he had spent some time there, he was at the surgery of a doctor who examined him for a complaint. The doctor said, *"My Dear Nguyen, I am sorry to have to tell you that you are suffering from Tuberculosis and that it is best if you go to Crimea so that you can recover from the disease there!"* After again returning to Paris, he took a ship to Bangkok, arriving there in July 1928.

He had the constant feeling of being observed and he was correct in this assumption. He wrote a letter to his wife. It said, *"Although we have been apart for almost a year, our feelings for each other do not have to be said in order to be felt."* The letter was intercepted by his enemies.

He lived in the Thai village of Nachok until late in 1929 before moving on to India and Shanghai. On a cold night in Hong Kong, in June 1931, he became drunk and approached a woman with the aim of having sex with her. She was the wife of a junior British clerk, and she took great exception to being approached by someone whom she considered to be inferior to her. She got up and walked to the police outpost which was a short distance from the hotel.

When she entered, she said to the desk sergeant, *"Sergeant, please go to the hotel and arrest a little brown monkey who is calling himself "Nguyen Ai Quoc, the little monkey seems to think that he is good enough for a British Lady!"* The sergeant answered, *"Very well my Lady, I shall attend to it."* Soon Nguyen was arrested and in order to resist French demands for his extradition, the British announced that Nguyen Ai Quoc had died before quietly releasing him in January 1933.

While speaking to some people near him soon afterwards, he said, *"I am going to Milan, Italy where I shall be working in a restaurant."* He did so and returned to the Soviet Union. After spending more time in Russia recovering from his tuberculosis, he returned to China.

There he served as an advisor with the Chinese Communist Armed Forces, which forced China's Nationalistic Government into exile on the island of Taiwan. At about 1940 Nguyen Ai Quoc began to use the name "Ho Chi Minh". This is a Vietnamese name, and it has the meaning of "Bringer of Light" This last name of Ho Chi Minh is the one that he is well known around the world by.

Destroyer of Enemy Forces is Born

On the 25th of August 1911 at the village of Loc Thuy in Le Thuy District of Quang Binh Province in Vietnam, the wife of Vo Quang Nghiem was in labour and after some more discomfort and pain, she gave birth to her new son. The midwife in attendance announced, *"Congratulations, you have a fine and healthy son! What name or names do you in mind for him?"*

The new mother answered with, *"My new son shall have the following names! Vo, after his father and also Nguyen Giap! You may think it strange, but I had a vision about him while I was in labour!"* The midwife answered with, *"No, I do not think that is strange at all! Many Vietnamese mothers have visions about their children and some of those visions appear to be true! So, can you tell me about the vision?"*

The new mother answered with, *"Yes, my vision about him is that he shall have a troubled life, with the French occupiers of our country making him an outlaw and that he will flee to China to escape from French persecution of him because he shall join the Communist Party and he shall become the right hand man for Nguyen Ai Quoc and that working together against impossible odds, he shall firstly inflict such a stinging defeat upon the French that they will leave the north of our country! That shall happen after these two men have taken other invaders, the Japanese to task and harassed them.*

After that, there will be new invaders called Americans and their allies from Australia, New Zealand, South Korea, and other places. My son's life will not be easy because the French will outlaw him. That will force him to live in exile in China and while he is in exile, the French will arrest and execute his wife, his father (my husband) and even his sister and sister-in-law!

His sister-in-law will be killed by the French on their guillotine, while the others will be court-martialled and then shot. In the vision, I have also seen my own death. The vision showed me that when I give birth to his new baby brother in just ten years from now, I will die in childbirth and the new son will then die soon afterwards. I wanted to see more, but then the vision ended!"

So, it was that Vo Nguyen Giap attended schooling lessons and in this he was helped by his father who not only encouraged him but also taught him. Some of his early feelings about Vietnamese independence came directly from the influence of his father, who was constantly saying to his son, *"Vo, the French colonialists are impoverishing the people of Vietnam! The entire peasant class and working classes of people are being forced to work for French rice estates and the Michelin Rubber Company for a small fraction of what the French workers are getting for salaries and wages! As you may or may not know, I am an active member of the revolutionary council for this area, and it will serve us well if you were to agree to become a messenger to our resistance units for us. So, my son, would you like to be a revolutionary?"*

The young Giap, now ten years old, jumped at this chance to prove himself. He said to his father, *"Father, I welcome this chance of proving my mettle and my worth! I shall be the best messenger that your revolutionary group of patriots ever had!"* Soon after this, Vo Nguyen Giap was running messages for the group of revolutionaries.

As he was ten years old, his mother was about to give birth again. She was experiencing more pain and discomfort than usual in childbirth, and she was running a high fever. The fact that she was running a high temperature alarmed the attending midwife, who managed to quickly get word of these events to Vo Quang Nghiem. Upon learning of this, he left where he was teaching and went to her side.

Arriving at his home, he went to his wife and said to her, *"My darling wife, I am here, what can I do for you?"* She answered with, *"My husband, I am glad that you are here. I am very weak, and I think back to the vision that I had of this new birth. The vision told me that this would happen at the tenth birthday of Giap and that neither I nor the new baby will survive this day. Promise me that you will always be there for Giap and our other children. In my vision of ten years ago, I saw that the French would exile Giap and also arrest you, our daughter, and the sister-in-law of Giap.*

The French will behead her, and they will also kill you and our daughter by firing squad after they have court-martialled you. It is very important that you make sure that young Giap attends the Lycee Albert-Sarraut in Hanoi. You must make sure that he studies for and obtains his degree in law and also make sure that he studies history, so that he can later on become a professor of history!

When he finally is old enough to do so, he will meet his wife, who will be called Minh Thai. She will be living in China where he will be in exile because of the French assaults upon his family and the fact that by then he will be an outlaw! Promise me now that you will make sure that these things happen even if I die in this childbirth, which my vision has told me will happen." Vo answered with, *"My Dear, you worry too much. I will always do what is necessary for my family, no matter what the cost is to myself!*

Our son shall go to the Lycee Albert-Sarraut in Hanoi, he will obtain his degrees in law and history! I shall be there to constantly teach him and instruct him in all things including revolutionary activities against the French invaders who are responsible for the low standard of living endured by most Vietnamese families!" His wife continued with her labour and eventually a baby boy was born. However, the infant died soon afterward.

Shortly after that the midwife came to Vo and gently said to him, *"Vo, she is running a high temperature and there is not much that you can do here for her. You have done the main thing of reassuring her that you will be there for the children and that you will make sure that Giap will obtain both his law and history degrees. That is very important as this will give her peace of mind if she is to die from this childbirth. I suggest that you go and resume your teaching and revolutionary activities. If there is any change in her condition, I will send for you. Now do something constructive and do not feel sorry for yourself about this!"*

And so, Vo Quang Nghiem left his home and returned to his teaching. While at the school where he was teaching and during a break, he spoke to some other teachers. He said to them, *"My wife is dying from complications resulting from the birth of my fourth child. He has been born but died soon after birth. I now very much fear for my wife because ten years ago, she had a vision that she would die from childbirth complications when Giap is ten years old. My friends, that means now. I have promised her that I will see to it that Vo Nguyen Giap completes his degrees in law and history at Lycee Albert-Sarraut in Hanoi as per her wishes!"*

The other teachers around him asked, *"Vo that this a very big undertaking, why are you potentially putting yourself in harm's way by doing this?"* He answered with, *"I am doing this because in her vision of ten years ago, she also saw that a man called Nguyen Ai Quoc would lead Vietnam to true freedom and that he would be greatly helped by my son, Vo Nguyen Giap! She told me ten years ago that these two men would be the leaders and heroes of Vietnam! That is already happening. A while ago, I heard Nguyen Ai Quoc speak. He was saying, "The British, French, and American capitalists are working together to keep the peasants and workers of Vietnam impoverished and they will continue to do so! I have joined the Communist Party because it Is the only political force it cares about the plight of the Vietnamese people!*

My son Vo Nguyen Giap is already running messages between meetings of revolutionaries and our patriots! Once he has completed his degrees of Law and the History of Vietnam, I expect that he will end up leading the armed struggle against all invaders, including the bloody French!"

His father's attitudes towards the French colonists were quickly taken up by his son, Vo Nguyen Giap. As he was growing up, he became more and more influenced by his father, Vo Quang Nghiem. He applied himself to his schoolwork and would ask for his father's assistance if there was something in his studies that he did not quite understand. That help was always given and Giap was promoted to the next level of learning. After successfully completing high school and university studies, he became a teacher of history at the Thang Long High school in Hanoi.

While he was still a student in 1926, he joined the Tan Viet Cach Menh Dang which was the Revolutionary Party of Young Vietnam. He was always quick to defend the people of Vietnam and just as fast in condemning the French colonial authorities whenever they were found to be unjustly persecuting the people of Vietnam. As a result, the young

Giap made enthusiastic speeches to all who would listen, and he was constantly demanding an end to French rule and for the French to leave his country!

In 1930, Vo Nguyen Giap was one of many supporters of student strikes. Typically, he would be seen in many various places loudly saying things like, *"See how the French invaders of our land are constantly making sure that we, the people of Vietnam, live in poverty in our country which is rich in many things and the French are simply taking what belongs to the people of Vietnam either for their own use or else to sell it for high prices to other foreign governments. The wages they pay to the Vietnamese workers of their timber getting activities in the forests of Vietnam, the obtaining and selling of salt and cooking spices and other things, such as the harvesting of rubber from the plantations owned by Michelin are so low that our people cannot survive on them. We all owe it to ourselves to overthrow the French colonialists and take back our country!"* His political activities of agitating for the overthrow of the French capitalist masters and his continuing support of student strikes soon came to the attention of the French authorities and French police in Vietnam.

The French commander of the Surete said to his men, *"Men, I want a well-known troublemaker called Vo Nguyen Giap arrested and bought in for punishment! Be on the lookout for trouble from the Little Brown Monkeys who make up the population of Vietnam. They may well try to stop you from arresting him because he appears to have some sort of hero status among the little brown monkeys!*

Do not take any nonsense from the Vietnamese and make sure that you have as many firearms and police personnel as may be necessary to help you make the arrest of this very dangerous man! We will even obtain assistance from the military units including the African units in the service of France or the French Foreign Legion if necessary!"

Giap openly said to people, *"It is my great mission in life to take our country of Vietnam back from the French invaders who must be made to pay for their crimes against my people! As you may know, I am studying Vietnamese Law and economy at the university of Hanoi! The French are robbing our people and things are so bad that the peasants can no longer afford to have salt or spices because of French activities against the people! I will soon have finished my studies and then I shall work as a history teacher and as a journalist. No matter what I do, I will always champion the cause of the Vietnamese workers and peasants, and I will always work to get the foreign exploiters out of Vietnam! As socialism appears to be the only way forward for the people, I am joining a new political party called the Communist Party!"* Soon after this, he was arrested and charged with things like sedition and treason for his roles in supporting student strikes.

The French magistrate hearing the charges against him summed up with, *"Vo Nguyen Giap, I find you guilty as charged of sedition and even of treason for your support of student strikes and your anti-French attitudes! No matter if you like it or not, it is the French Governor General of Indochina who has all power and legal standing in all French Indochina, while you only have the standing of a rebel and traitor! Do you have anything to say before I pass sentence upon you for the crimes of sedition and treason?"*

Giap answered with the typical bluster of an enthusiastic young patriot. He said, *"Oh how fucking* typical! Here you French are after having invaded my country and you have the unmitigated gall to say that I am guilty of treason! If anyone is guilty of anything, then it is you, the French arseholes who are guilty of taking the rice and other food items like salt and spices away from my people! You French are also guilty of making my people work for very low wages in the Michelin rubber plantations and the French owned rice estates which are yet again on Vietnamese land!

I have spoken to some English people, and they tell me that in England, you French are called frogs! This being the case, I call upon all French Frogs to get the hell out of Vietnam!" The French magistrate answered with, *"Vo Nguyen Giap, it does not matter what you think! You have broken the law, and you shall now pay the price! You are hereby sentenced to jail for eight years during which time you will be doing hard labour!"*

In 1931, after he had served thirteen months of his jail sentence, he was taken to the warden who said to him, *"Giap, for some reason French Headquarters in Paris has ordered your release. From now on be very careful in what you say and whom you say it to! Remember that we, the French masters of Indochina consider you people of Indochina to be no better than little brown monkeys with the only difference being that you have recently come down out of the trees!"*

That prompted Giap to say, *"How typical of French arrogance! The fact is simply that you, the French people are so backward that you were still living in caves at the time when the great civilisations of China and Angkor Wat were flourishing!"*

The French warden ignored what Giap had told him and said, *"I strongly suggest that you go into exile in China soon because France is about to completely outlaw the Communist Party. If we again have problems with you or any member of your family, including anyone whom you may marry and her family, then we will execute the person concerned. We may even behead such a person in public so that justice will be seen to be done!"*

Exile and World War Two for Giap

In 1939, Giap was attending a meeting of the Communist Party, when he noticed an attractive young woman. She was Nguyet Thi Quang Thai and Vo Nguyen Giap was strongly attracted to her. Vo went over to her and introduced himself. He said, *"Good day to you my beautiful lady! My name is Vo Nguyen Giap, and I would be greatly honoured if you consent to spending your life with me as my wife. I earn a living by teaching history and also, by working as a lawyer."* She said, *"Vo Nguyen Giap, I accept your proposal, and I will discuss things further with you after the meeting. My lodgings are close by and when the meeting has concluded, we can simply walk the short distance and discuss things in earnest. It that fine with you?"* Vo said, *"Yes."*

22nd of September 1940, Japanese Troops Enter Vietnam from China

Vo Nguyen Giap and Nguyet Thi Quang Thai married and soon afterwards went to China in order to escape French attention. One evening at their home, she said to him, *"Nguyen, this is my sister and she, like the two of us is a socialist who is working towards both Chinese and Vietnamese independence."* Nguyen then shook her hand

and said, *"My dear sister-in-law, I have heard much about you from Nguyet. She said that you are also a socialist working towards the betterment and freedom of our country and its people!"*

She answered with, *"It is a pleasure to meet you Nguyen, my brother-in-law! In a week from now, I will be attending a gathering which is being chaired by the famous Nguyen Ai Quoc who will be happy to take someone like you into the Communist Party!*

I would just love to be able to introduce you to him! So, would you like to come along and meet this already famous man?" Giap answered this with, *"For sure, I would love to meet him. Please remind me about this when things are closer to it happening so that I will be there ready to do whatever it is that this great man wants to be done!"*

His sister-in-law answered with, *"It pleases me, my brother-in-law that you feel that way about it all because the meeting is this afternoon at 14:00 hours. The venue for the meeting is the home where I have my lodgings."*

So, at 12:30 hours of the same day, Giap, his wife and his sister-in-law went to her home where the meeting was being held. After entering the home, Giap was introduced to Nguyen Ai Quoc by Nguyet Thi Quang Thai, who said to Quoc, *"Sir, this is my husband, Vo Nguyen Giap, whom you have heard so much about. He has been banished from Vietnam by the French invaders. He, my sister, and I have all been made outlaws by the French.*

Because of my revolutionary activities on the behalf of the people and the party, the French have offered rewards for myself and my sister. In the case of my sister, the French have already condemned her to death in her absence. If they catch her, she will be beheaded by the French using their guillotine. My husband is a passionate patriot, and I believe that he will better serve the people if you accept him into the Vietnam Workers' Party." (Communist Party)

She was answered by Nguyen Ai Quoc who said, *"I have heard of your husband and how he was expelled from schools and university studies for supporting student strikes while he was a student himself and that he was jailed by the French for eighteen months before they released him! I have also heard that despite these things he is a professor of history and has a law degree! He is exactly what our country needs, someone who has high intelligence and who is strongly nationalistic.*

I am happy to meet this man and then make him a member of the party. I can already feel that he will make a big difference for the Freedom of Vietnam Movement!" So, it was that Giap was introduced to Nguyen Ai Quoc who said to Giap, *"Vo Nguyen Giap, welcome to this meeting of the Workers' Party of Vietnam. At the moment, I am known as Nguyen Ai Quoc, but that will change to Ho Chi Minh (Bringer of Light) in the near future. As you may already know, the last name of my wife is Minh. By using this name, people will identify with it and much more support for our revolution against the foreign overlords will be the result! In order that people will rally to our cause, I would like you to join the party so the people will see that we both are completely here for them, and we will stand by our people!*

Once you are in the party, I will get you to address various meetings of people at various places and that should create a groundswell of people who support the revolution!" Giap answered with, *"Nguyen, please go ahead and make me a party member! I shall be happy to do whatever it takes* to free the people of Vietnam from the French and other foreign capitalist yokes! You mentioned that you tried to get support for our revolution from the Americans because they themselves went through the revolutionary process in order to stop them from being exploited by the British, yet they support the continued subjection of the Vietnamese people by France. It is therefore entirely up to the people of Vietnam to obtain our freedom.

The only countries willing to help us are the Soviet Union and its allies. Britain and her dominions as well as the Americans have stated that they completely support the French terrorists." (Many Vietnamese called the French colonialists terrorists because of the way that the French were imposing their laws and order upon the Vietnamese people) Soon afterwards at a Party Meeting, Nguyen Ai Quoc said, *"I hereby announce the formation of the "Vietnamese Independence League" (Viet Minh). There are multiple reasons for this. Most importantly, I have received word that the Japanese have entered Vietnam from the Chinese borders. The news is that the French army ran away from the Japanese like the scared chickens that the French are!*

Our country's armed struggle against the French starts now and this will also include military actions against the Japanese because they have told the French colonialists to maintain order in our country and ensure that everything is supplied to the Japanese forces as it was to the French. The military arm of the Viet Minh shall be commanded by Vo Nguyen Giap, and he will take the fighting directly to the Japanese as well as the remaining French colonialists. Both the Japanese and their French colonists are trying to govern Vietnam for the betterment of the French and the Japanese."

He went on to say, *"While we have been conducting revolutionary activities against the French, they have been successful in the arrest of the father of our General Vo Nguyen Giap who was agitating on behalf of the Viet Minh. The French have also arrested his sister, and his sister-in-law!*

All of them are awaiting the death penalty imposed upon them by the French. The French Court-Martial has decreed that his sister-in-law will be beheaded using the guillotine. Vo Nguyen Giap shall immediately begin to plan the removal of all Japanese and French occupiers of Vietnam from our country!"

Vietnam During WW2

The French were continuing with their arrogant occupation of the countries that made up Indochina. Typically, the racist French attitude towards the people of South East Asia was to consider the people to be no different from monkeys. Some officials openly called the people, *"Little Brown Monkeys"* Things were no different in the British colony of Burma, where the same sort of racist attitudes towards the people was practised by the British.

With the Higher Economic Council set up by the French to manage the economy of Indochina, the authorities in Paris set Indochina the task of providing France with three point five million tonnes of food, eight hundred thousand of tea, coffee, and sugar. All of this as well as three hundred tonnes of rope and six hundred tonnes of rubber had to be provided by Indochina. To cap all of this off, the working hours of the already underpaid and overworked people of

Indochina were increased from forty-eight hours to sixty hours for men and to fifty-four hours for women[12].

Politically, in Indochina all activities of the Communist Party were banned, and all organisations allegedly run by communists were dissolved and their documents were seized. Many Cao Dai sanctuaries were closed. Many prisons were built to keep political detainees away from Vietnamese society.

The French Governor General of Indochina, whose name was Catroux, declared, *"Communism and all other movements of national liberation shall be exterminated! Communism in particular must be eliminated to pre-empt the unrest in Indochina and to guarantee the loyalty of the people! I admit that my colonial administration has much to fear from the Communist Party.*

That party is the only one that has both maintained and increased its support. It is also very dangerous because it has a comprehensive programme to win government and take control! It is mainly active in the countryside where the military resources of my administration are thinly spread!" At a communist Party meeting in November 1939, it was decided to outline the situation and to complete tasks as follows: The war in 1939 was a war between the imperialist powers which aimed at a new dividing up of the world.

At Bac Son village, in July 1940, Nguyen Anh Dung was addressing a meeting of the local Central Committee of the Communist Party. He said, *"My Friends, The French colonial masters have suffered a major defeat within their own country. They were foolish enough and stupid enough to try to interfere with what their neighbours, the Germans*

---

[12] Vien, 2009

were doing and now they have paid the price for their arrogance! The French colonialist masters here in Vietnam are confused by what has happened.

The French here are the Vichy French who are subject to Germany. The Japanese have landed, and the French colonialists have just surrendered everything, and they are giving in to all Japanese demands! I have learned that Japanese troops coming from China's Guangxi province have wiped out the French garrison at Lang Son.

The survivors of the French garrison have fled to Hanoi along the Bac Son Road. If our people were to rise in revolt right now, we could clash with and wipe out the French garrison survivors! By taking and using the French weapons against them, we could capture the French post of Vo Nhai." He had barely finished speaking when Lanh Hao Quoc Spoke. He said, "Nguyen, I fully agree that we should attack the French right now while they are disorganised and confused! I also agree that we should use weapons captured from the French to wipe out all French colonists before they act together with these new Japanese masters to keep our people down! I hereby volunteer to lead the attack upon the French at Vo Nhai and indeed, any French that we find along the road between here and Hanoi!"

This was answered by Nguyen Anh Dung. He said, "Lanh my friend, I agree that you should take your small and highly mobile unit and do the things we have just discussed! However, I want you to be careful because our uprising is in its early stages and because we only have small, scattered forces, we are vulnerable to attack from more powerful enemy units. For those reasons, I want you to make sure that we do not attack enemy units unless we outnumber them by at least three to one."

So, it was that Lanh Hao Quoc took command of his platoon sized force and patrolled the road between Bac son and Hanoi. Soon Lanh was approached by a forward scout. He said, *"Sir, there is a small force of fifteen French soldiers running toward Hanoi, what do you want us to do?"* Lanh answered with, *"Quickly get all thirty of our men to go directly to this point on the map which is about one kilometre from here. Make sure that our men line one side of the road only and that everyone is hidden from view. Once you are all concealed make sure that you can see the road from where you are and prepare the ambush!*

Kill all French soldiers because if we kill all soldiers they send, they will stop sending them! Make sure that you take all French weapons, including whatever ammunition you can get your hands upon! Now go and kill the invaders of our country and the despoilers of our women!"

The forward scout quickly returned to his unit and told the others. Very soon the entire platoon of Vietnamese freedom fighters was running through the forest in order to make sure that they arrived at the selected ambush position long before the fleeing French soldiers got there.

Upon reaching the ambush site, the Vietnamese fighters hid themselves from view as ordered. Lanh now said to them, *"Men, in a short time, we will engage the French in battle! We shall not open fire until the leading French soldier approaches our last man in this ambush. He will spring the ambush by firing and killing the first of the French. You are all to select your targets before this happens and to keep your targets in view.*

If that cannot be done, you must select a different target. All Frenchmen must die!" Now that the orders had been issued, the Vietnamese kept on with making sure that they were concealed from view and awaited the arrival of the French. After some time had elapsed, the sound of heavy breathing and conversations in French could be heard. All of the Vietnamese were ready, and the last man of the unit had mounting excitement building up within him. Soon, he saw his French target and opened fire.

That resulted in the deaths of the fifteen French soldiers and that was followed by the Vietnamese patriots obtaining the French weapons and ammunition from the French bodies. They then buried the slain French soldiers. After that, the French outpost at Vo Nhai was attacked and taken.

The French were killed and most of the rank-and-file Vietnamese defenders then joined the Vietnamese patriots. New uprisings were suppressed, allowing the colonialists to concentrate their forces as these were required. The rebels withdrew into the mountains and formed the first guerrilla groups led by the Communist Party.

The French colonists had to deal with claims by Thailand demanding territory in the northwest of Cambodia's Tonle Sap and the right bank of the Mekong River in Laos. Japan backed the claims by Thailand. In order to protect their colonial interests, the colonists sent units of Vietnamese soldiers the fight the Thais.

Some of those units which were stationed in Saigon, rebelled against being sent to the front. That was part of a plan of action which formed part of the programme which had been put into place by the Communist Party Committee for Cochinchina. This plan actively prepared for the uprising as of June 1940.

The Insurrection of 23rd of November 1940

Being launched during the night, this plan looked likely to succeed, but some traitors wanted to enrich themselves and informed the French Colonial Administration of what was about to happen. As a result, the French colonists disarmed the mutinous units and therefore the Saigon revolt did not take place. However, uprisings took place in eight of Cochinchina's twenty provinces.

During the evening of 23rd of November 1940, a member of a unit of Vietnamese soldiers under French command was preparing his weapons and equipment for use on the following day when a messenger arrived to see him. Having located him, the messenger said, *"Dung Hung Lanh, I have just come from an urgent meeting of the Central Committee of the Communist Party which has urgent messages for you and all patriots of Vietnam! The Party wants you to immediately take yourself and your platoon of Vietnamese soldiers and you are to flee to My Tho province and there you are to again work against the French occupiers of our country!"*

The messenger waited for Dung to answer. Dung finally said, *"Nguyen my friend, what is it that has happened? My platoon and others have been waiting for midnight because it has been ordered that we should attack the French Colonists then. What has happened?"*

Nguyen the messenger answered with *"The Central Committee of the Party has been informed that some traitors have sold out our patriots to the fucking French and that the French are immediately moving to disarm all Vietnamese soldiers stationed in Saigon for use in action against the Thais! The French military, military police and civilian police units are at this moment arresting all Vietnamese patriots they can find. The Party wants you and your men to go to My Tho province as I have already stated to you! When you get there, you shall find that at least fifty-four of the one hundred villages of the province are willing and able to take part in the armed struggle against the French and the Japanese!*

The Central Committee of the Communist Party likes the new flag that you have helped to design, and the Party wants you to raise the red flag which is emblazoned with a gold star at the first village in My Tho province that you go to! The members of the Committee of the Party believe that it will become the rallying flag for our fight against the capitalist aggressors from France and Japan! Also, beware that the French colonists are under the direct command of Japanese and they are likely to be as ruthless and cruel as the Japanese. So, expect no mercy from either one of these foreign occupiers"

These things combined, and many villages were destroyed, resulting in over twenty thousand people being arrested or killed. In the first years of World War Two, the Vietnamese people under the leadership of the Communist Party had shown that they were willing and able to take on the foreign occupiers of their country, even though some of the early battles had been lost by the Vietnamese.

In early January of 1941 Dung Hung Lanh was thinking of how best to continue the struggle for freedom against both the French colonialists who were under the command of the Vichy French Government and also the Japanese. He now said to his sergeant, *"Sergeant, do you know of anyone in the colonial garrison at Do Luong village in Nghe Anh province?"*

His sergeant answered with, *"Yes Sir, I think that if you get word to my brother who is a sergeant in the French Colonial Garrison at Do Luong, that will help you to take the place over. You may even end up in a position to attack Vinh! I was at Do Luong recently and I saw that the garrison there has the new Japanese 75 mm Mountain Gun model 94! I saw three of those guns at Do Luong and I also noted that there is a large amount of ammunition for those guns stored there. It may interest you to know that this mountain gun can be towed or dismantled into six different parts allowing it to be carried elsewhere and reassembled.*

The weapon Is equipped with a bipod and ring rack with a panoramic telescope! Sir, my advice is that we obtain as many of these guns as possible as well and as much of its ammunition as possible because such an easily transportable weapon will be of great assistance to us against the foreigners!" Dung Hung Lanh considered what his sergeant had told him. He said to the sergeant, *"Sergeant, I think that your contacts are bloody marvellous! Please contact your brother at the garrison concerned and we will take over that area soon afterwards. It will be very good to have our new red flag with the gold star in the middle of it flying above what is currently a French outpost!*

This will signal our people that a revolution is in progress and that the foreign forces will be destroyed! In particular, your news of three Japanese mountain guns at the garrison at Do Luong interests me because having such weapons and their ammunition will greatly assist the freedom movement!" The sergeant did as he was asked and soon received a reply to the message he had sent to his brother at the colonial garrison.

It read, *"Brother, if you and your unit were to come here to Go Luong, you could simply walk in and take over. That would give you immediate access to the new Japanese mountain guns that we have here as well as one thousand rounds of the seventy-five-millimetre ammunition for them.*

When you come, please sound three long blasts on a bugle as the signal that you are on the way. Upon hearing this, my men and I will arrest our French officers and open the gates to the outpost. I have with me one of your national liberation flags of a red background emblazoned with a gold star. When you see this flag flying over the outpost, come in and take the three Japanese mountain guns and their ammunition away. See to it that your commander knows of this because I have spoken to my men, and they would all like to join the freedom movement against all foreigners!"

The sergeant informed Dung of this. *Dung said to him, "Very good sergeant, we will proceed to Do Luong at the morning twilight."* This resulted in Dung and his men being admitted into the French outpost of Do Luong when they saw that their flag was flying over it.

This pleased Dung and he said to his followers, *"Men, I have received news that the colonial French garrison at Vinh is now in open revolt and the men there have asked us for help because they fear that the French will bring both more troops and artillery to use against them!*

This is why is so good that we have captured these Japanese guns because we will use them against the French at Vinh!" Dung was quickly answered by his sergeant. He said to Dung, *"Sir, might I caution you against going into action against the French enemy too quickly? Even though you have good men, please remember that they are* experienced infantrymen who have little idea of how to use artillery pieces, in particular Japanese ones. It seems to me that in would be a good Idea to postpone the attack upon Vin until we get our personnel trained in the use of the Japanese mountain gun artillery!"

With the garrison from Do Luong now added to his platoon sized force, he marched towards Vinh. He was supremely confident that the colonial force at Vinh would also arrest its French officers and join the liberation movement. Huu had obtained an audience with the French commander of the Vinh outpost and spoke to him.

He said, *"Sir, Dung Hung Lanh and his force are coming here. They have with them three Japanese artillery pieces and ammunition which they captured from your outpost at Do Luong! They are seeking to wipe you out!"* That was answered by the French commander who said, *"So, the little brown monkeys are finally coming! Good, because they are walking into my trap. I have arranged three batteries of the most modern French artillery available to be in and around Vinh!*

All guns have been ranged in and have large distance markers for up to two kilometres to their fronts, sides, and rears. When the slant eyed little brown monkeys get here, they will all die! As for you, I sometimes use intelligence from traitors like you, but I cannot stand the sight of traitors! Accordingly, you will be taken from here to a place of execution and there you shall be shot. How do you like that you slant eyed little brown monkey?" So, it was that the traitor got his just deserts, but Dung and his men continued towards their objective of Vinh. As they moved ever closer to Vinh, they were observed by an alert French sentry.

He reported to his lieutenant saying, *"Sir, the Vietnamese force you have been expecting is approaching!"* The French lieutenant said, *"Great news private, just let the Vietnamese fools keep on coming. When the little brown monkeys get to where the ranging pegs are, closely observe them!*

When they are at three hundred and fifty metres from this position, see to it that you and the other sentries fire the flares you have been issued with. That will immediately result in all of the artillery batteries opening fire on the Vietnamese and we will just wipe them out. We should then be able to take back the captured Japanese mountain guns!"

However, the Japanese mountain guns were not with the Vietnamese unit. It had been decided that more training was needed before the Vietnamese patriots could properly use them. So, the guns were sent to other units of the freedom movement. That was just as well, because the Vietnamese were almost wiped out to a man, including all their officers.

As the unit of Vietnamese patriots was approaching Vinh, Dung was beginning to have mounting misgivings about attacking the garrison there. He constantly had the feeling that he and his small force of patriots were being watched. He could not shake off these feeling and it was bothering him greatly.

Therefore, he said to his men, *"Fellow patriots of Vietnam, we are small in number, and for some reason, I am getting premonitions about the coming attack on the French garrison at Vinh. It is bad luck that we cannot have the captured Japanese mountain guns with us at the moment, but our men must firstly learn how to use them. I am getting the constant feeling that we are being watched and that our doom awaits! If it turns out that these premonitions are correct, then we are in for a torrid time indeed!*

We shall have to make sure that we do everything to minimise our casualties! You all have emergency shell dressings with you, and you have all been taught basic emergency first aid. As well, I want you all to break up your silhouette shapes with leaves and grasses as appropriate. As we move forward, I need you all to keep your silhouette shapes invisible to the enemy by making sure that we always have either the backdrop of hills behind us or forest. There is to be no speaking, and you are to use the hand signals that I have taught you in order to communicate. By doing these things, we should be able to arrive at Vinh undetected."

The Vietnamese patriots kept on advancing. Suddenly, the ground shook and there was the whistling sound of artillery shells flying overhead. Next, a series of explosions took place among the Vietnamese patriots which resulted in many of their deaths and also the others were wounded. This caused Dung to yell, *"We are in a trap! The French have been watching us and noting our progress! We must retreat to our agreed battalion safe area. Get out of here now and may heaven be with us!"*

So, the patriots retreated as Dung had ordered, but it was too late for most of this small force consisting of his own platoon and the Vietnamese members of the colonial garrison at Do Luong. The casualties suffered by the Vietnamese force was extremely high with only Dung and four other wounded men escaping.

Living Under Two Foreign Yokes

From 1941 to 1945, Vietnam lived under the colonial government which was intensified by Japanese occupation.

The Vichy French Colonial Government and the Japanese agreed on the tapping of Vietnam's resources to the maximum and on the maintenance of order by both of these foreign occupiers against the revolutionary movement.

Economic exploitation was intensified to both meet the interests of the Vichy French and the Japanese. This required more control of the population. Accordingly, repression was intensified, and political manoeuvring increased in order to mislead public opinion and to rally reactionary or politically naive Vietnamese citizens[13].

To illustrate these things, let us consider the plight of peasants who were being systematically exploited by the twin yokes of both French and Japanese occupiers at the same time. Imagine that some peasants from the village of Dat Do in the province of Phuoc Tuy were talking. Nguyen Quan Trang was speaking to his friend and fellow peasant called Sinh Thao Thu. Sinh said to Nguyen, *"Nguyen my friend, I am at the end of my wits as to how to provide for my family! The main problem is that although the land gives me good rice and maize crops, my family and I are living in poverty, and we are all going about in clothing which is little more than rags!*

Let us face it, we are now in the year of 1944. No matter what some people may say, between 1940 and 1944, prices have risen by four hundred percent while my income has either remained stagnant or it has only risen by up by twenty percent. Although my good wife is always washing and mending our clothing, we have been reduced to the wearing of rags by the dual French and Japanese occupiers

---

[13] Vien, 2009.

of the bloody present administration! These sorts of conditions and injustices cannot be allowed to continue!"

Nguyen answered his friend with, *"Yes, my friend, those conditions are breeding discontent not only here, but also all over Vietnam. Discontent has also spread to the richer peasants as well as the merchants and industrialists who have been hit by shortages of both materials and equipment. Not only that, but the Vichy French administration has set up monopolies which are also forcing the prices that we receive for our produce down! The situation is intolerable!*

I was listening to a broadcast on the radio in which the man who is the only hope for the future of our country against the foreign occupiers of the dual French and Japanese administration was speaking. His name is Ho Chi Minh, and he said that he and other leaders of the resistance against foreign occupiers are concerned that some of our patriots have swallowed the lies put out by the Japanese! He warned that the Japanese are spreading illusions about the Japanese giving support to our people to rise up against the French Colonialists when in fact the Japanese are fully co-operating with them! He has therefore called upon all Vietnamese patriots to rise up and wipe out both the French and Japanese!"

The Vichy French Government had sent Admiral Decoux to Indochina as the French governor General. He carried out a dual policy of dictatorship and appealing to the peasants. At the end of 1940, he spoke to a handful of elected councils which gave the colonial government the façade of democracy.

To them he said, *"As of now, all elected councils and other impediments to French rule of Vietnam shall be abolished! All power shall from now on be only in the hands of the Governor General of French Indochina and also my security services!*

As of now, my administration will revive reactionary concepts drawn from Petainism and Confucianism. Quoc ngu, the transcription of the entire Vietnamese language into the Latin alphabet is working well, but any Vietnamese person found to still be using Chinese characters in order to write, will be executed! As well, there will be more organised literary competitions and painting exhibitions. All of these shall have prizes awarded and will be utilized at every opportunity to promote French cultural values!" His words caused concern to many of those present, but they remained silent and most opted to raise the matters of the loss of democracy with their local Communist Party Committees.

The Vietnamese people were made to ensure the compulsory delivery of rice to the Japanese. Even areas that were dangerously short of food, such as Tonkin had to deliver 130,205 tonnes in 1943 and 186,130 tonnes in 1944. They had to deliver this to the Japanese no matter if the harvest was good or bad.

The peasants had to provide sacks to the Japanese, who made the peasants stop planting rice and to plant jute in large areas. In 1944, American bombing disrupted the supply of coal to Saigon, resulting in the French and Japanese using rice and maize as fuel for the power stations and they hoarded rice for their own use. While this was happening, no improvements were made in agriculture and there was no maintenance of the hydraulic works. A natural disaster then caused a terrible famine, beginning in 1943 and getting worse from 1944.

The Japanese general in command in Vietnam said to his officers, *"Japan is in full agreement with the French colonialists about the exploitation of Indochina's resources to the utmost, as well as the putting down of all revolutionary activities! We will continue with our governing in the form of a dictatorship of an occupying power. The Vichy French Colonists are part of the Axis, and they will continue to enforce Japanese/French will upon the peasants of Indochina!*

I have promised the peasants that Japan will give the people of Indochina their national independence which they can achieve with our help and so have the solidarity of Asian peoples rising in revolt against the whites so that we will build a mutually beneficial and prosperous Greater East Asia!

My men are working to recruit supporters, with individuals such as Tran Trong Kim, Ngo Dinh Diem, and Nguyen Van Sam. Also, we are cultivating small, organised groups such as the Greater Vietnam Party in Tonkin."

So, it was that the Japanese experienced that it was more important to maintain order in Indochina with French help rather than to use puppet governments. Even in 1944, after the fall of the Vichy Government in France, the Japanese continued with that policy[14].

Birth of the Viet Minh

Ho Chi Minh convened the eight meetings of all members of the Party Central Committee at Pac Bo in May

---

[14] Vien, 2009

1941. He addressed the meeting saying, *"Fellow patriots of Vietnam. It is my considered opinion that the Vietnamese revolution must stand without hesitation in the international stage as an anti-fascist power of which the Soviet Union remains the nucleus!*

The Central committee believes that Hitler shall inevitably attack the USSR. That will bring about the collapse of fascism and the World War will end with the emergence of new socialist countries! It is in the light of these expectations that the strategy of the Vietnamese revolutionary movement must be decided, and you are here to hear about all of this and to vote upon it!

Our main objective is to liberate our country from the Franco-Japanese occupation. The national liberation of our country must come first, and the interest of all social classes is subordinate to this prime objective! A broad national union must be created in order to fight French colonialism and Japanese fascism, so we are setting up a national front which brings together all social classes, political parties, and even religious groupings. We shall confiscate all land belonging to imperialists and traitors.

The land will then be allocated to poor peasants. There shall be a reduction of land rents, loan interest and communal land will be shared fairly! All of these things shall be applied gradually in order to finally achieve the ideal of giving the land back to the tillers! This is the only way that the national union can be secured without neglecting the needs of the poor peasants!"

So, it was that the Party Central Committee decided to speed up preparations for armed uprisings, reinforcing of guerrilla and self-defence units, plus the setting up of guerrilla bases[15]. The Party Central Committee now issued the following communique, "The Pacific War and the Chinese peoples' resistance against Japanese aggression," the Central Committee resolution declared, *"This will be a favourable development for the Indochinese revolution. At this moment, by keeping our forces ready, we will be able to launch partial insurrections and win victory in various areas to clear the way for a general insurrection."*

Truong Chinh was elected General Secretary of the Party. The Viet Minh Front was set up, involving many workers, peasants, youth and women's organisations and guerrilla units that operated in the highlands. The Viet Minh rapidly gained support among the working class and its emblem was the red flag with a gold star emblazoned upon the centre of it. The situation of the working people was quickly getting worse under the dual French and Japanese yokes!

Meanwhile at Long Binh in the south of Vietnam, a local Vietminh leader called Nguyen Chien was becoming very concerned at the large number of Japanese tanks in the Long Binh area. He was speaking to other members of his platoon sized unit.

He said, *"We have the added problem of the Japanese in the Long Binh areas coming to the aid of the Vichy French Colonial Administration. Besides actively aiding the French occupiers, the Japanese in and around Long Binh have large numbers of small two-man crewed tanks which they use to enforce the Franco-Japanese demands for rice and other produce from our people. Does anyone at this meeting know of any way that we can combat*

---

[15] Vien, 2009

these tanks which are giving the Franco-Japanese aggressors the upper hand at the moment?"

His question was answered by the French born rubber and rice merchant known as Sacha Roussel, who had proved that he was indeed an able and willing patriot of Vietnam even though he was French born. Sacha said, *"Nguyen and others, you speak of your concern about the ruthless way the Franco-Japanese administration is using the two-man crewed Japanese tanks against us. As many of you know, I still have connections in the countries of French speaking Canada and in the USA!*

The answer to the problem of the small Japanese tanks is to use an American weapon called a Bazooka against them. The Bazooka is a portable rocket launcher that is fired from the shoulder. This weapon consists of a smooth tube which is five feet in length. (1.5m) Both of its ends are open, and this makes it recoilless. The weapon is equipped with hand grips, a trigger mechanism, shoulder rest and sight. It is designed for relatively close quarter anti-tank and anti-strong point assaults.

The rocket that It fires Is nineteen inches long and it weighs about 3.5 pounds. (1.6 kg) The rocket has eight ounces of pentolite high explosive, and it is a shaped charge meaning that the blast goes in a forward direction. It can penetrate five inches of armour (127 mm) if fired at a range of three hundred yards (127 m).

The main defects are its short range and Its inaccuracy. I am sure that I can procure these for you because the American arms manufacturers are true capitalists and so they will sell them to you as long as you pay them the money that they will ask for. So, would you like me to organise getting the Bazookas and the necessary rocket ammunition for you?"

That was answered by Nguyen who said, *"By heaven Sacha, you really are a blessing to the freedom movement! Yes, go ahead and organise things so that these new weapons and their ammunition are delivered here as quickly as possible. Do you know how to use the weapons yourself or is the supply of them as far as you can go?"* Sacha answered with, *"I can both organise the delivery of the weapons and their ammunition as well as training our patriots in their use for you. So how many weapons would you like in the first order and, how many of the rocket ammunitions should be delivered?"*

Nguyen said, *"We can lay our hands on sixty-eight thousand American dollars, how many of these Bazookas and their rocket ammunition will that get us?"* Sacha answered with, *"I think that may get you about fifteen Bazookas and about ten rockets per Bazooka."*

Nguyen said, *"Very well, go ahead and obtain these things. When the weapons arrive, I need you to personally train our patriots in their use, so also make sure that you obtain dummy rockets for training purposes. We will only use the real ammunition for combat purposes against the Franco-Japanese forces and tanks!"* Sacha then left for where he was to obtain the Bazookas and their ammunition.

Sacha arrived at Shanghai and met the American arms dealer. He said to Sacha, *"Sacha old friend, it is good to see you again. I accept your proposal for me to supply you with fifteen Bazookas and ten rounds of their rocket ammunition for each weapon! Give me the USD $28,000.00 now and another US$10,000.00 in a month's time and I get* them delivered to your address at Long Binh within a month!"

Sacha said, *"My friend I have anticipated that you would want another USD $10,000.00 and so, I have it here with the original USD $28,00.00 asked for. Now deliver the order on time! My associates depend upon it!"* As agreed, the shipment of Bazookas and their ammunition arrived at the Long Binh residence of Sacha a month later and another meeting of the local Vietminh Liberation Front was called for a week later.

At the meeting, Sasha said to Nguyen, *"Nguyen, the weapons and ammunition have arrived at my home in Long Binh. It is now high to train our patriots in the use of the weapons, using the dummy training rounds that I have also supplied! I would like to be in the lead of one of the units to attack the enemy as soon as we can do so!"*

Nguyen replied with, *"Good work! Take note everyone that we begin training in the use of the new weapons immediately. Sasha has been promoted to the level of platoon commander, and he will be training us! He has also been given command of the Long Binh Second Platoon"* And so, the Long Binh patriots trained in the use of the Bazookas until Sasha thought that they were ready for action using the new weapons.

Nguyen said, *"Good, I want you to take out your platoon to cover the areas to the north of here between Long Binh and Bien Hoa! I and my platoon will be doing the same things in the areas to the south of here and Bien Hoa. We move out into positions of ambush of the tank units now.*

Each of the five platoons has been issued with three Bazookas per platoon. That means that there are three bazookas available per platoon. It is now up to us to use these weapons against the French colonists and the Japanese occupiers effectively! The Japanese tanks are operating in groups of three. Therefore, a ten-man infantry section armed with a bazooka per section should be able to wipe out the tank units as long as they get close enough to the tanks!" That resulted in the wiping out of the Japanese tank units of the Long Binh area[16].

The Viet Minh did not just produce a programme and then stick to it. Above everything else, they tried to and were successful in drawing the masses of the population into action on the political and the military levels. A new type of action called "Armed Propaganda" appeared.

In 1943, the patriots were strong enough to re-establish the Bac Son-Vo Nhai base and fan out towards other provinces. By the end of 1943, Viet Minh armed propaganda units operated in much of Vietnam[17]. At the end of 1943, Viet Minh armed propaganda units were operating in several provinces in the mountainous regions north of the Red River. By 1944, liberation was well established in these provinces and networks of Partisans were set up in central Annam and Cochinchina.

In the border provinces of Cao Bang and Lang Son, the peoples' organisations prepared for armed uprisings. Nguyen Ai Quoc (later known as Ho Chi Minh) returned

---

[16] When I was serving in Vietnam with Australian army in 1969, we saw groupings of three and sometimes two small Japanese tanks in and near Long Binh. Years later, I was speaking to a former member of the French Foreign Legion about it, and he told me that the tanks were in those groupings because the Legion used them as target practice for Foreign Legion Bazookas after WW2. The tanks had been knocked out of action by the Viet Minh using newly acquired bazookas. He had been a member of the Wehrmacht during WW2.

[17] Vien, 2009.

from China, and he was convinced that an uprising at this point may be premature and postponed it in order to intensify political activity.

Nguyen Ai Quoc announced at a meeting of the Central Committee of the Communist Party in 1944, *"Patriots, friends, and comrades, I have been operating under the name of Nguyen Ai Quoc for some years now. It is critical that we win the hearts and minds of our people, otherwise the European Capitalists and their allies in the United States of America will just keep on with what the present Franco-Japanese occupation forces are doing in the enslavement of the people.*

An illustration of this is what their actions are doing in the subjugation of our people, our normally highly productive country cannot feed its own people because our rice and maize crops are being stolen from us by both the French colonialists and the Japanese. I am now a married man, and the last name of my wife is Minh. I am now going to change my name to Ho Chi Minh because this means, "Bringer of Light" and that will be really good for positive propaganda purposes!

We shall also set up the **"Propagation and Liberation Army."** *(sub-units were also known as Propaganda and Liberation Units) I have chosen that name to emphasize the political nature of the activities of this body! Now then, Patriots, friends, and comrades, I am most happy to announce that the commander of this Is Vo Nguyen Giap, whom you already know as the leader of the Viet Minh Forces!"*

In mid-December 1944 on the eve of the founding of the Propaganda and Liberation Unit, General Vo Nguyen

Giap received instructions from Ho Chi Minh. These were written on a small piece of paper inserted into a packet of cigarettes.

They read as follows: *"The Vietnam Propaganda Unit for National Liberation is the first one born. I hope many others will soon come into being. Its size is small, but its prospects are brilliant. It is the embryo of the Liberation Army and may have to move throughout our country from north to south.[18]"* Orders for the beginning of offensive action soon followed and resulted in General Giap calling for an orders group (meeting of soldiers) of his staff officers on 23rd of December 1944. He said to them, *"Gentlemen, we will launch the attack of our Liberation Army against the Franco-Japanese outposts of Phai Khat and Na Ngan. Move your sub-units and units into position while it is still very dark and completely surround the enemy!*

Use whatever you have in the way of weapons to make this work for you. I want both of those outposts of the foreign capitalist aggressors to be wiped out. You shall take both places beginning on 24th of December 1944 and I want the operations against the enemy to be successfully concluded by mid-night of the 25th of December 1944!"

So it was that two days after the founding of the unit, General Vo Nguyen Giap obtained his first two victories against the enemy. The two sudden attacks against Phai Khat and Na Ngan posts resulted in their annihilation by swift and victorious operations. As they took place between Cao Bang, Bac Can and Lang Son provinces, the news of the victory of

---

[18] Giap, 1971

the Vietnamese spread rapidly and stirred the three provinces[19].

A peasant who was a member of the Viet Minh called Phuc Sang Trang was seething with disgust at the attempted forcing of the people to plant jute for the manufacture of Japanese sacks at the expense of rice that he openly expressed his disgust at the foreign occupiers of his country He was one of many who thought this way.

He loudly said, *"The fucking French colonialists and their bloody Japanese allies, are making us starve in order for the Japanese to have sacks! Both the French and Japanese are constantly demanding and taking large amounts of harvested rice and maize, which they are burning to provide fuel for the generation of electricity in the south. We cannot continue to have our food taken from us! I call upon every man and woman to oppose the foreigners and to confront the bastards even if we are only armed with sticks and hoes when facing French and Japanese guns! Vietnam is for Vietnamese people and not for the cruel and greedy foreign capitalists who are making us stave!"*

In the cities of Vietnam, workers intensified the movement against the foreign occupiers. *"The Workers' Association of National Salvation"* was founded, and it urged strikes and demonstrations in support of pay rises and an end to brutality. These activities provided a stimulus for the active involvement of intellectuals and students. While all this was happening, the declaration by Charles De Gaulle promising to liberate Indochina was hardly noticed[20].

---

[19] Giap, 1971.
[20] Vien, 2099.

1945 – The Turning Point

In 1945 it was apparent that the Axis powers would lose World War Two. In France, the Vichy Government had fallen, while in China the Japanese were suffering defeats in China as well as in the Pacific. In Indochina, the Gaullists began to prepare to restore French colonial rule. On the 8th of February 1945 while visiting Brazzaville, Charles De Gaulle proclaimed, *"I hereby both proclaim and promise to the people of Indochina, a degree of autonomy."* What he did not say was the new French Government would deploy more French troops to safeguard the French presence in South East Asia.

The Japanese commander of the Indochina areas, called for an "O" Group (Orders Group) with his senior officers. He addressed them in the Officers' Mess at a base near Saigon. He said, *"Gentlemen, we are in a most difficult situation, and we are faced with a revolutionary movement which is gaining strength by the hour as well as the possibility of an about-face by the French colonial forces here. That could easily become a very dangerous situation for us all! I want you all to think about this and please let me have your suggestions of how best to deal this alarming set of situations!"* There was an almost stunned silence for a short time, which was followed by some of the assembled officers speaking.

A captain said, *"Sir, how about us leaving the French no room at all in which to manoeuvre. We can easily do this by disarming the French Colonial Forces! Those who do not wish to disarm will just be shot!"* The old Japanese colonel said, *"Thank you for this brilliant suggestion, captain! We shall strike immediately and disarm the French immediately and thus remove the threat!"* So, it was that on the 9th of March 1945, Japanese soldiers disarmed the French without meeting any resistance. The whole colonial structure collapsed overnight.

Meanwhile a major famine was beginning to take hold. The seizure and hoarding of rice and speculation considerably worsened an already bad situation. With the people ready to move in masses, the Viet Minh called upon them to intensify guerrilla activity and for the peasants to seize the stores of rice that were held by the Japanese.

General Vo Nguyen Giap was talking to people about promises made by the Japanese that they would guarantee freedom from the French colonialists. He said to them, *"My people, do not be deceived by the promises of the Japanese regarding the obtaining of independence by holding negotiations with the Vietnamese puppet government of the Japanese! The Japanese want you to hold negotiations with the puppet emperor Boa Dai and his prime minister of Tran Trong Kim. Due to having been occupied and very badly treated by the Japanese occupiers, who obtain much assistance from the French colonists, our country of Vietnam is right now in a pre-revolutionary state. The Viet Minh Front will now draw upon the people to launch a general insurrection and to seize power using three elements.*

- *Development of guerrilla activities in the highland.*
- *Action by the peasant masses in seizing rice stores.*
- *Political agitation in major cities."*

In 1945 at Saigon, the Workers' Sections for National Salvation had grown from three thousand to one hundred and twenty thousand members by March 9. The

Youth Vanguard led by people like Dr. Pham Ngoc Thac, and Thai Van Lung had two hundred thousand members in Saigon and one million in Cochinchina as a whole[21].

The August Revolution

In summer of 1945, the suffering and resentment of the Vietnamese people reached a climax resulting in revolutionary actions by both the political and military organisations of the armed struggle for freedom of the people and for freedom from hunger. Therefore, the rebellion spread throughout the country. The decisive force which led and co-ordinated these things on a nation-wide basis, was the Viet Minh Front. On the 13th of August 1945, Japan surrendered. On the same day, the Communist Party of Indochina held a meeting at the level of a national congress. It was decided to adapt the following slogans:

- End foreign aggression.
- Seize back national independence.
- Found the peoples' power.

On the 16th of August 1945, the Viet Mihn held a National Congress in order to bring together the delegates from many political organisations, religious and ethnic groups. Several speakers produced the same sort of conclusions.

Typically, it was stated, *"We are at the cross-roads of gaining the freedom and independence of our country. In order to be successful in gaining freedom for our country, we must firstly see to it that we seize power from the hands of the Japanese and the puppet Vietnamese Government*

---

[21] Vien, 2009.

before the arrival of allied troops in Indochina and receive in our capacity as masters of the country, the troops which come to disarm the Japanese The main problem with all this to pre-empt the Allies, Chiang Kai-shek, British, French and American, all of whom want to occupy Indochina for their own interests!"

This led the Congress to adopt a 9-point programme:

(1) Seize power and found the Democratic Republic of Vietnam on the basis of total independence.
(2) Arm the people. Strengthen the Liberation Army.
(3) Confiscate the property of the imperialists and traitors, and depending on circumstances, nationalise it or share it out among the poor.
(4) Abolish the taxes imposed by the French and Japanese and replace them with a just and non-punitive budget system.
(5) Guarantee the fundamental rights of the people: - human rights, - the right to private ownership, - Civil rights: universal suffrage, democratic freedoms, equality among the ethnic groups, between men and women.
(6) Share communal land fairly, reduce land rent and loan interest rates, postpone repayment of debts, and provide relief to victims of natural disasters.
(7) Introduce labour legislation: an eight-hour workday, minimum salary, national insurance.
(8) Build an independent national economy, develop agriculture, and set up a national bank. Develop a national education system: fight illiteracy and introduce compulsory elementary education. Build a new culture, establish friendly relations with the Allies and countries struggling for independence. Develop a national education system: fight illiteracy and introduce compulsory elementary education. Build a new culture, establish friendly relations with the Allies and countries struggling for independence.

The National committee for Liberation was elected and the functions of the provisional government were headed by Ho Chi Minh. He said, *"This hour is a decisive one for our nation's history. Let us all stand up and fight tenaciously for our own liberation. Many peoples of the world are rising up to gain their independence. We cannot lag behind. Forward! Under the Viet Minh banner (red background with a large gold star in its centre), let us march courageously forward!*[22]*"* A Tsunami of independence activities swept the country. That resulted in large numbers of people demanding change, and they were often backed up with armed groups of guerrillas. In most cases, that resulted in local authorities fleeing or handing power over to the revolutionaries.

Most garrisons of Japanese soldiers or the troops of the puppet Vietnamese Government in Hue, allowed themselves to be disarmed. A few cities remained under foreign occupation. One of these was Lai Chau which was re-occupied by a large French column on its way back from China where it had sought refuge during the Japanese putsch on the 9th of March 1945.

At the major large cities of Hanoi, Hue and Saigon, the swift victories won by the uprisings were celebrated. There were also pro-Japanese agents trying to stop the revolutionary tide. These tried to set up a National Salvation Committee with the aim of slowing or stopping the revolution, but they failed in that. On the 17th of August 1945, a rally which had been organised by some pro-Japanese supporting the puppet government in Hue was turned into a mass demonstration of support of the Viet Minh by the enthusiastic crowd.

On the 19th of August 1945, a general strike was called, and it was followed by more than one hundred

---

[22] Vien, 2009.

thousand people demonstrating in the streets of major cities. That forced the puppet government to resign and hand over power to the revolutionaries.

With it being the Vietnamese Royal Capital, Hue was also the place to site the pro-Japanese puppet government. On account of the Viet Minh trying to avoid unnecessary bloodshed, they tried to persuade the Vietnamese king named Bao Dai and his prime minister Tran Trong Kim to resign. There were also reactionaries in Vietnam who wanted to hang on to their power.

Accordingly, they were planning to ask the Japanese command to provide a guard of five thousand men. After hearing about this and wanting to stop it from happening, people like Thang Toan Trang contacted his friends and associates saying to them, *"Friends and fellow citizens of Vietnam, the puppet government of Bao Dai and their cronies are attempting to use another Japanese force of five thousand men to enslave us and to keep us down.*

We, the people of Hue and surrounding villages must put a stop to this, and we must stop it all now! We will all be accompanied by armed groups of Viet Minh soldiers where-ever we go, and we must take to the streets and demonstrate against all of this. At the same time, we must completely occupy various ministries!"

All those things were done and on 23rd of August 1945, Bao Dai abdicated and so the Tran Trong Kim puppet government collapsed. On 25th of August 1945, the delegation from the peoples' Government in Hanoi led by Tran Huy Lieu received the symbols of power from Bao Dai. The symbols of power were the dynastic seal and sword.

Meanwhile, in Cochinchina, the pro-Japanese formed a united National Front by 14th of August 1945. The king's envoy from Hue, Nguyen Van Sam, asked the Japanese to arm members of the front, but he was not able to withstand the popular pressure of the people.

Revolutionary power was set up by one million people from Saigon and surrounding areas marching through the city while they were protected by armed groups of Viet Minh. So, it was that the August Revolution in 1945 put an end to 80 years of French colonial administration, abolished the monarchy and re-established Vietnam as an independent nation[23]. Meanwhile, behind the scenes, there was much frantic activity by the Japanese occupiers of Indochina, beginning on the 5th of March 1945.

"O" Group on the 5th of March 1945

Japanese Lieutenant General Tsuchihashi addressed the meeting of officers and senior NCOs. He said, *"Gentlemen, it is now the 5th of March 1945 and during a raid in January of this year, American aircraft from their carriers sank twenty-four of our vessels as well as damaging another thirteen of them! We have a rather serious situation on our hands at the moment!*

The Vichy French Government that the French Colonists of French Indochina pledged allegiance to, no longer exists, and I fear that French Indochina and its French garrisons will become a direct threat to all Japanese soldiers stationed in French Indochina! It is highly likely that that they will in due course become part of the Allied push against our

---

[23] Vien, 2009.

Japanese homeland or even attack us right here, in French Indochina!

We must not let that happen, so, we shall strike first and so, nullify this threat! As well, when the American aircraft from the carriers attacked us, we managed to shoot down six of them. The crews from the aircraft were picked up by the French Colonial Authorities and they are currently detained in a Saigon Prison.

I have been in touch with the Vichy French commander called Decoux and I called upon him to surrender. However, he has declined to do so, and he is about to be replaced by Mordant. I have the Emperor's approval to use my judgement about this and we shall move against the French before they become a problem for us!

Lieutenant General Saburo Kawamura now spoke. He said, *"I also fear an attack upon us which shall be considerably aided by the French Colonists! I therefore completely support your plan to act first and stage a pre-emptive strike against the French by launching* **'Operation Bright Moon'** *, which is now the code name for the Japanese led coup d'état which will disarm the Vichy French Forces during or by the 9th of March 1945!*

The French have a long history of cowardly behaviour, and I strongly believe that they shall simply retreat when we attack them in order to safe-guard their rears! We should redeploy Japanese Forces right now so that we can stage the Coup d'état by the 9th of March!"

Coup d'état Against the French by the Japanese

During the first half of 1945, the French Colonial Forces still greatly out-numbered the Japanese in in south East

Asia, and they comprised some 65,000 men. Of these, 48,000 were locally recruited *"Tirailleurs Indochinois"* who were serving under the command of French Officers. The remaining French Forces were French regulars of the colonial army plus another three battalions of the French Foreign Legion.

However, since the fall of France in June of 1940, there had been no replacements of personnel or supplies from outside of French Indochina. That resulted in only 30,000 French Army Forces who could be described as being "Combat ready".

On the 7th of March Lt. General Tsuchihashi spoke to several of his sub-ordinates. He said, *"Decoux, the bloody leader of the French Forces in Indochina is wasting my time and he is just stalling in order to embarrass me! As well as embarrassing me, his stalling can easily result in either the British under Admiral Mountbatten or the Americans invading! I therefore order that an ultimatum be delivered to the French upstart called Decoux, telling him to surrender to Japan immediately!*

If he chooses not to comply, he shall find that Japanese Forces have moved into and now occupy every French centre! Fighting has taken place in Saigon, Hanoi, Haiphong, Nha Trang and along the northern frontier! As well, the 11th Régiment d'infantrie colonial based at Martin de Pallieres Barracks was surrounded and their commanding officer, Lieutenant Colonel Moreau was arrested! There has been small scale fighting in Hue! The Garde Indochinoise has been fighting us, and I expect them to fall in about eight hours from now!

As well, I have been informed that at the Lang Son areas near the Chinese border, the French under the command of General Emile Lemonnier are holding out against all Japanese attempts to take over the French fortress complex at Lang Son! That must be rectified immediately, otherwise our Japanese Forces will have enemies at their rears as well as possibly facing enemies from the front and sides!"

Battle of Lang Son

Now, came an interjection from a Japanese captain. He said, *"Sir, I am Captain Kayakawa, and I suggest that if you want to be successful in your coup d'état by the 9th of March 1945, it may be better to invite Lemonnier and other officers of the French Garrison at Lang Son to a banquet to be held at the headquarters of the 22nd division of the Japanese Imperial Army. If he chooses not to attend, we can still bring him to task. I also suggest that we put all of this into play immediately, because it is now the 7th of March, and you want the French to be overrun by the 9th of March! Therefore the time to act is now!"*

Due to French fears of invasion by Chinese forces, the French Colonial Army built a series of fortifications along the Sino-Vietnamese border. The main fortress was located at Lang Son, which is about eighteen kilometres from the border with China. The French named the main fortress as 'Fort Briere de l'Isle.' It had a garrison of four thousand men, many of whom were Vietnamese from the Gulph of Tonkin areas. Commanding the garrison was General Emile Lemonnier, who was also the commander of the border region. He was known to be patriotic and stubborn.

He had served in the French army in 1914 when he was a lieutenant in the 25th Artillery Regiment and during that time, he received several commendations. After the armistice of 1918, he transferred to the French Colonial Forces. As a member of that force, he served with distinction in various regiments of the 'Artillerie Coloniale.' Having impressed many others, he was made a Knight of the Legion of Honour in 1920. He continued to serve in French West Africa from 1925 to 1936. After returning to France, he left that country for the last time in 1937.

Lt General Tsuchihashi answered, *"Very well captain, go ahead and see if you can get that obstinate man to come to the banquet and if he does so, we can easily kill him! If he does not, we shall just have to take his forts by storm. One way or the other, we shall be victorious, and the French shall loose! In the meantime, I want all of the Vietnamese to be brought under our immediate control. No excuses shall be tolerated, just get it done!"*

So it was that Captain Kayakawa had an official invitation for the officers including the commander of the French force at Lang Son to attend a banquet at the 2nd division Headquarters drawn up and delivered. Upon being told of the invitation, it was immediately rejected by General Emile Rene Lemonier.

He said, *"So, the near sighted little brown monkeys called Japanese want me to go to their headquarters for a banquet? Bloody bullshit to that! It has all of the hallmarks of it being a trap! I am not stopping other officers from attending but be warned! Those of you who do attend this this bullshit banquet will be putting yourselves into harm's way! I fear the worst from these untrustworthy heathens called Japanese! The little brown monkeys are attempting deceive us! We can be certain that the so-called banquet is a trap from which there can be no escape!"*

Those French officers who had attended the banquet were arrested and taken prisoner. The Japanese captain Kayakawa demanded to know where the French general was. He was told, *"Sir, he never came. Apparently, he does not trust anyone who is not French, and even then, he is known to gather intelligence about that person before he sees him or her!"*

Captain Kayakawa said, *"So, it appears to we must take the French positions the hard way! Very well then! I want as much artillery as possible to be used against the French. Also, our Japanese battalions have the support of armoured units consisting of twenty-two light two-man crewed tanks! I want all of them to take part in our assault upon the French positions. We shall be victorious and have the French forts in Japanese possession by the 9th of March 1945. I will find the French General Lemonnier and he shall sign the document of surrender of all of his fortresses and men under arms!"*

The smaller forts surrounding the main French fort of Fort I'Isle were taken one by one until only the main fort was left. After sustained attack by Japanese artillery, infantry, and tanks, it also was about to fall, and that allowed Captain Kayakawa to find French General Lemonnier. Upon doing so, Kayakawa spoke to Lemonnier.

He said, *"Well, you arrogant French arsehole, you have lost all of your smaller forts and soon, we shall have this last one as well! Do something for the good of your men and order them to surrender. Also, I need you to sign the documents of surrender immediately."*

General Lemonnier answered, *"Go to hell, you jumped up little brown monkey! I shall never sign any document of surrender! Fuck you because you are a near-*

sighted little brown slant eyed monkey shithead!" Captain Kayakawa replied, *"You arrogant French arsehole! Both you and that other disgusting Frenchman called 'Camille Auphelle' shall be put to work in digging your own graves! While you are doing so, you shall be under the supervision of Sergeant Sato and his section.*

Be warned these men have just joined us after being transferred here from their previous posts as guards of Allied Prisoners of War who were building the Burma Railway. None of them will put up with any non-sense from the likes of you and you shall find that they just delight in watching white men like you, and other arrogant French suffer until you die!"

Having said that, Captain Kayakawa walked away while the two Frenchmen were left to the mercies of the brutal Japanese section. Sergeant Sato kept on at both men saying, *"Both of you lazy white men are working far too slowly! Get a move on with your work! You are only delaying the inevitable by being so slow and obstinate! Work faster and then you can die like men!"*

Both Auphelle and Lemonnier said to their Japanese tormentors, *"You want us to dig our own graves, therefore you can either dig them yourself or you can wait for as long as it takes, you fucking little brown monkey!"* Captain Kayakawa returned, and he was furious that there had been very little progress in the grave digging. He went to Lemonnier and said, *"I shall give you a final chance to redeem yourselves! Here is the official document of surrender of fort Briere l'Isle, sign it and you shall live!"* The French general replied, *"You little brown monkey, go and fuck yourself!"*

That aroused the fury of Captain Kayakawa who shouted, *"Sergeant Sato! You and your men shall now pinion the arms of both of these white men to their sides or better still, tie their hands together behind their backs! You shall then make both of them kneel. After that has been done upon my command of 'up,' you are to lift the hands of both men up high and hold them at the new height! Because they have their hands tied, that will result in them leaning forward with their necks sticking out. I shall then behead both of them with my sword!"* After the war, Kayakawa was tried for war crimes and executed.

Japanese Find the Viet Minh Hard to Fight

The Japanese attempted to disarm a group of Vietnamese patriots, (the newly formed Viet Minh commanded by Ho Chi Minh and Vo Giap). The Japanese thought that the Vietnamese nationalists would readily defect to the Japanese forces. Instead, when six hundred Japanese soldiers marched into Quảng Ngãi, the Viet Minh ambushed the Japanese.

The Viet Minh only lost three men killed In action (KIA) and another seventeen were wounded, but they killed one hundred and forty-three Japanese as well as wounding two hundred and fifty of them before they withdrew from their position. On the following day, a much bigger force of Japanese occupied the position after finding it empty.

At Haiphong, the Japanese assaulted the Bouet Barracks which also had the headquarters of Colonel Henry Lapierre's 1st Tokin Brigade. The Japanese used heavy mortar and machine gun fire. Attacking with ferocity, they took one French position after the other until the entire barracks fell, causing Lapierre to order a ceasefire. He refused to sign surrender papers for the remaining French garrisons in the area and chose instead to order the destruction of code books where-ever possible. That meant that the Japanese had to use force to subdue the other garrisons. Meanwhile, the Garde Indochinoise had fought for nineteen hours against the Japanese before their barracks was overrun and for the next three days they resisted the Japanese in spite of hunger, disease, and betrayals. After that, three hundred of them of which one third were French, managed to elude the Japanese and escape to A Sầu Valley.

There were also other actions against the Japanese in the north and in Laos. The Japanese attacks upon the French in the Northern Frontier was the scene of the heaviest fighting. Realising that they first had to take Lang Son, (strategic fort near the Chinese border with Vietnam.) the Japanese attack was delayed while they organised re-inforcements.

Independence?

Both before and after the Coup, the Japanese were trying to convince others that they had the interests of all Asian peoples at heart and they even said, *"We only invaded other Asian countries in order to remove the European and American white man from Asia. Stick with us Japanese, and together we shall make Asia great while we kick the whites out of the entire region! In order to do that, we will consult with you as to the best way forward in this glorious quest to remove the white man bully from all of Asia!"*

Due to instructions and orders that were sent by mail to the Japanese Chiefs of Staff commanding the conquered nations of French Indochina, an "O" among the Japanese General Staff was organised and put into place while the coup d'état was in the process of being carried out.

Present at the conference were Lt General Kayakawa, Lt General Tsuchihashi and captain Kawamura as well as many other Japanese officers. Also attending the conference were three men apparently not immediately connected with the Japanese. These were, Bao Dai of the Nguyen dynasty of the empire of Vietnam, King Norodom Sihanouk of Kampuchea, and King Sisavang Vong of Luang Prabang of Laos.

Proceedings were opened by Lieutenant General Tsuchihashi. He said, *"Gentlemen, by the grace of Emperor Hirohito of Japan, we shall now set up your independent countries! We have set up already, the new Empire of Vietnam which shall be headed by Bao Dai, the last of the Nguyen dynasty.*

Bao Dai shall have the continuous assistance of the Yokoyama Seiko, who is the Japanese Minister for Economic Affairs of the Japanese mission in Indochina. He shall be the key advisor to Bao Dai. We also want Bao Dai to appoint a government of which we approve and that must be headed by Tran Trong Kim. The Empire of Vietnam shall be free to make its own laws, but they must first be approved by Tokyo! All collected taxes must be paid to Tokyo!

As well, the people of Vietnam can forget about freedom of expression and freedom of speech! All people who are found to be critical of Emperor Bao Dai of Vietnam or Emperor Hirohito of Japan shall be deemed to be disrespectful. Those who are disrespectful and also are found to speaking against the ruling classes of either Japan or Vietnam shall be guilty of treason. King Norodom Sihanouk, we are granting you and your kingdom of Kampuchea freedom, but you shall be guided by Japanese officials at all times! Do you understand?"

King Sihanouk replied, *"I understand that you are granting my people a partial freedom which is always subject to Japan's approval! In short, you are saying that all three countries of Indochina shall look like they are free, but they will all have puppet governments that are subject to Japan! I think that is what you are saying!"* Lt. General Tsuchihashi replied, *"Yes, Your Majesty, that is correct! You and the other rulers of Indochina can govern your people, but the final word in everything shall came from Japan and taxes must be paid to Japan on time!"*

King Norodom Sihanouk said, *"No matter how you portray it, what you are offering us is in fact just a continuation of Japanese occupation and interference in the countries making up French Indochina. By you saying that everything must firstly be approved by Tokyo, you are telling us that we, the people of Indochina do not matter and that you shall always control everything about us! Instead of lying to us all of the time, why is it that you unwanted Japanese people do not just leave us alone and go back to Japan where you have originally come from? It is because of your actions that many people of the West are openly calling Japanese 'Little Brown Monkeys!' If you did not treat all other people with distain, then perhaps other people would take kinder views of the Japanese!"*

As soon as he finished saying that there was a loud voice agreeing with what he had said. That was the King Sisavang Vong of Luang Prabang (Laos). He said, *"I totally agree with what has been said by King Norodom Sirhanouk of Kampuchea! (Cambodia) He has correctly told you that the freedom that you say that you have given us is not freedom at all, so instead of continuing with typical Japanese lies, just leave French Indochina and leave us all alone. If you were to do that, you would find that much of the world opinion would start to favour Japan! So, just pack up* and leave from our countries! We, the people of Indochina are the only ones who have the right to be here!"

That in turn infuriated the Japanese overlords. Lt General Tsuchihashi now spoke. He said, *"Kindly get it through your thick skulls that it is only we, the Japanese who have the interests of other Asian peoples at heart! We are offering you and all Asians freedom if you join Japan to rid Asia of the menace of the Caucasian (white) race of oppressors! In order to achieve that, it requires you to do your part in ridding Asia of these European oppressors who take everything without asking and then just subjugate you!"* With that said, the meeting broke up and there was much distrust and bad feelings coming from it.

After Emperor Bao Dai, King Norodom Sirhanouk and King Sisavang Vong had left the "O" group, Lieutenant General Tsuchihashi spoke to the other Japanese officers who were still present. He said, *"Gentlemen, I do not trust that king of Kampuchea or the king of Laos at all! I gather by their attitudes, that they would much rather have the French back in control of South East Asia than Japan!*

It is because we cannot trust the kings of Kampuchea and Laos that I want contact made with the nationalist leader of Kampuchea. We must get him to come here and then we shall make him our puppet Prime Minister. King Norodom Sirhanouk shall have no say in the matter! He only rules in name and he shall remain loyal to Japan if he wants to or not!"

The Japanese then contacted the nationalist leader of Cambodia called Son Ngoc Thanh, who was living in Japan, having been exiled from his home country. The Japanese military contacted him, with Lt General Tsuchihashi saying, *"I want you to return to Kampuchea! We, the Japanese shall help you to take power! Kampuchea has King Norodom Sirhanouk as its head, but you can quickly become Prime Minister with Japanese blessings!"*

And so, he returned to Cambodia and became the Prime Minister. However, in Laos, things were not going so smoothly for the Japanese! King Sisavang Vong favoured a return to French rule and refused to declare independence and found himself at odds with his prime minister. By the 15th of May 1945, the coup d'état was complete, and the independent countries were set up. General Tsuchihashi declared the operations to be complete and that released several brigades for use on other fronts.

Aftermath of the Coup d' état of 1945

The coup had resulted in heavy French losses. 15,000 French soldiers were prisoners of the Japanese. Two French soldiers were discussing the current situation and what they thought had brought it all about. Pierre Montague said, "Hey Jacques, it has come to my attention that we lost fifteen thousand French soldiers as prisoners of the Japs! I began looking at the records of combat losses and I found that we only lost about four thousand and two hundred men killed in action (KIA).

Many more were executed by such things as beheading by the Japanese heathens after their surrenders. About one thousand men were lost during the fighting or else they were beheaded by the Japs! Over three thousands of our soldiers reached Chinese territory as part of the retreating French columns. Some of our native Indochinese soldiers managed to get away and re-join their original villages and towns in Indochina.

Meanwhile, in northern Vietnam, Ho Chi Minh has declared the independence of Vietnam and the formation of the Democratic Republic of Vietnam. His guerrilla army known as Viet Minh have started their campaign with the help of the American OSS (later to be re-organised and re-named as Central Intelligence Agency or CIA).

The Americans supplied the Viet Minh directly with arms, money, and training. In return the Viet Mihn attacked many Japanese outposts and managed to overrun some of them. It was from this time forwards that the Viet Mihn began their tunnels in order to remain an effective fighting force in spite of overwhelming numbers against them. The Viet Mihn established their bases without meeting much resistance from the Japanese. They kept on establishing bases throughout Vietnam and including tunnel systems which proved to be invaluable for them. A famine had begun, and it helped to cause resentment towards the Japanese and French overlords. The hate of the Vietnamese people spread to include the Americans when bombing by the USA contributed to the misery caused by the famine!

Viet Mihn Take-Over

Meanwhile, Japan surrendered when emperor Hirohito announced the surrender on the 16th of August 1945. Soon after, the Japanese garrisons handed control over to Bao Dai and the United Party. That allowed the nationalist groups to take over public buildings in most of the major cities. Meanwhile, the Japanese occupiers did not oppose the Viet Minh because they were reluctant to give the French a foothold in Vietnam again.

The entire French colonial system had collapsed overnight. Meanwhile a major famine was beginning to take hold. The seizure and hoarding of rice and speculation worsened an already dire situation. With the people ready to move in masses, the Viet Minh called upon them to intensify guerrilla activity and for the peasants to seize the stores of rice that were held by the Japanese[24].

Vietnamese Opposition to Chiang Kai Shek

There were serious external threats to the new nation, which were from countries outside of Vietnam. As part of the surrender agreements of the Japanese, all of Indochina was occupied above the 16th parallel by the armies of the Chinese Nationalist leader Chiang Kai-shek, while the south of Vietnam was occupied by the British Forces who were smoothing the way for the return of the French.

Chiang Kai-Shek's general Li Han called for an "O" group to be held on the 29th of December 1945. Addressing the Chinese Nationalist officers present he spoke. He said, *"I have orders from Chiang Kai-shek to take over in the north of Vietnam! Our leader wants the remnants of the former nationalist parties in Vietnam to be imposed upon people of Northern Indochina. By that I mean all of Indochina, meaning the countries of Cambodia, Laos, and Vietnam!"*

A Chinese major asked, *"And just how do you propose to do that sir? Northern Vietnam has an extremely popular set of leaders. In particular there are two of them that have significant importance. These men are known as President Ho Chi Minh and General Vo Nguyen Giap!"*

---

[24] Vien, 2009

General Li Han replied, *"By using the army of our leader Chiang Kai-shek to enforce our wills, we should be able to install the earlier nationalist leaders of Vietnam into power! They will not be able to do anything at all, they shall just be our puppets and enforce whatever we tell them to do! I have today sent an ultimatum the new Communist Government of Vietnam demanding the immediate sacking of all Communist Government Ministers and that the leadership of the government of the Democratic Republic of Vietnam is handed over to nationalist groups of Viet Cach and Viet Quoc. I also called for the immediate sacking of the President Ho Chi Minh!"*

The major said, *"Very amusing sir! Do you really think for just one moment that the people will do as you demand? If you actually believe what you have just said, then you are in for a rude awakening and that shall occur very soon, sir!"* Frustrated that he could not force the government of Vietnam to sack President Ho Chi Mihn and his ministers, the general called for eighty seats in the National Assembly of Vietnam be granted to Viet Quoc and Viet Cach. Ho Chi Mihn and General Vo Nguyen Giap were informed of that, and Ho Chi Mihn answered. He said, *"We shall counter what Chiang Kai-shek, and his army are doing! Chiang Kai-shek is a problem, but he is under threat from the revolution in his own country and he will find that even the continued support of the Americans cannot keep him in power! A far greater threat to the people of Vietnam and the other countries of Indochina, comes from the French colonists!"*

The Founding of the Democratic Republic

Because of being bought into power by an irresistible popular tide, the Provisional Government appeared before the people of Hanoi. On the 2nd of September 1945, members of the new government of the people spoke. At Ba Dinh Square, President Ho Chi Minh appeared before a great and enthusiastic crowd. To the crowd he proclaimed Vietnam's independence. He said: *"The French have fled, the Japanese have capitulated, Bao Dai has abdicated. Our people have broken the chains which fettered them for nearly a century, and they have won independence for Vietnam...our country has the right to enjoy freedom and independence and has become a free and independent country. The Vietnamese people are determined to mobilise their entire physical and intellectual strength and property to safeguard their freedom and independence[25]"*

In the streets of major cities and in the countryside, people were talking to each other with the joy that only full freedom can bring them. Typically, they said to each other, *"My fellow citizens and comrades, now, at last, after eighty years of foreign oppression and our revolutions, we the people of Vietnam finally have full independence. We will now have a new era beginning which will allow everyone to work towards the building of our new country!*

We have shown the world that we are prepared to shed blood, if need be, to defend that precious independence. We all know that our independence is being threatened from all sides and that we have no-one on our side. For those reasons, we must do everything ourselves! Added to this is the threat of famine which is everywhere in Vietnam. Some of this is caused by natural events like droughts, while much famine has been imposed upon us by the French and the fucking Japanese!

---

[25] Vien, 2009.

The British and French armies are about to land in areas around Saigon and in the north of Vietnam, the army of Chiang Kai-sheck is ready to invade us. We have no allies, and we stand alone against all who would yet again try to take us over! The only thing that we have on our side is the clear - and far-sighted leadership of the revolutionary party!"

On the 2nd of September 1945, the Central committee of the Viet Minh said, *"Our independence is still fragile. To seize power is difficult, but to preserve it is more difficult!"* Soon, the new government made the appeal of: *"At this moment, let all thoughts be turned to the struggle for independence, and each person's concern be the struggle against foreign aggression. Only at this price can we avoid annihilation and smash the yoke of slavery!*[26]*"*

Establishment of a National Democratic Peoples' State

Nguyen Khac Troang was in the company of some friends, and they were discussing events in Indochina and how things could be improved. Nguyen said to his friends, *"Comrades, it is peoples,' power that shall soon become the crucial factor that is safeguarding our independence and making sure that the revolution delivers what is has promised!*

The most important task is that of the defence of our country's independence and our borders. These things must take the priority at all costs! We must consolidate our national unity while we mobilize the great energy of our labouring masses! We must remain ever vigilant for

---

[26] Vien, 2009.

aggression from foreign imperialists who wish to again conquer us and to make us once again their slaves! We have to present a united solid front as a determined people, and we must be totally unwavering in our ideals, and we must use flexible tactics against all enemies! On the domestic front, we must win the fight against famine and press on with strengthening the Peoples' State and immediately put an end to illiteracy!"

His friends agreed with him and his friend, Quang said, *"The famine of 1944 has not yet been bought under complete control, and I have received word that the biggest flood in many years has or is about to hit the Red River Delta. Should that also happen, there will be series shortages of manpower, cattle, and seeds. We may even lose up to a third of our normal output of the November rice crop! Our new revolutionary government really has its work cut out for it!"*

The famine was a very Important issue and the major challenge for the new government. This caused Ho Chi Minh to speak to those in the conference with him. He said to them, *"Comrades, our people are starving and that is something which we must rectify immediately. I need your ideas of how best to solve the famine and I welcome all ideas! No ideas will be rejected out of hand and all ideas will be considered. I want your ideas of how we can rectify the situation in both the long and short terms!"*

His audience was speaking among themselves when a delegate said, *"Uncle Ho, I think that we must ration all rice and maize that happens to still be in Vietnam. Both the French and Japanese have taken much from us in food and a large part of that was used by the French to burn in order to generate electricity! In order to get the people to accept our orders of rationing of food, we, the leaders of the country must show our people that we also will be rationed like everyone else! When the people see us do this ourselves, they shall have complete faith in us. I therefore recommend that we launch a dual campaign against famine – for mutual aid and solidarity which will result in increased production. Over the long term, it is necessary to build more dykes and to maintain the present ones!"* So, it was that Ho Chi Minh announced these things.

His announcement caused hope and the excitement among the people of their newly found independence, inspired the people, with the result that they saved even tiny amounts of food and shared what they had with the neediest. All people cultivated even small plots of land. Short term crops, including sweet potatoes, cabbages and marrows were grown on all available soil, including public parks. Volunteers collected surplus food from homes and took it the neediest people.

Allied Take-over

Meanwhile, in Paris, the then French president Charles de Gaulle, was speaking to those around him. He was heard to say, *"France shall regain total control of French Indochina! Let no-one have any doubts about that! It is entirely the fault of the arrogant Americans and their even more arrogant British allies and partners in crime that the heroic French defenders of Indochina lost against the Japanese! The morons commanding British, and the USA forces did nothing to aid the French people of French Indochina during the Japanese occupation.*

It is because of the inaction of the British and the Americans that that all of French Indochina has been left in chaos by the Japanese occupation. I call upon the British and American governments to do something positive to return France's former colonies and territories back to France and to help France to install its will upon South East Asia in general!"

As result of that was joint discussions between the British and Americans about the best course of action in French Indochina. Jointly, they decided that the British Forces under the command of Admiral Mountbatten would pave the way for the return of the French Forces to Indochina! So it was that on the 11th of September 1945, British and Indian soldiers of the 20th Division under the command of Major General Douglas arrived in Saigon. This direct British interference in the affairs of the sovereign country of Vietnam was code named as **'Operation Masterdom'** by the British.

It was a post WW2 conflict mainly involving the British-Indian infantry forces and it was putting the French back into control in French Indochina. It did not matter to the British of how the feelings about the armed intervention by foreign forces were thought of by the Vietnamese, Laotian or Cambodian people! What is beyond dispute is that the British actions in Indochina paved the way for the return of the French Expeditionary Army Group.

As the French colonists returned to power in Indochina, they increasingly said to the local people, *"All of you people of Cambodia, Laos and Vietnam should now be thankful that France has recognised the monarchies and countries put into place by the Japanese. France shall continue to rule over all of Indochina, but each country within in shall have its own king or emperor.*

Each ruler shall have the power to conduct normal day to day running of their countries, but all laws passed, and all military alliances must be confirmed as legal by France! France shall always have the power to veto any law passed by any country! All resources shall be owned by France! French Law shall overrule all laws within all countries making up French Indochina!

In Vietnam Emperor Bao Dai shall continue to rule. He shall have the power to appoint who-ever he like as his prime Minister and other ministers! Rebellion against the Vietnamese Emperor and his officials shall be treated as rebellion against France and that is punishable by death!"

Those things were enforced, leaving the Vietnamese population more determined than ever to expel the foreign forces and those of the hated British and French in particular! While he was in command of the British forces in Saigon, General Gracey even re-armed Japanese Prisoners of War and then used them to enforce the return of the French Colonial Governments.

It was a similar story in Cambodia where King Norodom Sirhanouk undertook the role of being a puppet ruler for the French. While in Laos, King Sisavang Vong also had the power of being an absolute ruler, but always subject to French law and French interests. Over the years after World War Two, the American Central Intelligence Agency was to become increasingly involved in South East Asia.

Official American policy was to completely back-up the rule of corrupt officials in southern Vietnam after the Geneva conference on Indochina passed resolutions that wanted there to be a unification of Vietnam and stressed that free internationally supervised elections were to be held within a year from then. That did not suit the American aggressors. Instead, the Americans immediately set about the turning all of Vietnam below the 17th parallel into one huge American armed camp.

So it was that the administrations of the USA openly favoured telling Bao Dai what to do in order to rule in South Vietnam. The Americans then persuaded the French to put pressure upon Emperor Bao Dai to appoint Ngo Dinh Diem as his Prime Minister.

Bao Dai did as he was asked by the French and the Americans only to find that later, Diem was leading a plot to oust him and install himself as the first President of South Vietnam which was then called the Republic of Vietnam. That was organised by the CIA, and it had the backing of the entire Eisenhower Administration of the USA! One of the main supporters was the Vice President of the USA called Richard Nixon.

Meanwhile, the popular freedom fighting movement known as Viet Mihn had by now established the Democratic Republic of Vietnam. The Americans regarded that as a threat to American interests and so, what was only the people of a sovereign nation taking back their own country developed into a major but undeclared war!

It was a case of the super powerful USA, and its allies interfering where they had no right to be! It was the continuation of American hysteria about anyone or any country which had socialist or communist ideals. So, the "Cold War" between the West and the USSR began to have the potential to become ever hotter and the likelihood of World War Three and a nuclear exchange became increasingly probable!

Also, let us not forget the fact that China had deposed Chiang Kai Shek, and he was now taking refuge in the island of Formosa (renamed to Tiawan). China was mainly looking after its internal structure and was not a threat to American interests, no matter what the Americans say about this!

"The First Indochina War"

Things finally came to a head and resulted in the first shots of what became known as "The First Indochina War" being fired on the 23rd of September 1945 in Nam Bo and the uprising then spread throughout Vietnam like wildfire after 19th of December 1946. This was the result of almost one hundred years of exploitation by the French colonialists and their attempted enslavement of the Vietnamese people. This armed resistance to French rule was the most important concern of the National Liberation Front.

Although the task of liberating all of Vietnam was the main objective, the democratic rights of the people were no less important, in particular when you remember that that the struggle for freedom was led by a party of the working class and that the worker-peasant alliance made up the foundations of the united national front.

The resistance grew, as did the political and ideological consciousness of the masses. As that and the resistance grew, so did their class consciousness as well as their patriotism. All of that resulted in the need for increased material and manpower resources. The Vietnamese war of resistance against the French colonialism delivered a severe blow to the imperialist system. This resulted in the joining of forces by British, French and United States of America's imperialist systems which worked together to undermine the resistance.

The victory of the Chinese revolution and the founding of the Peoples' Republic of China in October 1949 altered the balance of power of the world's armed forces. In order to make up for its failure of policy regarding China, the USA triggered a war of aggression in Korea and began to openly intervene in Indochina. With the attention of the USA being focussed on Korea and other places, Vietnam was geographically isolated and therefore the fight was between the Vietnamese people and French colonialism[27].

Battles at Hanoi and Lo River

At the French Command Headquarters, senior officers were conferring with the French High Commissioner, who had the name of Bolaert. He bluntly said, *"Gentlemen, I hereby declare that the French military forces shall have a say in all matters of the entire Indochina region and that includes the way the people of the region live and play. The job of you gentlemen and of all French armed forces in South East Asia is to swiftly destroy the poorly armed and inexperienced Vietnamese forces and to quickly capture the resistance group leaders. I want you to immediately use our clear superiority in all armaments and the capacity of French regular troops to wipe out the rebels and to bring their leaders to trial by Court-Martial!*

After the leaders have had a fair French trial by Court-Martial, they will be taken to a place of execution and shot as the sentence for committing treason against France! Do not take any excuses for not doing the job of bringing the inhabitants of Indochina to heel. Just look at the difference in forces! We have the cream of the French and indeed, the world's finest forces which includes the French Foreign

---

[27] Vien, 2009.

Legion. The Viet Minh have inexperienced and poorly armed guerrillas, so there can be no real contest! French forces will win!"

Pitted against the French forces was the Vietnamese resistance which although poorly armed, was based upon political superiority and heroism of the people. The people had complete confidence in their government to wage and win a drawn-out war. Because the entire population took part in a total war which covered all domains, this was called a Peoples' War! A popular slogan was, *"The resistance is bound to win!"* In 1946, vast liberated areas formed powerful rear-guard bases. The Viet Bac, a mountainous region between the Chinese border and the Red River, was the cradle of resistance. However, even in enemy-held areas guerrilla activity existed; people sheltered partisans and dedicated activists. The bases were always developing and threatened the French from the rear.

At a Party meeting held to discuss the brewing war of independence from French colonialism, a delegate said, *"The problem of the Viet Minh is the development of armed forces which are particularly suited to peoples' war. In this regard, I suggest that we use local self-defence forces made up of guerrillas operating in their villages while continuing their farm work. As well, regional forces which must cover large areas and well-trained regular forces which are capable of mounting full-scale operations against the enemy troops must be set up and both armed and maintained!"*

That was immediately voted upon by the Party Central Committee, which approved this plan. Next a platoon commander of the Viet Minh forces spoke saying, *"Comrades, those of us who happen to be in units which take on the French army must have good reliable and modern* weapons as well as a plentiful supply of ammunition for them. The is now little likelihood of us being able to obtain weapons and ammunition from the European Allies or the USA.

Therefore, we must get our weapons from other socialist countries such as USSR! I would like us to have the M1941 and M1943 82 mm mortars which we should be able to get from USSR. Also, it would be nice to obtain the Russian 7.62 mm Degtyarev Light Machine gun and possibly the Russian Ak 47 or the Simonov 7.62mmm semi-automatic carbine. If we could have Russian rocket launchers similar to the Bazooka, that would be marvellous!

We have managed to obtain many 75 mm Japanese Mountain guns which are ideally suited to being dismantled and transported to other areas using pack animals or humans as the means of transport. I suggest that we use the captured Japanese mountain guns in assaults against the French. We have both many guns and a plentiful supply of ammunition for them!"

The Central committee of the Party discussed what he said and approved everything that he was asking for. With it being known that political and ideological education of the armed forces was the heart of the resistance, much time was devoted to these things as well the training of the Viet Minh soldiers to be completely ready and to know the cause of their country. All of these things were bought together and used effectively right from the first major battle, the Battle of Hanoi. The French command from General Leclerc downwards boasted, *"Our superior French forces can wipe out the resistance within twenty-four hours because they are only backward heathens and uncultured, unlike us, so we will soon put them to the test!"* The test when the French began to put it into place did not give the result the French were expecting.

For two months the *"Regiment of the Capital"* was supported by the population and had dug in behind houses while they also operated in the streets. They were successful in tying down a well-trained army of six thousand five hundred men supported by forty tanks and armoured vehicles plus thirty aircraft. The patriots inflicted severe losses upon it, killing five hundred French and wounding a further one thousand five hundred. This resulted in a two-month delay which considerably slowed down the French strategy while also giving the resistance time to organise.

More reinforcements arrived over time which allowed the French Expeditionary Corps to extend its control. In particular in the major cities which the resistance did not try to hold. Some towns were destroyed by the inhabitants in order to prevent enemy troops from occupying them. All over the country of Vietnam French soldiers were harassed by guerrillas.

Operation Condor

This was the attempted weakening of Viet Minh artillery assaults against the surrounded French garrison at Dien Bien Phu. The French general Cogny, Captain Jean Sassi and General Navarre were discussing operations during an "O" group held to discuss ways of getting the Viet Minh out of their high ground positions overlooking the French Garrison at Dien Bien Phu.

Captain Jean Sassi spoke. He said, *"My dear generals, I know that I can break through all of the enemy positions and with my men assisting, we shall create havoc for the Viet Minh! They shall lose their prized high ground positions as a result of what I can do to them!"*

That aroused the interest of General Cogny who now spoke. He said, *"Do you really have a solution to the Viet Minh holding the high ground and having concrete casements built upon it for their artillery and mortars?"* Jean replied, *"Yes, you had better believe it! I shall lead the GCMA Malo-Servan commando unit which consists of Méo partisans through the jungle and cause havoc among the Viet Minh positions! First, we need to be air dropped about fifty kilometres away from Dien Bien Phu, after which we can walk through the jungle until we get to our objectives of the Viet Minh gun positions on the high ground surrounding Dien Bien Phu.*

Among my objectives shall be to force a breakthrough with the help of French Union soldiers based on Elaine Hill in order to surround the coolies supplying the Viet Minh combatants and to suddenly attack those weak "Little brown monkeys" using the element of surprise! When we achieve that, it will create much confusion among the enemy Vietnamese! In order for my commando to get close to the Vietnamese, my men and our Hmong partisan friends shall be wearing the black clothing of the Viet Minh, and we are equipped with sub machine guns and rifles."

General Navarre said, *"Assuming that all will work out for the best, when can you have you force ready for action, Jean?"* Jean replied, *"We can be ready for action on the 30th of April, why do you ask?"* The general replied, *"If you can be ready by then, that is good! However, I do not think that you have let yourself enough time to get everything ready, after all, it is the 27th of April today!"*

Jean's commando units consisted of several teams. The Sam Neua team was in the advanced position and closer to Dien Bien Phu. As it got closer to Sassi's team, they showed the way to the outpost. (that involved tying tape to trees, so that other groups of soldiers could find their way to attack Bien Dien Phu outpost by simply following the tape tied to the trees in order to get through thick jungle and find the objective at Dien bien Phu.) However, unknown to Jean, the Viet Minh had been actively carrying out aggressive patrolling and discovered the tape tied to the trees, and simply reversed the direction shown. That resulted in the Hmong partisans becoming lost and Operation Condor was added to the growing list of French failed operations against the Viet Minh. They were only a few kilometres from Elaine Hill, but they could not reach their objective, and Elaine Hill fell to the Viet Minh on the 31st of April.

First of March 1947

With the wind blowing hard during a storm, Edeltraut Zimmermann began her journey from her home to 1054 Olpenner Strasse in Cologne, West Germany. Underway, she was wishing that the wind would die down and not push her little car around so much, as it was becoming difficult to control. Finally she arrived and rang the doorbell of the large house. Anna Kramer (nee Ahrens), the mother-in-law of Hildegard Kramer received her warmly, and ushered her to where Hildegard was in labour.

Edeltrout sized up the situation and then felt around Hildegard and she pronounced that this was going to be a breech birth. That meant that the child was positioned the wrong way and was about to be born feet first instead of the normal head-first birth. It was just as well that Edeltrout was experienced in assisting during such difficult births. As Hildegard pushed, she found that things were becoming more painful constantly. As the baby finally emerged, Edeltraut rotated it. Soon afterwards, there was the sound of an infant crying. Edeltrout then cut the umbilical cord and washed the baby before she handed it over to Hildegard. She said, *"Congratulations, Mrs. Kramer you have a fine and healthy son!"* Hildegard accepted her new boy with great love and relief.

Hildegard was born a Prussian, and therefore, she followed her family's Prussian tradition of giving the first son four Christian names. She named her son as Michael Georg Kaspar Friedrich Kramer. Many years later, that was to become a problem for Michael.

From now on, I will refer to Michael by his preferred name of Mick; that is also the name that most people who came into contact with him knew him by. His father, Friedrich Wilhelm Paul Kramer will from now on simply be referred to as Fritz the younger, in order to not confuse him with his father of the same name.

Michael's mother, Hildegard Kramer, was industrious and skilled in knitting and sewing of clothing. These skills were of great importance to the Kramer family in postwar Germany, in particular during 1947 to 1949, when there were shortages in the community of many items, including footwear and clothing. So, after recovering from giving birth to Mick, she began to jumpers and pants for her infant son. After she had consistently worked on making new items, she finally decided that she had made enough clothing for her son. She then enrolled Mick into a kindergarten and went to work on the reconstruction effort that was evident throughout Germany.

Due to the huge number of buildings that were little more than the shells of walls and the fact that these were a constant danger to the public because of the high likelihood of people being injured by falling masonry, many people formed work-gangs to demolish the bombed out buildings and to re-use the material for new buildings. That was to mark the beginning of what people around the world termed as "The Economic Miracle of West Germany." The Chancelor of West Germany during this time was Conrad Adenauer.

On the twenty-eighth of November of 1948, Andreas Christopher Kramer was born. He was a healthy baby, and his birth occurred without any complications. Once again, his birth took place in the home of Fritz Kramer the elder at 1054 Olpenner Strasse Cologne. By now, some of the difficulty in obtaining things had eased and Hildegard was able to purchase a well-made pram which had large wheels.

Hildegard walked into the Cologne CBD on a regular basis, after first catching a tram running between as tram stop located four hundred metres from Olpenner Strasse in a neighbouring street. The city-scape of Cologne was a scene of destruction with the damage caused by the war still plainly evident. Even now in 2025, Mick remembers what the streets of the CBD of Cologne looked like in 1949.

That was the scene when Hilgard took her two sons into the Cologne CBD on the 18th of December 1949. Mick, who was now a toddler, could walk quite well. So, Hildegard took him, and his brother Andy, who was in the pram to the kindergarten where both boys would spend the day until they were collected by their mother. They were almost at the kindergarten, when an unknown woman approached them and began screaming at Hildegard.

She screamed, *"You fucking high-class arseholes are all alike! You live in a totally undamaged house which is large enough to accommodate other people and it has heating. You could easily let other people like me live there, but you will not do that because you are too busy with your superior airs and graces to let other people like me live in your house.*

It is because of the likes you and other people like you, that others like me have to live among the bombed out ruins of the city. On top of all of that, you, and the others like you have the nerve to look down upon other people like me, you are a rotten high-society bitch!" Hildegard, being the daughter of a Prussian financier and banker, immediately said, *"Yes, I am High of High Society, and in total control of my destiny unlike lower-grade people such as yourself. Yes, I live in a totally undamaged house and the likes of you can never enter it! So, instead of bemoaning your fate, get on with your life you low-grade person, and return to the gutter where you belong and let the diligent people of the city get on with rebuilding it and their own lives, you low-grade gutter bitch!"*

Hildegard's husband, Fritz Kramer the younger, had just returned from the assembly line of the now General Motors car known around the world as Opel. He worked for the company as one of the production line supervisors.

When Hildegard told him about the encounter with the strange woman in the CBD of Cologne, he said, *"Well, my dear, I personally think that you have done the correct thing and to hell with the stupid bitch! I am sure that we can expect a lot more of this kind of thing to happen. The simple fact is that many people are desperate to have good shelter and heating.*

They are also likely to be very envious of those people, like us, who have those things. I shall inform my cousin who is a lieutenant in the Cologne Police Force about this this. We should also keep an eye on this situation and if this sort of thing continues to happen, then we must consider various alternative solutions to the problems."

Hildegard was thrilled by that response, because she took it as a hint that Fritz was considering leaving Europe. For a long time, she had wanted to leave Europe and its petty international squabbles and the possibility of war because of them.

She wanted to be free of the threat of war consuming her children and she also wanted her sons to grow up in a country which had little likelihood of experiencing war directly. So, she said, *"Fritz, I have been investigating the possibility of us all leaving Germany and moving to another country. I firmly believe that we must live in your birthplace of Swakopmund, Australia or Canada. So, Fritz, where do you think we should go?"*

Fritz answered, *"If we go to German South West Africa, it will be like returning home. However, we must remember that after World War One, the victorious British have taken over everything there, including my father's two diamond mines. They are now owned and operated by British owned or approved companies.*

Even though Swakopmund has a whole suburb named after my father, I suspect that the British authorities will not take kindly to a German returning to Swakopmund, in particular now that the full atrocities of the NAZI Government of Germany have become common knowledge. We must be practical. Let us face it: if we stay here, we have a substantial home with heating, food, clothing, and footwear.

We do not have to learn a foreign language and we can stay among our own people! As well, I have a responsible work position right here, and there is no guarantee that I could even obtain work in another country. Therefore, I favour staying here in Germany, even though things may become difficult for the next few years."

That did not suit Hildegard at all. She said, *"I want my sons to grow up in a country where there is little likelihood of it becoming involved in a war! I do not want my children to experience war, no matter what the circumstances. Fritz, you are very good at speaking many foreign languages and I know that you already speak fluent English, so how about us migrating to Australia?"*

Michael's father, Fritz Kramer the younger, replied, "Hildegard my Love, are you really serious? Already we live in a very large and comfortable home which is large enough to accommodate us and our expending family. I have a responsible position at Opel, and it pays me good money. All we have to do is to keep on going and in time, all will be well! Cologne is already rebuilding, and it is just a matter of time before all of this war damage is just a memory.

I am really against us leaving Germany. It will be hard for us in English speaking countries because of World War Two, but if you still feel this way about it all in a year from now, then perhaps we should consider it. We shall need to consider all financial matters, including the probable cost of both building and the purchase of existing houses. We must also consider how we will be received by the populations of where-ever we go to! It will not take the local *people long to realise that we are Germans! Consider that Germans are not very popular people anywhere in the world at the moment!"*

Hildegard became alarmed that the idea of leaving Germany may be shelved, so she forcibly said, *"Fritz, you have a choice, either start doing what is necessary for us to migrate to Australia or Canada, or I will do so own my own and take my children with me. The choice is your's to make!"*

Although the idea of migrating to another country seemed totally crazy to Fritz, he contacted the Australian Immigration Department Office in Cologne and found out about assisted passage from Germany to Australia and what that required of him and his family.

Operation Vulture!

Meanwhile, the French forces surrounding Bien Dien Phu were almost in a state of panic, as they discussed the background and that the Viet Minh forces commanded by general Vo Nguyen Giap had surrounded the French at Dien Bien Phu. The Viet Minh could hardly believe that the French forces had been placed into a very compromising situation by having their forces sited into a flat area surrounded by high ground. That flies in the face of well-known tactics of *"Take and hold the high ground at all costs!"*

The French arrogantly thought that the Viet Minh had no artillery or mortars. However, the Viet Minh had captured Japanese Mountain Guns of 75 mm calibre. These guns were easily dismantled into component parts such as the breech, mountings, bipod or tripod, barrel, and wheels. These could then be easily transported to where they were required for use and re-assembled. As well, they had 81 mm and 82 mm mortars which were also used against the French with devastating effect! The Viet Minh attacked the French as of the 13th of March 1954.

The French tried to control things and even tried hitting back using their artillery and aircraft. These aircraft included thirty US supplied C-119 flying boxcars which had been converted into bombers which could drop napalm upon the Viet Minh artillery positions, and they were flown by American pilots! They were directly employed by 'Civil Air Transport,' which was the name of this mercenary air unit. It was commanded by Major General Claire Lee Chennault, who had commanded the WW2 *'Flying Tigers'*.

Dien Bien Phu could only be supplied by air drop and the drop zone was shrinking fast because of Viet Mihn gains of French territory and their artillery having a dramatic effect upon the French, many of whom were now either wounded or dead.

At an "O" group called to discuss the worsening supply and combat situations of the French, a colonel of the French forces called Jean Louis Nicot spoke his mind. He said, *"I am the officer in charge of aerial resupply, and I know that it is too dangerous for our pilots to be dropping resupplies from low altitudes. Therefore, I am ordering that all resupply drops from now onwards shall be changed from 2,000 feet to 8,000 feet altitude! That shall apply immediately! There shall not be any change to that command!"*

It was because of the raise in the altitude of the dropping height that accuracy declined, and many supplies fell into the hands of the Viet Minh. With these events causing near panic among the French based in Saigon, they pressed for the Americans to launch overwhelming airstrikes to save Bien Dien Phu.

Meanwhile, back in Paris, the French leader, Charles de Gaulle, was in conference with his military advisors. Addressing all of them he said, *"What is it about warfare that you clowns do not understand? Why is it that the cream of the French forces is bottled up in Bien Dien Phu which is in the far north-west of Vietnam and it is almost in Laos. Why is it that none of you clowns cannot beat the rag-tag army made up of the 'Little Brown Monkeys'?"*

That was answered by the French Chief of staff, called General Paul Ely. He said, *"President de Gaulle, the Viet Mihn whom many people including the British, French and Americans like to call 'Little Brown Monkeys', have both artillery and mortars which they use with devastating effect against all French forces at Bien Dien Phu. Part of the reason for that is the location of the Bien Dien Phu battlefield is surrounded by high peaks and the Viet Minh have been successful in getting their artillery to the top of those peaks which allows them to pour fire directly into the French base on the plain below them."*

De Gaulle could not believe what his ears were hearing. At first, he was stunned and after recovering his composure he said, *"God almighty! Am I surrounded by fucking idiots? Do you really mean to tell me that the entire French forces are on a plain overlooked by high ground upon which the VietMinh have placed their artillery which you told me they do not have?*

Are you people fucking mad or are you just stupid? All of you are senior officers of the French Defence Forces and none of you blinking idiots appear to know the fact that upon going to an area and setting up any type of base, you must firstly take and hold the high ground! God, save me from you fucking fools!"

General Paul Ely said, *"Cursing us will not improve the situation sir! The only way forward for France is for me to travel to Washington and plead the French case for American help directly to the American policy makers. I have arranged for me to be in Washington for just that on the 20th of March 1953!"* Charles de Gaulle replied, *"Well do not just fuck around this time! This time you must get things done!"* And so, General Paul Ely of France had a closed meeting in Washington with the US Secretary of State John Foster Dulles and the chairman of the joint Chiefs of staff, Admiral Arthur W Radford.

During the meeting, Admiral Radford said, *"General Ely, you worry too much! We have a plan which we shall give the code name of 'Operation Vulture.' Using this plan involves the use of sixty B29 bombers based in the Philippines and escorted by fighters from the Seventh Fleet. They shall bomb the fuck out of the Viet Mihn positions besieging the French at Dien Bien Phu!"* Accordingly, General Ely came away from the conference with the impression that the Americans would intervene on the French side, and he reported to Paris that he had the co-operation of the USA.

Operation Vulture – the Plan

On the 24th of March 1953, the Secretary of State of the USA, called John Foster Dulles said, *"Indochina is the top priority in foreign policy, being in some ways more important than Korea because the consequences could not be localised but would spread throughout Asia and Europe!"*

During a discussion between the chiefs of the General staff of the USA, involving what should be done about the freedom fighting activities of the people of Indochina. Vice President Richard Nixon was heard to say, *"So, you are telling me that the slope-headed Gooks want and deserve freedom! Well, let me tell you how that will affect both the American and the British peoples! Firstly, by letting the people of Indochina become free and letting them decide what is or is not right for them and for the betterment of their people, we can expect that all of Asia will become a communist armed camp! That must not be allowed to happen! Already, the British are fighting insurgents in the Malayan states of, Singapore, and in the outer Malaysian states of Sarawak and Sabah which are located on the island of Borneo. That area is now a problem in so much as the rest of the island of Borneo belongs to Indonesia and the president of that country, Doctor Sukarno has official ties to the communist government of the USSR!*

We can therefore colour all of Indonesia either pink or red which shows that the Indonesians are extremely likely to either be or about to become communist or socialist! If the countries of French Indochina become free and decide to join with their Indonesian neighbours, the whole of Asia, other than Japan and South Korea will be aligned with communist governments or supporters of the communists! Secondly, the Indochinese people must not be allowed to have independence from France because the French are keeping those slope-headed gooks in their place! They must never have freedom, and they must always be controlled by western powers!

At the moment, the French are in difficult circumstances in the north-western part of Vietnam at a base area called Bien Dien Phu. The French commanding General has been foolish enough to site his base area on a large flat plain which is surrounded by hills and mountains!

The French are so arrogant that they believed the Viet Minh could never obtain neither mortars or artillery and even if they managed to do so, the Viet Minh could never get those weapons up the hills and mountains through thick jungle. However, not only have the Viet Minh obtained artillery and mortars, but they have also placed them upon the high ground surrounding the French base at Dien Bien Phu, which is now in great peril!

Accordingly, I propose that the USA joins with Britain and that together, we apply all of 'Operation Vulture,' which will result in the Viet Minh being wiped out in their positions surrounding Bien Dien Phu and the French Forces shall thus be relieved! That will be the end of our current problem! I also favour the immediate sending in of American infantry and other ground troops to aid the French efforts in Indochina! So, gentlemen, let us get 'Operation Vulture' up and running before we all end up being sorry for not acting decisively when we had the chance do so!"

John Foster Dulles, the USA Secretary of State entered the conversation. He said, *"Vice President Nixon, I am most glad that you have this hawkish view as to what the USA must do in Asia to ensure French victory against the god damned gooks! I support completely your idea of sending American ground forces to Indochina to help the French maintain their sovereignty there!*

The only thing we lack is the will of the American people to enter another war, because World War Two is still fresh in the minds of many Americans who lost members of their families who died while fighting for the USA, and we are already fighting the North Koreans and Chinese in South Korea! I am hoping for the British to join us in implementing 'Operation Vulture,' which will end the plans of the little slant eyed monkeys to become independent!"

Admiral Radford said, *"Gentlemen, I also support the immediate implementation of both the entire Navarre Plan and also that we implement 'Operation Vulture' in its entirety! It will be good to see those Viet Minh slope-heads wiped from the map and for the French to maintain control of the gooks!"*

Next, President Eisenhower spoke! He said, *"Whoa gentlemen! We must not act too hastily! For all of 'Operation Vulture' to be implemented, the USA must not act alone as world opinion will be decidedly against us! We do have the means to do this militarily, however, unless we are joined in 'Operation Vulture' by the British, we must abandon the whole idea! I have been having strategic discussions with the British leaders about all of this and I must admit that the British are luke-warm about the idea of us invading yet another Asian country without justification or provocation at best! Our British allies have told me that if the USA goes ahead and implements 'Operation Vulture' without consulting the British, that we shall be entirely on our own!*

Their reason for having such a timid approach to the problem is that 'Operation Vulture' calls for using nuclear weapons against the Viet Minh positions or else using aerial bombing of those positions with napalm. The US Army Chiefs of staff are against the use of 'Operation Vulture' because of the likelihood that American soldiers will be drawn into a bottomless pit into which we shall be pouring the lives of thousands upon thousands of Americans! Therefore, as president of the USA, I rule that unless Britain joins us in 'Operation Vulture,' it must be called off! Not only that but consider that fact that 'Operation Vulture' has several versions!"

Plans were draw up for the Americans to help out the French by suppling and crewing U.S. B-29 bombers, some of which were armed with nuclear weapons. Officially, the were no American ground troops or combat pilots actively assisting the French in Indochina. However, that does not account for the fact that American adventurers were active as pilots for the French through their connection with 'Civil Air Transport,' the mercenary unit which was flying the thirty US supplied 'C-119 Flying Box Cars' which had been converted into bombers which were to drop napalm upon the Viet Mihn positions.

(1) This alternative version of 'Operation Vulture' required the sending of 60 B-29 bombers based in Gaum or the Philippines and supported by up to 150 fighter aircraft from the US Seventh fleet. This plan included the option to use up to three nuclear weapons on the Viet Mihn positions in support of the French colonial forces! That was supported by Admiral Radford, the chief of Staff of US Forces. As well, American adventurers were serving as either outright mercenary soldiers or they were members of French units such as the French Foreign Legion. The USA was supplied the money for the French aggression against the people of Indochina, even though the USA was officially neutral. The USA directly supplied American arms and war materials to France[28]. In fact, America supplied 900 combat vehicles, 15,000 other military vehicles, 2,500 artillery guns, 24,000 automatic weapons, 75,000 small arms, 9,000 radios[29].

America also provided 160 F-6F Hellcat and F-8F Bearcat fighter aircraft, 41 B-26 light bombers and 28 C-47 transport planes. Pilots were also supplied but covertly, using the 'Civil Air Transport' mercenary unit as a cover. Even so, the Viet Mihn noose around Dien Bien Phu was tightening and the alarmed French sent General Ely to

---

[28] Readers wanting more detail on this should go to "A Gracious Enemy & After the War Volume One."
[29] Vien, 2009.

Washington in order to lobby the US administration to send US bombers to help lift the siege of Dien Bien Phu. Some of the US administration agreed with the French General Ely. Among them were Vice President Nixon, who wanted American ground troops to be sent in. As well, the Chairman of the joint chiefs of staff, Admiral Arthur Radford and the US Air force Chief of Staff, Nathen F Twining pushed for 'Operation Vulture' to be fully implemented.

Advising against it was the US Army Staff General Mathew Ridgway. He was heard to say, *"We must not become bogged down in a land war against the Asian people, it would become a quagmire into which American units will sink without clear victories against the enemy! As to 'Operation Vulture,' I think we should cancel it because it is likely to involve us in direct combat with either China or the Soviet Union and therefore, World War Three!*

We must not let that happen. When talking about taking on the Asian peoples now, America must get rid of the old delusive idea that America can do things in the cheap and easy way! I urge our president to consider that air power alone cannot defeat the Viet Mihn, they are fighting to take their own country back!

When the day comes for me to face my Maker, and account for my actions, the thing I would be most proud of is the fact that I fought against and perhaps prevented the carrying out of one of the most hare-brained tactical schemes that would have cost the lives of thousands of men!" Eventually common sense prevailed, and 'Operation Vulture' was called off mainly due to British reluctance to proceed with such an aggressive idea!

Interference in the Affairs of Indochina Since 1950

There were many meetings between the American President and the general staff of the American Armed Forces which also included the entire USA cabinet. Of great concern, the continuing problem of the wars of liberation in South Eastern Asia! It was during one these meetings that Vice-President Richard Nixon spoke.

He said, *"Mister President, you have been asking me and the other members of the cabinet of the United States of America to not spend so much money on the Indochinese War and to make sure that the USA has the correct outcome from the Indochinese liberation wars that fits in with our hard-line policies of supporting right-wing governments of whom we approve! It is now the year of 1950, and I want a military mission from the Armed Forces of the USA to immediately go to Indochina and actively advise the French Colonial Forces on all matters. That must also include increasing amounts of direct US military aid in the form of supplies of ammunition, weapons, vehicles, and radios which shall be directly supplied to where they are needed by the French in Indochina!*

It is very clear that the USA must Immediately obtain strong and legal footholds within Indochina that shall give us the right to permanently have US run and staffed bases within countries such as Vietnam. In that country, we have the Japanese installed and French approved puppet ruler, the so-called Emperor Boa Dai! He is weak willed, and he is a push-over for anything that the USA wants done! However, I know that the Vietnamese freedom fighters called Viet Minh are also aware of that and they are likely to court his favour as well! We cannot let that happen!"

So it was that Richard Nixon was answered by President Eisenhower. He said, *"All of what you have just said is all very well to say, but Richard, please tell me how you are proposing to accomplish it without getting us into a war with the Soviet Union or China?"*

Richard Nixon replied, *"I want to see the USA propose and implement a legal treaty of "Economic Co-operation" directly between Emperor Boa Dai of the southern region of Vietnam and the USA! The agreement must include the USA to having the right to equip, train and control a new armed force. In order to help us to effectively control things in southern Vietnam, I want to see Emperor Boa Dai appoint a staunch anti-communist like Ngo Dinh Diem as the replacement of Prime Minister who is currently the Japanese installed puppet called Tran Trong Kim Just remember that he was installed by the Japs!*

As well, I recommend that we send a high-ranking mission made up of myself, General Daniels, John Foster Dulles, and support staff to sign, seal and deliver the "Economic Co-operation" agreement between Emperor Bao Dai and the USA which must contain clauses that allow the USA to do whatever we Americans think is correct, no matter how the Indochinese people feel about it! We must stop communism spreading! In time, we shall invade and conquer the north of Vietnam which is now called the Democratic Republic of Vietnam! Only then will we in the west be able to relax!"

Accordingly, the *"Economic Co-operation Treaty"* between Washington and Emperor Bao Dai was signed in 1951. Four years later, in 1955, Ngo Dinh Diem ousted Emperor Bao Dai and became the first president of the Republic of Vietnam, a country which came into existence as a front for what was to become one huge American armed camp after fake referendums were held which were supported by newspapers in Australia, Britain, France, and most of English-speaking world.

That resulted in much pressure being applied upon the French Administration which allowed the American agents to be installed into the Boa Dai puppet administration in return for vastly increasing amounts of military aid. By 1953, the USA granted the vastly increasing amounts of aid to the French administrators in return for the full implementation of the Navarre Plan which allowed American General O'Daniel to lead missions in Vietnam.

The Navarre Plan

US aid to the French in Indochina rose to 385 million dollars in 1953, covering 60 percent of the expenditure on the war. By 1954, this had risen to 80%. American arms totalled 25,000 tonnes per month in 1953 and 88,000 tonnes by July 1954. American missions led by high-ranking officials included the Secretary of State John Foster Dulles and Vice President Richard Nixon. Nixon participated directly in working out France's military strategy. Airlifts were organised in France, the Philippines and Japan to supply the French Expeditionary Corps and American pilots took part the operations against the Vietnamese people[30]!

Washington tried to prevent the holding of the Geneva conference on Indochina and failed in that attempt. The Americans then concentrated on undermining the accords and agreements reached at the conference and supported moves by the agents of the puppet Bao Dai administration for the unconditional surrender of the Vietnamese resistance and the grouping of imperialist and local reactionary forces in South East Asia into a coalition which would have allowed them to continue the war. The scheme failed and the Geneva Conference closed on the 20th of July 1954 with the drawing up of agreements putting an end to the war. Meanwhile, the American administration in

---

[30] Vien, 2009.

Washington had managed to persuade the French to accept Ngo Dinh Diem as Bao Dai's prime minister in June 1954.

Repression and War

The Americans were not prepared to accept the peace agreements and immediately began to set-up a new strategy. The objective of which was clearly aimed at turning southern Vietnam into a new type of US colony which allowed the Americans to have a political and strategic base from which the USA could dominate South East Asia. In September 1954, a South East Asian Military Organisation, (SEATO) was set up. That included (USA, Britain, France, Australia, Pakistan, New Zealand, Thailand, and the Philippines and was used as later excuses for unauthorised military aggression by the allies against Indochina.

On the 28th of April 1956, French soldiers finally left Vietnam, but the French side-stepped their responsibilities of implementing the Geneva agreements which provided for general elections to achieve a peaceful re-unification of North and South Vietnam. The French approved of and used the Japanese installed puppet emperor called Bao Dai and in 1954, the Americans got him to appoint Ngo Dinh Diem as Prime Minister of South Vietnam.

Having helped their puppet rulers of southern Vietnam set up an illegal armed force, the Americans decided to train it as well as equip it. The insignia of the ARVN, (Army Republic of Vietnam, meaning South Vietnam) were all originally based upon French designs. As the war dragged on, The Americans decided to change the rank structure of the ARVN as well as the insignia to resemble USA ranks more closely in 1967.

Migration Agreement with Australian Government

Meanwhile, Fritz Kramer the younger, had applied for migration to Australia, in accordance with the wishes of his wife, Hildegard Kramer. He signed the undertaking; - I, Friedrich Wilhelm Paul Kramer of 1054 Olpenner Strasse, Cologne, in consideration of the Government of the Commonwealth of Australia having agreed to make free grant toward the cost of my passage to Australia having agreed to make free grant to the migration agreement made between the governments of the Commonwealth of Australia and the Federal Republic of Germany on the 29th day of August 1952, do hereby convent with the Commonwealth of Australia in the manner following:-

That I shall remain in employment approved by the Government of the Commonwealth of Australia for a period of two (2) years from the date of my arrival.

Should I require for special reasons to depart from the Commonwealth of Australia before the expiration of two (2) years from the date of my arrival, I will prior to my departure, pay the Commonwealth of Australia a sum equal to the amount that was granted to me by the governments of the Commonwealth of Australia and the Federal Republic of Germany as well as any international organisation towards the cost of my passage to Australia pursuant to the Migration Agreement here-in referred to.

That while in Australia, I shall use every endeavour to learn the English language, and I will regularly attend the nearest free of charge night class made available by the government of the Commonwealth of Australia for the purpose of providing migrants with instruction in the English language.

Dated this .... 19th of January 1952

Signed   ………. Witness signature ……….

It was now that ASIO completed the investigation of Fritz Kramer the younger, and it was found that de-Nazification had not been carried out. Fritz was considered to be useful to the Australian Intelligence Service, and so, his application for immigration to Australia was approved.

On a sunny day in June 1953, the family comprising Friedrich and Hildegard Kramer plus their two sons of Michael and Andy boarded the Australian Ice Breaker "Nelly Dan" at Bremen Haven. The "Nelly Dan" was normally in the service of the Australian Antarctic Expedition, but she had been temporarily reassigned to the Australian Department of Immigration and Citizenship (DIAC) to help in transporting suitable immigrants to Australia.

There were many people seeing off their friends and relatives who were leaving Germany for Australia. Some of the migrants had brought rolls of paper streamers which they threw from the decks of the "Nelly Dan" towards their friends and relatives on the wharf below them. The people on the wharf below caught the streamers and held them until the ship moved off from the wharf. The breaking of the streamers symbolised a break in their relationships due to the great distance between them. As Australia was twelve thousand miles away from Germany, the journey to Australia would take a month and pass through the Suez Canal.

Mick still remembers the voyage to Australia, in particular, the passage through the Suez Canal. He later said, *"Both sides of the canal were lined with people who dark toned skins and who were wearing white robes. This was the very first time that I had ever seen people who looked different to me!"*

The Kramer family had a cabin to themselves on board the "Nelly Dan" and found that the voyage was a comfortable one. The ship arrived at the Australian port of Melbourne on the 20th of July 1953. The immigrants were met by officials from DIAC and placed on board a train bound for Albury/Wodonga. Upon arrival at the Wodonga Railway Station, the migrants were all placed upon Australian Army trucks and transported to their new temporary homes at the army base of Bonegilla in the state of Victoria.

It was now that the Department of Immigration and Citizenship (DIAC) again made contact with the migrants. Fritz was informed that he was to immediately go to work for the Snowy Mountains Authority, which was constructing a series of dams and hydro-electricity power stations that became known across Australia as "The Snowy Mountains Scheme."

Operation Boa Dai

Meanwhile, back in Indochina, things were becoming worse for the French, and they launched an extensive political campaign in an attempt to set up a new *"National Government"* after making some vague promises of autonomy. Meanwhile, in France, the Marshal Plan had been adopted and a plan for getting rid of all communists from the government had started. With *"Operation Boa Dai"* taking place in Vietnam, major military preparations were under way.

Five infantry regiments, half a brigade of paratroops, several artillery batteries and two engineering battalions supported by forty aircraft and eight hundred vehicles plus a flotilla of motor launches, conducted a major offensive against the Viet Minh hoping to destroy the leadership of the resistance. It was thought that the Vietnamese would be caught between two armed columns. One of which was up the Red and Lo Rivers while the second column was airborne troops. So it was that General Leclerc was speaking to others in the Officers' Mess.

He said, *"The Vietnamese will be taken by surprise – they cannot win! We are launching the French version of Blitzkrieg upon them!"* No-one told that to the Vietnamese patriots who closed with the French column sailing up the Lo River where the French were badly knocked about with heavy losses.

The French lost three thousand three hundred men who were killed in action (KIA) and another four thousand men were wounded. As well, the French lost eighteen aircraft which had been shot down. Also, they lost thirty-eight river vessels, and two hundred and fifty-five vehicles had been destroyed. This marked the first major victory for the resistance and the failure of the French attempt at blitzkrieg strategy.

Heyfield

Meanwhile, Fritz Kramer the younger and his family had been living at Ocean Grove, before they all went to Heyfield because Fritz the younger had received an order to report to the State Rivers and Water supply of Victoria based at Heyfield. Th family soon found that things were vastly different in rural Australia compared to what they had been used to in Germany. They now had to totally rely upon themselves for everything, including housing.

So, as the family was new in the country, and only the boys of Andy and Mick or their father could speak English fluently the family lived in a single quarters at a local sawmill for a few months until Fritz the younger could afford to buy two of these huts and a small acreage close to the saw mill.

Next, the family dug holes and placed the necessary stumps and other foundations ready to place the two huts that the family had purchased next to each other and that formed the first home owned by the family in Australia. Next an outhouse toilet and a kitchen was added to the now two-bedroom home.

Mick was enrolled at the Heyfield Primary school immediately Andy followed in the next year. The State of Victoria Primary School at Heyfield during that time shared a common boundary with the local Catholic School. There was some rivalry between these two schools resulting in the students at the State School taunting the students at the Catholic School with, *"Catholic dogs, sitting on logs eating the maggots out of frogs!"* That had various results: sometimes the Catholic students would answer with their own version of taunts and many times they would remain silent. Other times, they complained about the activities of the State School students to their teachers and that resulted in the State School teachers scolding their students.

On the 25th of April 1954, both Andy and Mick were at school. In those days, there was not a public holiday for ANZAC Day. ANZAC Day is the commemoration of the war dead of Australia and New Zealand. ANZAC is the abbreviation of Australian and New Zealand Army Corps. This was the first time that either Andy or Mick had ever heard of a war or that Germany had been the enemy of Australia and the British empire!

Hildegard went into labour at 2:00 pm on the 20th of January 1956. Fritz immediately put her into the newly acquired family sedan and drove to the Heyfield Bush Nursing Hospital. The only daughter to Hildegard and Fritz was born at 3:30 pm on the 20th of January 1956. Hildegard wanted her daughter named as Angela Melanie Sarah Kramer and she asked Fritz the younger to see to it that this was done. Fritz, being a practical sort of man, did not like the idea of people having more than one name. So, he simply recorded the name of his daughter as Angela Kramer, and that caused friction between him and Hildegard. However, Angela was happy about her name and years later, she said, *"Thanks for simply naming me as Angela, Dad!"*

The Strengthening of the Resistance

Meanwhile, back in Indochina, the French were facing the prospect of a protracted long war. Therefore, they decided to strengthen their rears by *"Pacifying"* the areas they had already occupied. They even planned to make the Vietnamese fight Vietnamese and to "Feed war by war." At the Offices of the Headquarters of the French Expeditionary Corps, General Leclerc was speaking to his fellow officers.

He said, *"Gentlemen, we shall be conducting swoops upon the "Little Brown Monkeys all over Nam Bo and southern Trung Bo. We will construct a complex network of watchtowers along the communication routes. In Bac Bo, I have ordered that we extend the French occupation to the provinces of Ha Dong, Lao Cai, Son La and Cao Bang.*

In Trung Bo our soldiers are launching many attacks upon the Vietnamese located in the provinces of Quang Binh,

Quang Tri and Thau Thien. The rebels will not be able to even breath without a French soldier or his officers knowing about it! I have pleasure in in announcing that the strength of the French Expeditionary Corps has been boosted to One Hundred and fifty thousand men and that expenditure for our war in Indochina has been increased to three hundred billion francs per year."

Two members of the Viet Minh platoons were discussing the way things were going for the country and the Viet Minh in general. Dac said to Huu, *"Our Vietnamese resistance has defined its political and military direction in early 1948. Guerrilla attacks remain the main form of action, while the regular troops try to switch to mobile warfare. Our regular army units have been turned into "detached companies" in order to train and support the regional army and self-defence forces, also to help set up regional branches of power and peoples' organisations where the enemy has been found to be extending their occupation.*

"Armed Propaganda" units infiltrated the enemy's rear base and launched effective resistance. We are ready to begin important battles at places like La Nga, Tam vu, Soc Xoai and Moc Hoa as well as along Highway 4." Huu said to Dac, *"Dac my friend, that is good news, as you know, I have just returned from major welding job at the armament's workshops, and I can tell you that the production lines are close to being fully operational. When that is completed, we will have the capacity of making recoilless rifles and heavy mortars which will allow the Viet Minh to engage in military operations of a vastly increasing scale. By the end of 1949 and the beginning of 1950, the French will be facing ever increasing difficulty!"*

In reality, the French command tried to send more reinforcements to Bac Bo to strengthen and extend their occupation of the Red River Delta. They also had in mind to conduct operational sweeps using mobile groups. Lieutenant Vincent Rousseau was in command of a mobile group consisting of two trucks and a command jeep.

He said, *"Men, we are going to conduct operations against the enemy by sweeping towards the military posts along the Sino-Vietnamese border. The fucking Vietnamese have no idea of how to conduct a modern war and we shall crush them all! On the other hand, our French military posts along the entire border have been reinforced. The size of the puppet army has been increased to one hundred and twenty-two thousand men! So, you see, the Vietnamese cannot hope to win!"*

The reality was that the resistance hit back very hard; guerrilla battles flared, fortified villages spread like mushrooms and French stores and communication lines were repeatedly attacked. This led to over two hundred fortified French posts being seized from 1949 to 1950, resulting in the French having ten thousand dead soldiers.

The problem faced by the patriots was ensuring the supplies of food and munitions to their armed forces. These were things which the French were trying to destroy. In order to ensure French victory, the French encircled Vietnamese held areas. They blocked the movement of rice, medicines and tools into the Vietnamese liberated zones and sent luxury goods there instead. They wanted the Bank of Indochina to impose its piastre on all areas to criminate the Vietnamese currency (the Dong)[31].

---

[31] Vien, 2009

Actions Against the People by Government in South Vietnam from 1954

As we have seen, the Americans through the 'Hawks' among them, including Vice President Richard Nixon, Admiral Arthur Radford and the Chief of staff of the US Air Force Nathan F Twining had managed to get Emperor Boa Dai to appoint Ngo Dinh Diem as his Prime Minister.

In direct violation of the Peace Agreements reached at the Geneva Conference of the First Indochina War, the Americans advised Ngo Dinh Diem to set-up a separate South Vietnamese State with its own National assembly and constitution. At a conference held between the Americans and Diem, it is believed that the discussion went along these lines:

General Daniels said, *"So, get the fake referendum going and when it is over, just say to the World Press, the following statement, "At the referendum held to determine if the people wish to join their northern neighbours in freedom, the people of South Vietnam have overwhelmingly opted to remain independent of the North and to continue with their American relationship!"*

And so, a fake referendum was held, and that enabled the Americans to get rid of Bao Dai and install Ngo Dinh Diem into power after he had led a coup d' ĕtat against Emperor Bâo Dai.

By 1954, the main policies of the American neo-colonialist policy became very clear. These were (1) to do away with the French presence, (2) take over South Vietnam, (3) set-up a puppet dictatorship that was entirely dependent on Washington, (4) liquidate the national revolutionary movement in Vietnam, (5) eventually invade and conquer North Vietnam.

The Diem regime applied systematic terror with the help of US advisors, almost as soon as it was in power. Using the fascist methods of the Nazis and the medieval methods of Vietnamese landowners and mandarins, terror was applied in order to eliminate opposition. Diem called for a conference with his sub-ordinates. That was held and Diem addressed the vassals before him. He said, *"I want a repressive machine controlling the whole country from the capital down to the most remote villages! You shall apply massacres, torture, deportations mass imprisonment and constant raids! You shall make the population so fearful of this government, that no-one will ever dare to become a revolutionary or other kind of outlaw!"*

Not content with this, Diem said, *"As of now, we shall have an apparatus of depression using strong-armed forces and police. The Police shall wear starched white shirts, grey trousers, and a grey peaked cap. They shall be armed with colt 45 pistols, and they shall have whistles for sounding alarms and calling for help. They shall hunt down all of those who were formerly opposed the French Colonial presence. Any person who has played even a minor part against the French shall be termed "A communist."* All charges of communism were punishable by prison, deportation, and death by torture and/or firing squad.

Tiger Cages

He went on to say, *"Also, I want to have the communists "Re-educated" by placing them into small 'tiger cages' and for them to be kept under those conditions for as long as is necessary the change the minds of these terrorists who call themselves patriots of Vietnam or Viet Mihn! After they have had a lot of this done to them and have seen their people and towns wiped out by my police and army, they shall not have the will to fight me anymore!"*

Diem was praised by Richard Williams, an agent of the American CIA operating in Vietnam. He spoke to Diem by saying, *"Sir, I have authority from the government of the USA to help you set up a prison system for use against anyone at all who can be shown to have even just sympathy for the communist or socialist causes! I can offer you full funding if you were to set up a system of 'Tiger Cages' measuring five (5) feet high by 9 feet in length.*

Those who are imprisoned in the 'tiger Cages' will not be able to stand up because of the low height of the 'Tiger cages.' By incarcerating the socialists, freedom fighters and all communists, including those who only have sympathy with the Viet Minh, you shall become very feared and that is what the USA wants to happen. We want you to establish the system of imprisoning communists in these 'Tiger Cages' and we want that to take place at the site of the old French prison on Con Son Island. We want the prisoners to be miserable, not have enough food to sustain themselves and we want the guards to splash caustic substances onto the skin of the prisoners on a regular basis. We want word about that prison to get out to the communists so that they will know that there shall be no mercy for all for those who have communist, socialist or any other viewpoints which could result in them becoming rebels sir!"

Diem answered, *"Excellent Mister Williams of the CIA, please inform you superiors at Langley in Virginia USA, that I have authorised you to establish this 'Communist Detainment System' you have told me about. The 'Tiger Cages' shall be put on Con Son Island as you have suggested and there shall be at least three hundred men in the cages as well as at least two hundred women constrained within the*

'Tiger Cages.' I shall even put children into the 'Tiger Cages' and I shall tell the newspapers in Vietnam about it so that the Viet Mihn shall be informed. That way, terror will spread though Vietnamese society, and no-one shall ever dare to cross my government because of what could happen to the person caught being a socialist or communist!"

So it was that the American presence in Vietnam was beginning, and right from the start, the Yankee and his South Vietnamese puppet officials were guilty of inflicting war crimes upon the people of southern Vietnam and later, also the upon people in the north of the country. The war crimes were committed by the government agencies of the South Vietnamese, the American Forces in particular, and even the Australians[32].

Attitudes of American People & Politicians

Many Americans believed that it was fair to deny the people of foreign countries their freedom on the basis of these people were communists and that it somehow made them evil people because of the American hysteria about socialism or communism. The simple fact is that Americans tend to be completely paranoid about the rights of anyone who has the political outlook of socialism or can be said to be different from American ideals. The US President Nixon had inherited the war from Johnston who had inherited it from John F Kennedy.

In the case of the US President Richard Nixon, it was said that he was heard to say, in 1969, *"Fucking Gooks, they have liberated their own country, and they have gotten rid of the French colonial masters who were oppressing them!*

---

[32] Australian "War Crimes mainly relate to the apparent deliberate shelling of South Vietnamese civilians who were herding their cattle between Hao Long and other places such as Long Phuoc. (12) times. (Ham, 2007)

They shall not continue to have freedom because they are communists and therefore, they are the enemies of the United States of America! I shall work against the communists of Asia, and we shall bring them down! I have been working upon this glorious quest to wipe out socialism in Vietnam since 1950 when I was the Vice-president of the USA!"

The victory of the Chinese revolution and the founding of the Peoples' Republic of China greatly increased the already strong impetus of Vietnamese resistance[33].

Border Campaign Strategies – New Franco-American Plan

The Chinese thought of Vietnam as a bulwark which was helping to protect them from the particularly aggressive United States of America. As we have already seen, the major western powers of Britain and the USA simply wanted the French to maintain their presence and colonial system in Indochina as a means of containing communism, it not mattering if the people of Indochina were subjected to cruel and inhumane practices by the French or not!

The new government In Vietnam was in dire straits because the Bank of Indochina's actions concerning Vietnamese currency and other factors bought about by not being recognised by countries outside of its borders. Then, in early 1950, the Democratic Republic of Vietnam was given full recognition by the Peoples' Republic of China and the USSR and that was followed by recognition by other socialist countries. This allowed Vietnam to stop being isolated as it had been until the recognition began.

---

[33] Vien, 2009.

Due to the emergence of a new factor of open intervention by the United States of America in the Indochinese affairs, more and rising tensions resulted in a US naval squadron arriving in the waters near Saigon and anchoring there. On the same day, that was being discussed by the Vietnamese living in and around the Saigon area. Trung was speaking to Nhat while visiting him Saigon.

Trung said, *"Look at that Nhat, the French have bought up yet even more naval ships with which to bombard us in order to try to keep their colonies operating here and to keep us subjected!"* His friend called Nhat knew more about what was happening due to his work position with the USA company of Coca Cola which was setting up in Saigon. Due to his position of being a supervisor, he knew that the naval squadron was in fact an American one. He therefore said to his friend, *"Trung, what you can see on the waters around Saigon is the United States of America Navy. The USA has decided not to support our struggle for freedom and instead, to openly support the foreign occupiers even though the Americans went through the same sort of revolutionary struggles against their former British occupiers.*

For some reason, the Americans are paranoid about anyone, or anything called either socialist or communist. They think that socialism is a threat to their existence. That is false, but it is typical of the lies being spread about us by the British, French and American Capitalists! If we allow these American naval squadrons to be here, they will just come in and completely support the French, which is no good for our people. We must make these new foreign invaders and their supporters leave immediately!

I think that the best way for us to do this is to immediately organise mammoth demonstrations against the

Americans and their French allies. I want you to go around all waterside areas of Saigon and speak to as many people as possible about organising this huge demonstration against the presence of the US Navy, while I go into Saigon city itself and organise the same things there."

The resulting huge demonstrations in Saigon forced the American warships to leave. That was followed in June of 1950, by the USA beginning the war in Korea. While that was happening, an American military mission was sent to Saigon to help the French command. The US gave France considerable financial and material assistance to help it to intensify the war against the Vietnamese patriots! The French sent reinforcements to seal off the Chinese-Vietnamese borders and to reinforce the French garrisons at Lang Son, Dong Khe, That Khe and Cao Bang which is situated on highway 4, which runs along the northern border.

In mid-September, General Giap and the Vietnamese High Command were in conference, discussing the military situation that they now found themselves in. General Vo Nguyen Giap said to his officers, *"I want the French outpost at Dong Khe to be taken by our Viet Minh Forces immediately! Also, at the same time, attack and wipe out the French at Cao Bang, we will remove the French bully from our lands, or I am not Vo Nguyen Giap!"*

The Viet Minh units were always both alert and active, being under orders to remove the French from the Dong Khe post and others, a Viet Minh platoons' commander was in position with his unit and others to launch the attack on the French outpost on the 16th of September 1950. Nguyen Anh called an "O" group with the members of his platoon while it was still dark.

He said, *"Gentlemen, we will be going into action against the French garrison at the Dong Khe post in about an hour from now. We have infantry support from other platoons to our right and left sides. We also have artillery support from the batteries which have been equipped with the Japanese mountain guns. A half hour before the morning twilight, the artillery will launch a barrage upon the French at Dong Khe.*

As soon as I receive the order to do so, we will attack and wipe the French out! Our order to attack will be made by the relaying of bugle calls because we do not yet have good portable radio communication devices. Now, if everything is clear, get some rest, or if not, ask questions. We must all be absolutely clear as to what is required."

At 05:50 hours of Vietnamese time, the first artillery shells were heard as they whistled overhead. That sound was immediately followed by the sounds of explosions coming from the French positions. Soon after that, the expected bugle calls were relayed and heard everywhere. This was the signal to launch the platoon sized infantry attacks by all platoons involved.

Upon hearing the bugles, Lieutenant Nguyen Anh sprang up and shouted. He yelled, *"On your feet! Take off your backpacks for now and put them into marked and secure areas which shall be guarded by two of our men."* That was done and then he said to his platoon, *"Using platoon 'Fire and Movement' tactics, we are attacking the French now! All sections of this platoon are to advance upon the enemy until we get close enough to wipe out the French arseholes! Charge!"* That resulted in the complete wipe-out of the French at Dong Khe and the post being taken by the Viet Minh. The surviving members of the French garrison fled to Cao Bang, but there the same sort of things happened, forcing the French to withdraw to That Khe.

A French soldier said to his companion, *"Do not worry Thibault, there should soon be another column from That Khe which will reinforce this column from Cao Bang. When our forces get here, we will be stronger than the Indochinese!"* What no-one in either French column knew is that the Viet Minh were their way to attack both French columns. Back at the Viet Minh positions, Bao was speaking to his friend, Chinh. He said to Chinh, *"Our units are going into prepared ambush positions and once we get into our positions, we shall await the arrival of the two French columns. When they come, we shall close with them and kill all of them if at all possible! We shall be supported by both the 82 mm mortars and the captured Japanese Mountain Guns. With that sort of close support, the French shall not have a chance of survival!"*

That was not quite what happened, but on the way, both of the columns were attacked by Viet Minh forces. The results of that was that the loss of eight thousand men who were killed or else taken prisoner. Included in that figure was the French commanders. The French quickly retreated and that caused Bao to say to Chinh, *"Look at how the French masters are running from the people whom they consider to be no better than monkeys! See how they have got the fuck out of Lang Son, Lao Cai, and Hoa Binh! The border between our country and China now lies wide open and the French plan to create "autonomous territories" for ethnic minorities in mountainous regions has ended in failure! Our border victories have thrown the enemy into disarray.*

I have read that the anti-war movement in France, led by the Communist Party, has grown in strength! Some

French people have suggested that France withdraws from Indochina in order to save the French colonies in Africa! According to reports in a French newspaper, the French government has chosen to become subordinate to the policies of Washington, as far took as Indochina is concerned! This worries me because it makes it very likely that we shall be fighting the Americans and their allies in due course, as well as the French!"

Meanwhile, France's General De Lattre de Tassigny had visited Washington and received American instructions on conducting the war against the Viet Minh arrived in Vietnam and took over the French Expeditionary Corps and he was eager to re-imposed French domination over Indochina!

De Lattre took a series of measures aimed at:

- increasing reinforcements from France in terms of men and military equipment, especially aircraft.
- building up Bao Dai's puppet army.
- creating a no-man's land around the Red River Delta, destroying all houses, and building concrete bunkers everywhere.
- intensifying the "pacification "efforts in areas occupied by the French.

At the Officers' Mess of the headquarters of the French Expeditionary Corps, General De Lattre was in conversation with other high-ranking French officers. He said, *"Defend the free world against the communist threat! Also, to build support for a puppet government of a "Free Indochina", which we French can easily control! By July of 1951, we will have bullied and coerced the puppet Vietnamese Emperor called Bao Dai into signing a decree* on general mobilization! Also, to build support for a puppet government of a "Free Indochina" which we French can easily control!"

He was answered by a young second lieutenant who asked, *"Sir, how will the French bullying and coercing of the puppet emperor help us?"* De Lattre said, *"He has command of a large and expanding puppet army which we can have him send into battle against the Viet Minh on our behalf. It is far better for France if the "Little Brown Monkeys" making up the population of the countries making up French Indochina die instead of French gentlemen. This way, we keep French casualties to a minimum and we maximise French political events by simply saying, "The atrocities being committed in Indochina are being committed by the army of the Vietnamese Emperor called Bao Dai, and not French soldiers!"*

The lieutenant said, *"Yes Sir, I see!"* he then went back to the group of young officers which he was a part of. A French major now spoke to General De Lattre. He said, *"Sir, you have said that we must create a no-man's land in the Red River Delta! You also have expressed your desire to completely "Pacify" our Vietnamese enemy! In order to be successful in completing the completing the "Pacification," and to make it look like everything that we do is entirely the fault of the Vietnamese, you should order Emperor Bao Dai to take extreme action against the population of the Red River Delta! Our French Forces could simply be in the background while the army of Emperor Bao Dai does your will. Get him to immediately conduct a series of extremely cruel operations against our Vietnamese enemies!*

I think that you should get the puppet army to go to the villages of all areas around the Red River Delta and have them firstly burn entire villages to the ground, followed in some instances by wiping out the civilian populations. You should see to it that all survivors are herded into concentration camps. Meanwhile our French soldiers should protect the puppet army from attack by the Viet Minh!

By conducting operations against those "Little Brown Monkeys" and making sure the population of Indochina does French bidding and restricting the French Forces to the role of protecting the puppet army of Emperor Bao Dai, you can keep France out of the spotlight which be put upon Indochina as soon as word of the massacre of Vietnamese civilians and the burning of their villages gets out into the international community! You will be able to blame the puppet army for herding the Vietnamese into concentration camps and thereby keep the Americans ignorant of what is really happening here! While the puppet army is doing this the French forces protecting them could be put to work in the construction of a ring of the bunkers which are needed to pacify rear base areas!

As all of that is being done, I think that you should order the French forces to systematically destroy all crops and food reserves. That will both starve the Vietnamese into submission and deny food to the Viet Minh! In order to completely subjugate the half-human "Little Brown Monkeys" French soldiers should shoot the buffalos and all other animals which are vital for the cultivation of rice! I also think Sir, that the setting up of reactionary local administration to control the local populations would be a good idea!"

General De Lattre was delighted with this conversation. He said to the major, *"Fucking hell major, I like the way that you think! As a reward for your outstanding suggestions, I shall immediately promote you to the rank of colonel without the necessity of you going through the rank of lieutenant colonel first. I am appointing you to oversee the full implementation of what we have just discussed with emphasis on both wiping out the "Little Brown Monkeys", burning their villages and destroying their crops!*

I in particular like your ideas of getting the French soldiers to protect the puppet army while they do exactly what I want! I also just love your idea of using French soldiers to shoot the easy targets of buffalo and all other farm animals necessary for growing rice! We shall also set up the reactionary local administrations you speak of, and the Vietnamese will obey France!"

At the end of 1951, General De Lattre was in conference with his officers, receiving a report of progress on what he had ordered earlier. The conference was being briefed by a lieutenant. He said, *"General De Lattre, I have the pleasure of informing you that your orders have been carried out! The entire Red River Delta has been encircled by a ring of two thousand and two hundred bunkers.*

Many villages have been burned to the ground and their inhabitants have either been killed or else moved into concentration camps in secure areas! Our Vietnamese puppet army has increased in size to one hundred and twelve thousand men! We have been taking delivery of dozens of aircraft and hundreds of armoured vehicles as well as artillery pieces which have been supplied by the United States of America! As well, we and our American allies have launched a Franco-American propaganda campaign which is full of praise for your leadership while also claiming that you are leading French colonialism to victory!" The French general answered, *"With this propaganda campaign you have spoken of, does it tell the truth about the ways things really are here, or can we put whatever we want into it?"*

The lieutenant said, *"It is my understanding that we can put whatever we want into the propaganda campaign. I therefore suggest that we blame the Viet Minh for all of the Atrocities committed by both the French and the puppet soldiers!"* The French general said, *"See to it that the Viet Minh and the Vietnamese Communist Government of Vietnam get the blame for everything that is done by France and its Vietnamese puppet solders! The rest of the world including the Americans in particular must always think that the atrocities are always carried out by our enemies and never by French forces or our allies and puppet soldiers!"*

I want you to organise press releases which always show the world the French side of things and always makes us look like the good fellows and not the aggressors. Write such good press releases that even the stupid Americans and their allies will believe that France is doing everything to make sure that the Indochinese people will be granted autonomy and freedom under French guidance. Make sure that you put out the story that the Vietnamese government cannot be trusted to bring in democracy on their own because they are communists! The Americans just love to swallow that sort of rubbish because it fits in with what they think about the world. So, feed those idiots as much false information and garbage as possible, because they will believe every bad thing said about communists. All we have the do to keep the good reputation of France is to keep going in the way we are!" The Lieutenant answered, *"Yes Sir, it shall be done!"*

Meanwhile in France, the opposition by the French people to against the Indochina War was growing. The lawyer for Henri Martin, the French sailor who had refused to fight the Vietnamese people, was speaking at a meeting called for the campaign to release him. In front of a vast crowd, the lawyer stated, *"Friends and comrades, see your parliamentary representatives and make them listen to our demands to have Henri Martin released. Henri quite rightly both said and wrote that actions of France in Indochina were as bad as the actions of the bloody NAZIs in France!*

We must make sure that no French persons are ever justly accused of becoming such a low-life as to be justly accused of being NAZI-like. Please come forward and obtain petitions which I want you to take into the community and get as many people as possible to sign these petitions for the immediate release of Henri!"

As well, cracks were beginning to appear the Franco-American alliance with American imperialism starting moves to get rid of the French colonialists. Though these things all had a bearing upon what was happening but the main obstacle to De Lattre's strategy was the great growth in strength of the Vietnamese resistance, on the military, political and cultural areas.

New Gains by the Resistance

No matter what the French or the government of the USA may have thought about it, following the declaration of Independence by the Democratic Republic of Vietnam, there was recognition by socialist countries of the new republic. Following its victory in the Border Campaigns there was rapid advancement of the resistance. In February 1951, the Communist Party of Indochina was split into three national parties each of which took leadership roles in the fight for national independence in its own part of Indochina. The

Vietnamese Party took the name of Dang Lao Dong Viet Nam (Workers' Party of Vietnam). This had Ho Chi Minh as president and Trung Chinh as the General Secretary[34].

Ho Chi Minh addressed his fellow members at a meeting of the Central Committee of the Vietnamese Workers' Party (Communist Party) in 1951. He said to his audience, *"Ladies and gentlemen, our new republic needs to forge new external relations with other countries. This is totally necessary for our great Peoples' Republic to gain recognition from different and forge new external relations with other countries. It is totally necessary for our great People's Republic to gain recognition from different countries, and we shall constantly expand our missions and delegations to other socialist counties as well as other countries which are capitalists!"*

Dien Bien Phu

Dien Bien Phu is a plain about eleven miles long and between three and five miles in width, depending upon where you happen to be on this plain. It is the largest and also the richest of the four plains in the mountainous region close to the Vietnam/Laos border. Dien Bien Phu has the capacity of being an infantry base and an air base of extreme efficiency which makes it strategically very important.

Many thousands of people joined the army and supplied units which operated far from their bases. They also built roads through dense forests while undergoing fierce bombing by the French Air Force. These things combined and this prompted General Vo Nguyen Giap to write, *"From the military point of view, The Vietnamese Peoples' War of Liberation proved that an insufficiently*

---

[34] Vien, 2009.

equipped peoples' army fighting for a just cause can with appropriate strategy and tactics can combine the conditions needed to conquer a modern army of aggressive imperialism![35]"

The High Command of the Vietnamese army was meeting for an information and orders briefing. After some discussion among the general staff, the supreme commander, General Vo Nguyen Giap made an announcement. He said, *"Comrades, during the November of 1953, our Vietnamese forces shall attack in the northwest of Vietnam. We will liberate the provincial capital of Lai Chau, thus compelling the French command to send relief forces to that area!"* In response, the French commander of the Expeditionary Corps, Navarre spoke to his general staff.

He said, *"Gentlemen, the Viet Minh are threatening the areas of the provincial capital of Lai Chau. We are therefore compelled to send relief forces to that area. In response, I have ordered that six battalions of our fine men shall parachute into the isolated base deep in the forests of the northwest called Dien Bien Phu and that this shall happen on 20th of November 1953!"*

Written orders were sent by the Vietnamese High command to all units in order to back up what was being ordered orally. These orders said, *"The aim is to liberate as much of the northern provinces as possible. Vietnamese army units are to closely co-ordinate with the Pathet Lao soldiers and launch attacks in central Laos where they are to liberate Kham Muon province and the town of Thakket."* On 21st of November 1953, the Vietnamese forces did as they had been ordered. That caused Navarre to speak to his

---

[35] Giap, 1970.

subordinate officers. He said to them, *"The combined forces of the Vietnamese and the Pathet Lao have successfully attacked Kham Muon province, and they have taken the town of Thakket! We must immediately rush several battalions to Laos in order to reinforce the Seno base!"* These events were followed in January 1954 by the joint Laotian/Vietnamese forces liberating the town of Attopeu as well as the Boloven Plateau[36].

At a conference of the French General Staff, that situation was discussed. Navarre said to his officers, *"Gentlemen, like yourselves, I am getting a strong impression that the Vietnamese offensive has lost its momentum. In our earlier discussions, you have informed me that we have on hand, twenty infantry battalions, four artillery battalions and three mobile battalions! I am sure that with these forces at our command, we can launch "Operation Atlante."*

The French plan was countered by a directive from the Party Central Committee. This order read, *"Only a small number of regular forces are to remain at fixed locations to resist the enemy's advance! The main body of the Peoples' Army shall launch an offensive in the Central Highlands and liberate Kontum Province!"* The written orders were carried out successfully and Navarre had no choice but to quickly send thirteen battalions to try to rescue Play Cu. Navarre discussed the situation that the French were finding themselves in, looking for solutions to the problem. He said to others, *"Gentlemen, while the Vietnamese forces are trying to kill us and we are trying to kill them, we must destroy the enemy forces. This can best be done by drawing*

---

[36] Vien – 2009.

those *"Slant eyed little brown monkeys" into a trap for them at Dien Bien Phu!"*

Unknown to the French, the Vietnamese High Command under General Vo Nguyen Giap was meeting. During the conference, the general suddenly said, *"Enough of all of this procrastination! The French have too big an number of forces at Dien Bien Phu. We shall wipe them out at that location when the time for us to take the position is right, but not right away. Between now and when the time is right, the Vietnamese forces shall advance towards upper Laos. Once there, we shall threaten Luang Prabang.*

That should make the French once again quickly send relief forces in order to defend the city and that area of Laos! As well, I want our Vietnamese revolutionaries to begin major attacks in Laos, Cambodia, and southern Vietnam as well as here in the north of Vietnam. I know that Navarre wants to concentrate his crack units in northern Vietnam, but by our soldiers and patriots attacking all over Indochina, the French will again be forced to disperse their army to all corners of Indochina!

That will make the task of beating French forces locally much easier because there shall be fewer of them! I also want guerrilla attacks to be stepped up in both the Mekong and Red River Deltas. Our units will constantly ambush and attack Highway five which links Hanoi with Haiphong and is the main supply route for the French Expeditionary Corps. As well, I want our special force commandos to silently slip into Cat Bi and Gia Lam airfields and destroy the aircraft stationed there. That will deal the French forces at Dien Bien Phu a stunning blow!" On the other side, the French, who actually believed their own propaganda, remained optimistic. The French Expeditionary

Corps had a news bulletin called "Carevelle." It reported the following: *"The Viet Minh command has to move its units and supply them over enormous distance through rugged terrain poorly served by transport routes. A campaign conducted in these conditions can only turn in our favour[37]"*

For the Viet Minh forces, the reality was that things were difficult because of the distance between the plains where their supply bases were located, and Dien Bien Phu was located about five hundred kilometres of tracks through forests and across mountains. The tracks were repeatedly bombed by the French Air Force.

In order to launch attacks upon the French, the Viet Minh had to move down the mountains to the heavily fortified French positions while under heavy artillery and tank fire. In February, the US General O'Daniel decided to visit the camp at Dien Bien Phu. Arriving at Dien Bien Phu, the American general reportedly said, *"I am enthusiastic about the prospects of the French for the coming battle of Bien Dien Phu!"*

With the French command still being optimistic about its chances of beating the patriots of Indochina, it ordered that new units be landed on the central Vietnam front of Quy Nhon as part of "Operation Atlante"[38].

At the beginning of operations at Dien Bien Phu, only ten French battalions were present, however, these were reinforced gradually in order to cope with the offensive launched by the Vietnamese patriots. When the Vietnamese

---

[37] Vien, 2009.
[38] Vien, 2009.

units attacked, the French forces totalled seventeen battalions and ten companies.

These were made up of both Europeans and Africans. There were also units of highly trained paratroops. As well, the Dien Bien Phu camp had three battalions of artillery, one battalion of sappers, one armoured company, a transport unit of two hundred trucks and a permanent squadron of twelve aircraft: totalling sixteen thousand and two hundred men.

The forces were set-up in three sub-sectors which could support each other and comprised forty-nine strong points. Each had defensive autonomy, several of which were grouped in "Complex Defence Centres" and equipped with mobile forces and artillery. These were surrounded by trenches and barbed wire entanglements which were hundreds of feet wide.

The most important was the central subsector situated in the middle of the Muong Thanh village. This was the main town of the Dien Bien Phu plain. Up to two thirds of the French garrison were concentrated there. It had several connected defence centres which were protecting the command post, the artillery and commissariat bases, and also the airfield.

To the east, the hills and mountains were the most important defence system of that sub-sector. Dien Bien Phu was considered by the French to be an unassailable and impregnable fortress. The central sub-sector did have strong forces, and the mountains to the east could not be attacked easily. Besides, the artillery and armoured forces could break every attempt at intervention through the plain.

A system of barbed wire and trenches permitted the French to decimate and repel any assault. The mobile forces formed by the battalions of paratroops would combine with that of the defence centres could counter-attack and break any offensive. The northern sub-sector comprised the defence centres of Him Lam, Doc Lap and Ban Keo. The very strong positions of Him Lam and Doc Lap were there to stop all attacks of Vietnamese soldiers coming from Tuan Giao and Lai Chau. The southern sub-sector, also known as Hong Cum sub-sector, had the role of breaking any offensive coming from the south and to protect the communication routes with Laos.

Their artillery was divided between two bases: one at Muong Thanh and the other at Hong Cum, arranged in such a way as to support each other as well as supporting all the surrounding strong points. Dien Bien Phu had two airfields, the main one being at Muong Thanh and a reserve airfield at Hong Cum. They linked with Hanoi and Haiphong in an airlift which used between seventy to eighty transport aircraft on a daily basis.

The reconnaissance aircraft and fighters of the permanent squadron constantly flew over the entire region. The planes from Gia Lam and Cat Bi airbases had been assigned the task of strafing and bombing the Vietnamese units[39]. Navarre asserted, *"We have such powerful forces and so strong a defence system that Dien Bien Phu is an impregnable fortress!"* the American Lieutenant General "Iron Mike" O'Daniel also shared that opinion. The French occupiers of Indochina and their American allies even concluded that the Vietnamese patriots had little chance in an attack upon Dien Bien Phu and that a Vietnamese attack

---

[39] Giap, 1970.

would present them with the opportunity to inflict a resounding defeat upon the Indochinese people.

Meanwhile, following the liberation of Lai Chau, the attack upon Dien Bien Phu was on the agenda. The general staff of the Viet Minh held a conference just after their forces liberated Lai Chau to decide whether or not to launch attacks upon the Dien Bien Phu base. They considered how well the base was defended and that it also had vulnerable points.

General Vo Nguyen Giap said, *"Gentlemen, the French base is very well entrenched, but it also has weak points! In attacking the base, we shall face difficulties in strategy, tactics, and supply. All these things can and will be overcome.*

Having analysed the situation and given due consideration to the pros and cons, I have decided that we must attack Dien Bien Phu using the method of taking no risks. Our tactics shall be to attack each enemy defence centre, each part of the entrenched camp, in order to create conditions for the launching of a general offensive to annihilate the entire base.

Our soldiers have succeeded in liberating the surrounding regions, thus isolating Dien Bien Phu, thus obliging the enemy to scatter their forces and thereby reduce their possibilities of sending reinforcements to the battlefield. We have made roads for use by trucks, cleared tracks to haul up artillery pieces, built casemates for our artillery, prepared the ground for the offensive and encirclement.

In short, we have transformed the relief of the battlefield terrain with a view to solving the tactical problems! We called upon our local compatriots to supply food, set up supply lines hundreds of miles from Thanh Hoa of Phu Tho to the northwest, crossing very dangerous areas ad very high hills. We have used every means to carry food and ammunition to the front. Both our troops and voluntary workers ceaselessly went to the front and participated in the preparations while under attack from enemy aircraft.

In the first week of March, the preparations were completed. This resulted in artillery having solid casemates, and the operational bases were completed as well as food and ammunition being available in sufficient quantities. We set up a programme of educating all officers and soldiers in the aims and the significance of the campaign, they were filled with a very strong determination to wipe out the enemy. They knew that only the destruction of the Dien Bien Phu entrenched camp would bring the Navarre plan to complete failure.

On 13th of March 1954, the Viet Minh troops received the order to launch an offensive at Dien Bien Phu. We had planned for the campaign to proceed in three phases: in phase one, we destroyed the northern subsector; in the second, the longest and bitterest one, we took the heights in the east of the central subsector and tightened our encirclement; in the third, we launched the general offensive and annihilated the enemy[40].

The First Phase: Destroy the Northern Sector

Beginning on 13th of March 1954 the First Phase ended on The 17th of March 1954. On the night of the 13th of March 1954, Vietnamese forces wiped out the very strong defence centre of Him Lam which overlooked the road from Tuan Gio to Dien Bien Phu. General Vo Nguyen Giap wrote:

---

[40] Giap, 1970.

"The battle was very sharp, the enemy artillery concentrated its fire and poured thousands of shells on our assaulting waves. Our troops carried the position in the night. This first victory had very deep repercussions on the development of the whole campaign.

During the night of 14th of March 1954, we concentrated our forces to attack the defence centre of Doc Lap, the second strong defence of the northern subsector which overlooked the road from Lai Chau to Dien Bien Phu. The battle went on till dawn. The enemy used every means to repel our forces, fired scores of thousands of shells and sent their mobile forces protected by tanks from Muong Thanh to support their position. Our troops fought heroically, took the strong point, and repelled the enemy reinforcements.

The third and last defence centre of the northern subsector, the Ban Keo post, became isolated and was threatened by us. This was a less strong position, manned by a garrison chiefly made up of puppet soldiers.

On the 17th of March 1954, the whole garrison left its positions and surrendered. After the loss of the northern subsector, the central subsector, now exposed on its eastern and northern flanks, was threatened."

A Viet Minh lieutenant was speaking to General Giap and some other higher-ranking officers. He said, "Gentlemen, the fighting of the first phase has proven the soundness of our tactical decisions and the good organisation of our defence. Our artillery fire, which has been very accurate, inflicted heavy losses upon the enemy. For the first time, our anti-aircraft batteries have been in action and shot down enemy planes! Above all, it was by their heroic spirit and their high spirit of sacrifice, coupled with their will to win that our soldiers have distinguished themselves during these battles[41]."

Despite their heavy losses, the French enemy still believed in the strength of their forces. The French even believed that the Vietnamese patriots would suffer heavy losses and be forced to stop their offensive. As well, they thought that the French could cut the supply lines of the Vietnamese thus forcing the Vietnamese to withdraw.

The Second Phase: Occupation of the Hills in the East

General Giap was speaking to his officers during an *"Orders Group"* he was holding to discuss the Dien Bien Phu campaign and to generate ideas. He said, *"Gentlemen, we are now about to launch phase two, which is the most important part of the campaign! We must deal with the central subsector, in the middle of the Muong Thanh plain. Our soldiers will have to work hard and actively to complete the operations required to form them.*

They shall have to dig a vast network of trenches, from the neighbouring hills to the plain. That is to enable us to encircle the central subsector and cut it off from the southern subsector. This advance of our lines will be made at the cost of fierce fighting. By every means, the enemy shall try to upset our preparations using the fire power of their air force and artillery. I therefore want our troops to draw closer to enemy positions and to take them using their irresistible power developed during the course of uninterrupted fighting."

A lieutenant of the Viet Minh forces was speaking to the members of his platoon. He said, *"Our army is launching*

---

[41] Giap, 1970.

The Full Circle for Mick

a large-scale attack of long duration to annihilate the French at the heights in the east and some strong points in the west in order to tighten our encirclement and to hamper and cut off supplies to the garrison. On this night of March 30, we shall concentrate forces to attack simultaneously the five fortified positions in the east. The rest our company has the jobs of taking the hills of D-1 and C-1. We have been chosen to take hill E1, and we are moving into position right now! You all have ten minutes to check your equipment, supplies and weapons." Ten minutes later, the lieutenant had gathered his soldiers and was leading them towards the French army's strong point located at the top of hill E-1".

It was a pitch-dark night with no moon and the Viet Minh platoon moved silently forward. After having moved forward for over an hour, the Lieutenant called his forward scout over to him and they discussed their location and the approximate distance to the strong point. The lieutenant said, *"Nguyen, I am most grateful that you are in my platoon. Your night vision is so good that even the cats must be jealous of you! We have been moving steadily forward in an uphill direction, and I estimate that we must now be somewhere close to the French strong point that needs to be wiped out. I need you and your most trusted companion to move cautiously forward and to see if you can locate the strong point."*

Nguyen answered with, *"Sir, I will take Duong with me, and we should be back here in about an hour and a half from now. As you know Sir, I a very good at making bird sounds, so I will make the sound of a peacock as we are re-approaching this position."* The Lieutenant answered with, *"Very good, that is the sort of thing that I like to hear."* And so, the forward and second scout left the area of the platoon and moved out into the darkness, on their way towards the French strong point. At the strong point, a group of French soldiers were complaining.

The French sergeant was saying, *"Fucking snakes, fucking grasses and bloody forest and mountains are all that this part of the country is! Pass the coffee pot Lois!"* That was overheard by Nguyen and his second scout who now went back to the platoon position they had left earlier. As they got closer to the platoon, Nguyen made a very loud peacock's call. The Lieutenant called out, *"Is that you, Nguyen?"* Nguyen answered, *"Yes, keep your voices down, we are closer to the French strong point than you may think!"* The lieutenant said, *"Hurry up and come in and give me your report."*

The two scouts went Into the platoon's position and Nguyen reported as ordered. He said, *"Sir, we are in fact quite close to the French strong point. Duong and I were able to get close because there is no moonlight, and the French soldiers are both complaining and also bored! By moving silently, we can get close enough to lob grenades into the strong point/bunker system."*

The Viet Minh lieutenant said, *"Excellent! We have Bangalore torpedoes with use, as well as some plastic explosive and grenades. We shall get as close as possible to the bunker and place the Bangalore torpedoes and grenades through the openings in the defensive system while at the same time other platoons' members shall go to the rear of the strongpoint and look for entry points. We will kill all the French there because prisoners will slow us down!"*

Next, the platoon moved towards the bunker and put the plan of attack into action. With sections one and two of the first platoon putting grenades through the slits in the bunker and section three of the same platoon locating the entrances and forcing their way into the bunker system, The French were quickly overcome with all of them killed. On Hills D1 and C-1, it was the same story. However, the Vietnamese could not take the most important location of Hill A-1.

That was the key to the entire defensive system of the central subsector, therefore its loss would mean the fall of Dien Bien Phu. So, for these reasons, the fighting was the fiercest. In particular on Hill A-1, this was the last height which protected the command post. Every inch of ground was fiercely fought over and because it appeared a stalemate situation had been reached; a conference of platoon and company leaders was called for. The captain said, *"Sir, I think that I may have the means of taking Hill A-1 from the French! However, I will need complete back-up and intense covering fire from infantry platoons, from our mortars and artillery. By having intensive fire upon Hill, A-1, I will be able to get my sappers in close to the bunkers and they will be able to use their flame-throwers and, other sappers can blow open any closed doorway openings in the defensive system."*

The major said, *"Thank you captain, that is what we shall do!"* so it was that although there was fierce hand to hand fighting, The Vietnamese patriots finally occupied half of the trenches, while the enemy continued to resist in the other half. That was followed by a French commander calling for volunteers to assault the Viet Minh. This was quickly organised and on April 9, the enemy launched a counterattack to re-occupy Hill C-1. The resulting battle went on for four days and nights. At the end of which half the position was still occupied by the French colonial forces and the other half occupied by the Vietnamese.

The positions of both sides were drawing closer together as time went on and at some points were only fifteen yards from each other. From the occupied positions towards the battlefields towards the west and the north, Vietnamese artillery and mortars pounded the French colonial forces without stopping. Fighting was carried out by both day and night. The French colonial forces became exhausted from being constantly harassed. Their strong points were falling to the Vietnamese forces attacking them one by one and combining nibbling attacks with full scale major assaults.

In mid-April, several enemy positions in the north and west were taken by the Vietnamese forces, which allowed them to reach the airfield, thus cutting it off from the north and west. The Vietnamese encirclement was becoming ever tighter, and the fighting became fiercer. The French commanders were now concerned that they might lose the Dien Bien Phu base and the quickly launched several violent counterattacks supported by tanks and aircraft. Their idea was to take ground from the Vietnamese patriots and to make them loosen Vietnamese encirclement of the French.

On the 24th of April 1954, the French forces launched their most violent attacks yet. The idea behind this was to drive the Vietnamese off the airfield. The result was that the French forces suffered heavy losses, but the Viet Minh stayed in control of the airfield.

Due to repeated and constant attacks by Vietnamese forces, the territory occupied by the French enemy shrank in size every day until they were driven into a square mile area. That was constantly threatened by artillery and mortar fire.

With the zone held by the French enemy now being narrow and surrounded, the only way the French forces could obtain resupplies was to have them dropped by parachute.

The foreign pilots greatly feared the anti-aircraft fire of the Vietnamese and therefore refused to fly low, resulting in many of the parachutes which had food and ammunition, falling into Vietnamese hands. That resulted in the Vietnamese pouring the artillery fire supplied by French air-dropped ammunition upon the Dien Bien Phu camp. Throughout the second phase, things were difficult due to Americans interfering by sending more bombers and other aircraft to support the Dien Bien Phu base[42].

The Third Phase: Annihilation of the French Enemy

The Viet Minh General Staff were holding an "O" Group, (orders group during which things like tactics are discussed and orders were given) and the Commander, General Vo Nguyen Giap was speaking. He said, *"On May 1, the third phase shall begin and if necessary, it will go on for the six days between May 1 to May 6 and beyond if necessary. Our forces shall do whatever it takes to win, and we shall be successful! Following several successive attacks, we have occupied Hill C-1 and Hill A-1 which was the key to the last defensive system of the central subsector. Also, we have taken other strong points from the foot of the hills to the east to the Nam Gion River and also some positions in the west."*

The attack was launched and at the next "O" Group, held on May 8, Giap said, *"The enemy has been driven into an area of one square mile and is constantly exposed to our artillery and mortar fire. They now do not have fortified*

---

[42] Giap, 1970.

heights to protect them. They are experiencing what it is like to have grave supply problems. Their situation is now critical! As many of you already know, during the afternoon of May 7, we launched massive and devastating combined attacks upon the enemy headquarters at Muong Thanh. As you already know, at several French posts, the enemy hoisted a white flag and surrendered. At 17:30 hours, we seized and occupied the headquarters. That resulted in the capture of the French General de Castries and is entire staff!

That was followed by the remaining forces at Dien Bien Phu surrendering. The resulting prisoners of war have been well treated by our troops! The "Determined to fight and to win" banner of our army flutters high in the valley of Dien Bien Phu. Believe it or not, on this very night, we have attacked the south subsector. This has resulted in the entire garrison of more than two thousand men being captured!

The historic Dien Bien Phu campaign has ended in our complete victory. Our troops have fought with unprecedented heroism for fifty-five days and nights. In the enemy rear in the Red River Delta, our patriots destroyed one after the other, many positions and they have also seriously threatened Route Number Five. In the Fifth Zone they have wiped out the French Mobile Regiment and liberated Ân Khe. They have penetrated deep into the region of Cheo Reo and threatened Pleiku and Ban Me Thuot. Our troops have also been very active in Hue and in Nam Bo.

In middle Laos, our men and Laotian units increased their activity on Route number nine and advanced southwards. On all fronts, we have put out of action one hundred and twelve thousand enemy troops and either shot down or destroyed upon the ground, one hundred and seventy-seven enemy aircraft. These great victories of the

Vietnam Peoples' Army and the people as a whole at Dien Bien Phu and other places have smashed the Navarre plan and stopped the attempts of the Franco-American imperialists to prolong and extend the war[43]."

Talks at the Geneva Conference

By the end of 1953, the fighting and the French setbacks caused deep divisions in French public opinion. That in turn, caused opposition to the wars in Indochina reaching even the traditionally right-wing areas. There was the conservative strong pro-American attitude of, *"Fight-to-the-bitter-end"* ideal was expressed by the Laniel-Bidault, but this view was becoming more and more isolated as the international opinion was deeply concerned and demanded peace.

President Ho Chi Minh said to those around him, *"Ladies and Gentlemen, we have the propaganda machines of Australia, Britain, Canada, France, India, South Africa, and the United States of America against us! The propaganda machines of those countries are spreading outright lies about our struggle for independence and they are openly on the side of the French capitalists and their colonial bullies! This is a situation that we must no longer tolerate because it is impacting upon our currency and foreign relations with other countries!*

In answer to all of that, I am attending an interview with the Swedish newspaper called Expressen, on the 26th of November 1953." During the interview Ho Chi Minh said, *"If we have drawn the inevitable lessons from these years of war, they are that the French Government desires to conclude an armistice and resolve the Vietnam issue through*

---

[43] Giap, 1970.

negotiations, then the people and the government of the Democratic Republic of Vietnam are ready to examine French proposals... The fundamental basis for such an armistice is that the French Government must truly respect Vietnam's independence[44]."

Meanwhile, at a conference between representatives of American arms manufacturers, elements of the United States of America's Government and also elements of the Laniel-Bidault cabinet of France, the discussions were on how to stop any meaningful conference which may have resulted in the Vietnamese resistance obtaining any representative status. It had become known that the USA and its allies planned to replace the pro-French agents in Vietnam with pro-American people who could continue the war.

It was the resounding successes of the Vietnamese forces which stopped all of these manoeuvres. On the 8th of May 1954, which was twenty-four hours after the fall of Dien Bien Phu, the Geneva conference on Indochina began. Mean-while, in Washington, the US President Eisenhower and his staff were discussing the Indochina situation.

His advisors told Eisenhower, *"Sir we have a probable critical situation in Indochina! The Vietnamese have been successful in wiping out the French Colonial Forces and Expeditionary Corps which were sent there to keep the people of South East Asia in line. By the USA and its allies entering the war there, we can keep up the status quo and therefore keep up our arms sales to all parties. The sales of arms in these wars have the potential of making the*

---

[44] Vien, 2009.

USA and other arms manufacturers many millions of dollars!

This will also bring about much needed stimulus of investment in industry and result in a very low unemployment rate in the USA and most of its allies. Besides all of the former, our American Administration can hide behind the myth of "The Domino Theory" which says that because Vietnam and China have become communist countries, so will all of South East Asia. That is in fact pure bunkum, but if we tell that to the public of the USA and all of its allies, the people will believe it all and we will be able to just keep on making much money from the misery imposed upon the Asians!

So, Mister President, we must torpedo the peace conference taking place at Geneva in particular because the Laniel-Bidault French Government has been replaced by the French parliament. The new government of Mendes means that France is leaning towards signing peace accords which are no good for our business or strategic interests!"

Although the Americans tried to stop the conference, they were unsuccessful, and agreements were signed which put an end to the Indochina War on the night of July 20. Eight countries were at the conference which included: The Democratic Republic of Vietnam, France, the Soviet Union, Britain, the Peoples' Republic of China, the United States of America, Cambodia, and Laos, as well as a representation of the puppet Bao Dai Government.

You may be wondering why China had the key role at the negotiation table, it was because Vietnam was receiving foreign aid exclusively from China. The peace conference was constantly being under threat of sabotage from the United States of America which only wanted to further their own interests in things like arms sales and also because Americans were becoming alarmed at the spread of communist ideals in Asia!

This was supposedly also a reason for the imperialist forces blockading the coasts and ports of Vietnam. For the fifteen days between 8th of June 1954 to the 23rd of June 1954 the French delegates refused to hold discussions with the Vietnamese representatives. They did, however, hold long negotiations with the Chinese. This resulted in the two parties agreeing on the main elements of a compromise that was acceptable to both of them. That resulted in the southern part of Indochina, which comprised southern Vietnam and Cambodia remaining under French influence, while the northern half of Vietnam and the two Laotian provinces of Sam Neua and Phongsaly would be controlled by the Vietnamese and Lao patriotic forces. China's southern borders would therefore be protected by forces that Beijing believed it could easily handle.

The Vietnamese delegates had to fight to have the principles of respect for the independence, sovereignty, unity, and territorial rights of the Indochinese countries enshrined into joint statements, but they were not able to prevent the partition of their country or to secure an autonomous re-grouping zone for the Cambodian patriotic forces. It seems that Zhou En-Lai had abandoned the Cambodian resistance, possibly because Laos has no common border with China.

The signed agreements included military and political provisions. Militarily, it was decided to put the forces of each side into two different zones, north and south of the 17th parallel, keeping separate the two armies. A three-hundred-day deadline was agreed on for achieving this.

Politically, the delegates had recognised the independence, sovereignty, and territorial integrity of the three Indochinese countries. The 17th parallel was not considered as a political frontier. Free elections using secret ballots were to be held in July 1956 at the latest. These elections were to give Vietnam a free and unified government. After nine years of war which were a total disaster for France, the French imperialists admitted how futile it was for France to attempt the reconquest of Vietnam.

From the years of the war, General Vo Nguyen Giap concluded and wrote: *"Our people and army have defeated a powerful and well-equipped enemy because our compatriots and our troops were motivated by a firm determination to fight for and win national independence, for the distribution of land to peasants, for peace and for socialism. The enemy confronted a united front from all social classes and all political and religious affiliations. Our Marxist-Leninist Party headed by President Ho Chi Minh implemented the mastery of the right political and military policies.*

We are, moreover, living in an era in which the imperialists can no longer dominate completely. A whole system of socialist countries with great political and material strength, and a national liberation movement swelling like a tidal wave are creating extremely favourable conditions for the struggle of oppressed nations. A people's war waged by a people's army may rightly be considered as one of the most decisive achievements, more important than any weapon for the countries of Asia, Africa, and Latin America. By liberating themselves, the Vietnamese people are proud to have contributed to the liberation of fraternal peoples. I believe that in the present era, no imperialist army, however powerful it may be, and no imperialist general, however talented he may be, can defeat a people, even weak and small, who know how to rise up resolutely and unite in struggle along the right political and military path.

Our experience had shown that no illusions should be harboured as to the good will of the imperialists. Colonialism in its new form is more dangerous than ever, and the people should be prepared to fight it. People should not be overawed by the power of modern weapons. It is the value of human beings which, in the end, will decide victory.[45]"

The Geneva peace accord said that it recognized the nationality and fundamental rights of the Vietnamese people including their sovereignty, their territory and unity. Due to the Geneva Conference allowing the imperialist combined forces of the Franco-USA coalition, on the one hand to hold South Vietnam under the 17th parallel and allowing the National resistance by the People of Vietnam to hold the north on the other, it stopped the Vietnamese from completely liberating their country[46].

The agreements stated that the south of Vietnam would be handed over to a provisional administration after two years at the most and that general elections would be held in 1956 at the latest, giving Vietnam a single and united government. That did not suit the Right-wing politicians in Washington who began to set up a neo-colonist regime in

---

[45] Giap, 1970.
[46] Vien, 2009.

south Vietnam with the full blessing of the Previous French Masters! The Americans wanted the new regime to have American approved counter revolutionary movements in South Vietnam which would allow them to turn the country into a colony and military base of the USA. Military and police apparatuses were set up in order to serve as an instrument of the enslavement of the south and to reconquer the north.

The Second Indochina War – Enter the USA and its Allies

John F Kennedy (President Elect) was at the White house in order to confer with his predecessor Dwight Eisenhower. He was told to wait while the President of the United States of America attended to some necessary items. After a time, John was escorted into the Oval Office, and he found himself directly in front of the out-going president. So it was that the conversation between two of the most powerful men on earth began.

Eisenhower said, *"Jack, we have a situation in South East Asia which I find to be intolerable! There have been a number of successful revolutions in places like China, African countries and in Vietnam which has declared its full independence from the previous colonial masters, the French. As well, the probability is that other South East Asian countries will follow the lead of Vietnam and start revolutions and pro-independence activities!"*

Kennedy replied with, *"What is wrong with the people of South East Asia and other places wanting to be free from interference by outside powers? It seems to me that the United States of America was itself built upon the blood* and sacrifice of the patriots who fought the war of independence against the British.

Before you say anything about this, just consider what may have happened if France had not supported us against the British. The simple fact is that the French did not give a damn about the people of America then and they still do not! We do not owe the French anything for their support against the British, because that was only given because the French King Louis wanted to embarrass the British who were his enemies at the time! You must know that the French have carved themselves an empire of colonies in Asia, Latin America, and Africa. Do you not realise that the conduct of the French in their colonies and in Indochina in particular is like that of an extreme right-wing oppressor? What the French colonists are doing In Indochina is akin to what the bloody NAZIs did during World War Two!

We Americans defined war criminals as those who actively and totally wage war upon others and that is exactly what the French are doing in Indochina! The French even transcribed the entire Vietnamese language into Latin script and made the people of Vietnam learn it. They also forbade the traditional use of Chinese characters that the Vietnamese had used prior to French colonisation for writing. They did that in order to take away the identity of the Vietnamese people!"

That was answered by Dwight Eisenhower, "For fuck's sake Jack, things are very different now! The situation in South East Asia is that in the former French colony of Vietnam, in the northern city of Hanoi, the Vietnamese leader calling himself Ho Chi Minh has declared the full independence of his own country, and he is encouraging the populations of the rest of South East Asia to rise up in revolt against the French and British.

If we allow that to happen, it will pave the way for a complete take-over of all South East Asia. The major problems are that the new governments are very likely to be communist ones! We must not allow that to happen! Regarding the Indochina War and the uprising in Vietnam in particular Jack, you have to go in!

As well, there is the angle of the USA earning big money from supplying all sides of these revolutions in Asia, Africa and even Latin America to consider. I have just concluded a meeting with the American arms manufacturers of Lockheed, McDougal/Douglas, Boeing, and Colt. These companies all want in on the possibility of supplying weapons to all sides of these conflicts! The arms manufacturers stand to make millions of dollars from the wars of independence.

Not just that, but if you were to colour red every country which either has or is likely to have a communist government, then you will see that the Soviet Union, plus "The Peoples' Republic of China," plus all of South East Asia, including Burma and Thailand, plus Malaysia would all be a red colour right down to Singapore! America and its allies cannot afford that to happen, so you have to go into the war of independence in Vietnam on the side of the French colonialists!

By doing that, it will generate demand for American weapons and our arms manufacturers will do very well. That will cause high rates of employment which is currently at a low ebb!" Kennedy said, "OK Dwight, I see what you mean, you are talking about the 'Domino Theory' which states that *if more states in South East Asia were to fall, the entire Asia region would become Communist!*

OK then, to appease the American arms manufacturers and those Americans who like you think that people should not have independence just because their colonial masters are the fucking French, I can see that we must not let that happen, because that sort of bullshit is the view of the right-wing majority like yourself! What a pity that happens to be the case! There should be justice in the world and all people must be both equal and free!

However, by siding with the French and helping them to impose their will upon other sovereign nations, the USA will come out of all of this very badly, at great expense and many totally unnecessary casualties due to our generals living in the past and even wanting to use the idea of large armies and huge battles in order to wipe out an enemy which has a very high degree of popular support.

That will be the case even before we end up with a huge number of casualties from what the public will eventually see as unjustified interference on our part against other sovereign nations purely because they may end up with a different political system to that of the USA! Therefore, I suppose the clearly corrupt and unrepresentative Government of South Vietnam must be supported by America and our allies solely because as you have pointed out, it is in the business and strategic interests of America to do so!

So, soon after today my administration of myself, Bobby Kennedy, Lyndon Johnston, Bob McNamara, Dean Rusk, Walt and the two Bundy brothers, will announce that we all share a belief that we have a crusading faith in the power of politics to create a better society.

A society in which all men are created equal before God and that all men have the right to live in freedom. We will say that we govern for the greater good of all people to live in freedom. In reality, we will continue with the present policies of your own administration and things will go on as they always have.

To make things look really good, we will make it look like we are enforcing full equality among all Americans by doing minor things like enforcing the rights of Americans of Negro decent to attend the same schools and universities as Caucasian students. As well, I will speak against such things as the Ku Klux Klan and other racist groups!

After that has had time to filter through the American community, I will announce that I am sending in American advisors to help the army of the Republic of Vietnam (South Vietnam). The announcement of the commitment of US combat troops will have to wait until after those things because if we do otherwise, we will be committing electoral suicide!"

The young President Kennedy had a close interest in guerrilla warfare. That allowed him to see that jungle combat skills of a counter-revolutionary war in fact was a new challenge to the USA forces. He tried to get his views imposed on a very reluctant Pentagon but found that he was resisted. The American generals could only think in terms of large armies and huge battles.

They believed or hoped that an enemy who chose to hide in jungles and tunnels would quickly be flushed out by American firepower and then die in open battle. Feeling frustrated, he was heard to say, *"Bloody fucking hell! You call yourselves generals when you are living back during the*

WW2 times which only means that you will get beaten if you try using those old tactics against an enemy which has close and popular support among the people of Vietnam. You are short-sighted fools who will cost us many American lives! Why is it that you cannot see that you are facing new types of warfare as has already been written about by both Moa Tse Tung and General Vo Nguyen Giap? You cannot see the woods for the trees! We will get many casualties!"

Australian Involvement in Indochina

Meanwhile, the British had announced that they would leave all British bases east of Suez Canal. That caused great concern to the Prime Minister of Australia, Robert Menzies, who immediately went into discussion about this with cabinet ministers. One of these was Malcom Fraser, who was to become the Minister of Army. Bob Menzies said, *"Malcom, I note that the British are pulling out of all bases east of the Suez Canal! That means that we will be left high and dry without back-up because the British shall be leaving their bases in Singapore and Malaysia!*

That will bring about a most serious situation for Australia, we have a coastline that is over twelve thousand miles in length, and we cannot defend it with our present small population of ten-point four point eight million people! I need you to see John F Kennedy in the USA and offer him the unrestricted use of Australian soldiers who shall be under American command for use in the new American war in Asia on the condition that we get a direct alliance with the USA coming to our aid in the event of an armed attack upon us!"

Malcom Frazer said, *"Hang on there a moment Bob, do you realise what you are asking? The defence forces of*

Australia are entirely made up of volunteers. We now have a peace-time army which is one regiment in size. (Three battalions) One of these is on active service against the fucking Indonesians in the Malaysian States of Sarawak and Sabah in Borneo. That means that already we have one third of the army on overseas duties!"

Menzies answered with, *"Do not give me a hard time Malcom, just offer the Yanks the expertise of our jungle fighting soldiers. At first, we will only send the advisers and if the war escalates into something bigger then it is at the moment, I will send in the first of the infantry battalions!"* The future Army Minister now argued, *"Bloody hell Bob, don't you get it? We already have an infantry battalion deployed in war-like operations in Sabah/Sarawak as well as elements of our special forces! We do not have more men to spare! We have over a third of the entire Australian army involved in hostilities already! Once we start taking causalities there will be no stopping of public anger about this and our government will be tossed out on its ear!"*

That made Menzies say, *"Malcom, we have announced the imposition of National Service for twenty-year old Australian males. When reporters ask you if the National Servicemen will be sent to Vietnam, just say, "If we still have the Vietnam commitment in a year from now, then they shall be sent there to fight, but only if they happen to volunteer for this! If you answer like that, it implies that this Vietnam War shall be over with very quickly. It does not matter if that is the case or not! What matters is that you return from seeing Kennedy in the USA with an alliance to keep us safe!"*

Next, the future Australian Minister of Army went to see Kennedy in the USA. At the meeting, it was pointed out that there was already in existence, a defence treaty between Australia and the USA called the ANZUS treaty. An advisor to Kennedy called McGeorge Bundy sent a private memo to President Kennedy. This said, *"Australians have tried to interpret our ANZUS commitment as a blank check, but Menzies has never made this mistake. He knows that we are good allies, but the exact shape of our action under the treaty will depend on your judgement as president at every stage.[47]"*

In May 1962 Rush was in Canberra attending the first ANZUS Treaty council to be held outside of America. Rush was there solely to extract a commitment from the Australian Government to send military advisers to South Vietnam. Meanwhile, Malcomb Fraser had returned to Canberra.

When he spoke to Bob Menzies, he said, *"Well Bob, with reference to the ANZUS treaty that was signed in 1951, we have an alliance of sorts. However, do not get excited about it for it is hardly worth the paper it is written on!*

The facts are these: (1) In US eyes, ANZUS has a chameleon-like quality. (2) America will decide when and how the treaty applies, if at all. (3) Australia is not a US defence priority and that is demonstrated by the USA fence-sitting over the Indonesian and West Papuan Circes!

In fact, the Americans consider that Japan is far more vital to US commercial interests than is our country! I strongly suggest that we cover up this almost useless treaty because if the opposition were to get hold of it, they will launch a campaign which will see the Liberal/Country Party Government in opposition!"

---

[47] Ham, 2007.

I remember that the newspapers of the time were broadly in favour and gave support to Washington. There were some exceptions to that rule, and one of them was the Courier-Mail which warned that South Vietnam could easily become the battleground of a new world war.

Meanwhile, Frank Hopkins the US consul general in Melbourne sent a message to Washington saying, *"After nearly two centuries of economic and psychological dependence on Great Britain, Australians are shocked by the thought that they may now have to stand on their own two feet and rely primarily upon themselves...They feel that Britain is letting them down and that the United States is failing to appreciate their plight... It remains to be seen whether Australians can find the courage, the confidence and willpower to work out their own destiny under much less favourable conditions....[48]"*

Australian Advisers Arrive

On the 6th of June 1962, after flying to South Vietnam, the Australian Army Colonel named as Francis Serong stepped out of his aircraft and onto the tarmac at Tan Son Nhut Airport (Saigon). He bore himself with confidence and he had the air of a man who knew his own mind and was very determined. He was met upon the tarmac by Lieutenant General Richard Weede, chief of Staff to the US General Paul Harkins, who commanded the newly formed US Military Assistance Command Vietnam.

The Australian Colonel was on a private fact finding and intelligence gathering excursion. After spending some weeks in Vietnam, he had visited the headquarters of the US Military Assistance and Advisory Group, the demilitarised

---

[48] Ham, 2007.

zone, Da Nang, and the Central Highlands. Having seen these areas and the state of progress of the undeclared war against the Vietnamese patriots.

He was thinking to himself and concluded, *"Fucking hell! Things are much worse than I have been led to believe, and they are getting worse! The progress of this undeclared war is dismal! I partly blame the Saigon Government of President Ngo Dinh Diem, which has failed to draw up a strategic plan! South Vietnam Government Plan? – that only exists on paper and there is little to nothing in fact! Saigon's ARVN soldiers who are US trained are as useless as using a bucket to put out a raging bushfire!"*

After having these thoughts, he wrote, *"If Australian troops were to join this war, we will probably lose some, tactically. We may lose the lot strategically!"* His tough minded-minded approach and willingness to speak his mind won him the respect and hatred of Australian, South Vietnamese and US armies as well as the ears of Presidents Johnston and Diem[49].

As of early 1963, Colonel Serong now focussed on his important task in Vietnam, that of being the first commander of the Australian Army Training Team Vietnam (AATTV). He had chosen the first thirty members of his unit from a list of a hundred officers and two hundred warrant officers. The training at the Australian Army's School of Torture prepared the men for what was to come, and they coped with the feared jungle training course at Canungra with ease after this. After having pre-embarkation leave, the men left for Vietnam on a Qantas flight to Saigon. Their locations were strictly classified.

---

[49] Ham, 2007.

As they stepped upon the tarmac at Tan Son Nhut airport, they were described as, *"Hatchet-faced professionals"* by an American officer. Although a British counter-insurgency expert called Sir Robert Thompson wanted them sent to the delta, that was overruled by Serong who insisted, *"My team are all jungle fighting experts and specialists – they operate in the jungle and not in bloody rice paddies!"*

There is little doubt that *"The Team"* was little more than a cog within the US war effort, however, a thousand members of the Team were in due course sent to Vietnam to serve there with distinction. They raised and even led small units of Vietnamese and indigenous Montagnard soldiers and with them, they fought a series of amazing operations against the enemy. The efforts members of the Australian Army Training Team Vietnam were such that it was the most highly decorated unit of the Australian Army for the entire Vietnam War.

The First Australian Infantry Battalion Sent to Vietnam

After World War Two, the Australian army had been re-organised into its peace-time army status. The army was primarily three battalions which together with supporting units, formed a regiment and the battalions making up the regiment were identified by both their number and the title of the regiment. This meant that the First Battalion Royal Australian Regiment was identified by the initials of 1RAR. The two other battalions were identified as 2RAR and 3RAR. At the height of Australia's commitment to the Vietnam War (Second Indochina War). Australia had a total of nine battalions which were later called the First Division. Many people seem to think only in terms of those who do the fighting when it comes to armies.

In fact, the soldiers involved in combat duties are outnumbered greatly by those in support. With the American Army, for every man at the "Sharp End" there were ten others in support. The Australians were having a smaller and less mechanised army had the ratio of six in support for every man at "The Sharp End."

As Australia's involvement in Vietnam grew, so did the requirement for more Australian soldiers who not were involved in the Malaysian States. Now Australian politicians from the conservative Liberal/Country Party Coalition Government were actively considering ways to send a force of combat troops to bolster the activities of the Australian Army Training Team Vietnam. The hawks among the Menzies Government demanded that Australia send an infantry battalion to South Vietnam which would be subject to American command.

This in turn now meant that Australia's professional army of three infantry battalions would have two thirds of its strength on overseas combat duties because out of the strength of three battalions, one was on active service in Borneo and another one would be serving in South Vietnam. These things demanded that Australia increase the size of its army and by the end of the Vietnam War, the strength of the Australian army was at nine battalions and supporting units or one division.

Menzies and his cronies knew that there would be opposition to the announcement that Australian combat troops would be deployed to South Vietnam in 1965. Menzies discussed things with some of his cabinet including Malcom Frazer, the future Minister of Army.

The Full Circle for Mick

Menzies said to Frazer, *"Malcom, today is Monday, 26th of April 1965 and I need some ideas on how we can announce to the Australian Public that we are sending Australian troops to the war in Indochina in such a way that we do not lose votes! Come on Mal, produce a strategy which will allow us to send the troops and still maintain our electoral advantage over the Labour Party!"*

The future Minister of Army answered, *"Bob, I thought that you would have been an astute and clever enough a politician to think of this yourself, but seeing how you have asked me, I suggest that you wait until eight in the night on Thursday 29th of April 1965 to announce that Australia will send the First Battalion Royal Australian Regiment to fight in South Vietnam.*

By you waiting until the evening of 29th of April 1965 to announce this in Parliament, the labour opposition leader of Arthur Caldwell and his deputy leader of Gough Whitlam should be absent, as will be most of the entire parliament, because the following day is the beginning of a long weekend. You are legally not required to give advanced warning to the house, so you can easily get away with this! I know that you are keen to involve us in the Indochina war, and I completely support you in this.

In order to sell it to the public we can simply tell some half-truths which are almost impossible to be exposed as outright lies, even though that is what we will be using! You can bullshit on about the danger of the red tide of yellow-coloured Asians to our north possibly invading us and how we need to maintain American support to stop that danger from happening. By us saying that we need to do this in order for the Yanks to support us under the ANZUS Treaty, we should be able to carry the day and even have the gullible Australian public swallow what we say!" Menzies replied with, *"Malcom my boy, you are a genius!"*

So it was that the Australian Prime Minister, Mr. Robert Gordon Menzies waited until after 8 pm of Thursday, 29th of April 1965 to announce to an empty parliament, *"The takeover of South Vietnam would be a direct military threat to Australia and all of the countries of South-East Asia. It must be seen as a part of a thrust by Communist China between the Indian and Pacific Oceans."*

He declared, *"The Australian Government is now in receipt of a request from the Government of South Vietnam for further military assistance. We have decided – and this has been in close consultation with the Government of the United States – to provide an infantry battalion for service in Vietnam... This decision represents the most useful additional contribution which we can make to the defence of the region at this time. The takeover of South Vietnam would be a direct military threat to Australia and all countries of South-East Asia. It must be seen as part of a thrust by Communist China between the Indian and Pacific Oceans!*[50]*"*

That statement and others like it, made it appear that Menzies had in fact lied his head off! Doubts about the Australian troops in South Vietnam decision provoked claims that the Menzies Government had misled Parliament, and Menzies kept up the pretence that Australian soldiers had been asked for by both the American Administration and the Prime Minister of South Vietnam, Phan Huy Quat.

In reality, Quat did not want any foreign troops in his country because he was a member of Dai Viet (the

---

[50] Ham, 2009.

Vietnamese Nationalist Party), and he had deep misgivings about the use of more foreign troops and how their presence would hand the propaganda arm of the Viet Minh (renamed to Vietcong by the Americans) a propaganda coupe.

So, the Australian Cabinet were in discussion and Menzies said, *"Gentlemen, we have problems, I have stated in public that Australia has been asked to provide combat troops for use in South Vietnam by both the South Vietnamese Government and the USA Government.*

At the moment, Quat is bloody refusing to take more foreign troops into his country for fear that the resulting propaganda by the Communists will cost the South Vietnamese Government dearly. We must coerce the South Vietnamese Prime Minister to formally request Australian soldiers before the fucking Labour Party can find out that we have been telling a series of lies to the Australian Parliament and people! Now come-on people, if it becomes public knowledge that our government is a pack of liars, we will be in deep shit! We will therefore coerce Prime Minister Quat into asking our government to send Aussie troops if he likes it or not!"

The seventeen days before the announcement of the Menzies Government that an Australian Battalion would be sent to Vietnam was a worrying time for everyone in the cabinet. The fact remains that neither the South Vietnamese Administration of that of the USA had asked for Australian soldiers to be sent to Vietnam. Menzies asked Australia's ambassador to Washington, Keith Waller to arrange a special meeting with Secretary of State, Dean Rusk.

That was done, resulting in the Australian ambassador sending a telegram which said, *"I asked Rusk if*

I could inform the Australian Government that is the President's desire that Australia should supply a battalion for use in South Vietnam…Rusk said that I could inform you and that the sooner the battalion was supplied, the better.[51]"

That had been the easy part of things. The hard part was getting the South Vietnamese Prime Minister to accept Australian soldiers. The whole idea appeared to be causing him pain. It was now three days before the scheduled statement by Menzies. The Saigon Government had not agreed to the proposal of using Australian soldiers and it did not make any request to do so!

A sense of near panic was among government ranks because on the day before Menzies was to make the announcement of Australian troops being necessary to serve in South Vietnam, there still was no formal request for Australian Troops from the Government of South Vietnam. As well, things were messy because of an article by Alan Reid about the dispatch of Australian soldiers to South Vietnam was imminent.

As this crisis was deepening, Menzies finally found a way out of the problem. Menzies had received a quickly drafted thank-you note from President Johnston. This stated, *"Dear Mr. Prime Minister, I am delighted by the decision of your government to provide an infantry battalion for service in South Vietnam at the request of the Government of South Vietnam"*

The simple fact about this was that no such request was ever received by the Australian Government. Therefore, it appears Menzies had lied and misled the Australian

---

[51] Ham, 2007.

Parliament by implying that he had received a written request for military help.

During the dead of night on 26th of April, the members of 1RAR were on board the HMAS Sydney which had formerly been an aircraft carrier and now was used as a troops transport ship. The battalion was commanded by Lieutenant Colonel Ivan Brumfield, and he was thirty-eight years old at the time. After being transferred from HMAS Sydney onto landing crafts, the Australians finally stepped ashore upon the beach at Vung Tau. Many Australians experienced a sense of unease, a sense of being watched by unseen eyes. All of them had their nostrils assailed by the stench of rotting vegetation, the smell of fish in the markets as well as drying fish and the sense of despondency which was prevalent.

Many Australian soldiers experienced what they later called *"Culture Shock."* After being transferred onto road transport, the battalion arrived at the American airfield at Bien Hoa. There were Vietnamese signs saying *'Welcome Australians'* and *'Long Live Australian-Vietnamese Anti-Communist Spirit'* at the gates to Bien Hoa Airbase[52]. So began the involvement of Australian infantry combat soldiers in Vietnam. Meanwhile, Mick was working in the Northern Territory of Australia.

Choice of Mick's Nationality

Hildegard and Edgar were upset that they had repeatedly been subjected to a number of anti-German comments from various people in the community. Their relatives in Germany had asked them to return there and they were both enthusiastic about the idea of returning to their

---

[52] Ham, 2007.

original homeland. Unknown to their children, they had organised travel back to Germany. They then informed their children. The two oldest ones were Andy and Mick. Both of them rejected the idea of leaving Australia. When their parents informed them of the decision to return to Germany, Andy was the first to speak.

He said, *"Mum and Edgar, I am staying here and completing my apprenticeship as a baker!"* On the other hand, Mick said, *"Mum and Edgar, even though at times my life in this area has been like living in hell due to anti-German attitudes of many people, most of that happened at Mount Burr, the home of cretins! Since starting work at APCEL, I am accepted as an Australian.*

If you need to return to Germany, then you should do so, but I am staying here! Yesterday, was Monday the 13th of July 1964. At 10 am of yesterday morning, I became a naturalised Australian Citizen (British Subject) and there is nothing that you or anyone else can do about it! I was asked if I would serve in the defence of this country during times of war and I have given my undertaking to do so!

I shall in fact be proud to do so! The registration number of my Naturalisation Certificate is E.M. (1) No.177701 and I think that will be printed in the local newspapers. When she read that Mick had been naturalised as an Australian, Hildegard scolded Mick. She said, *"I did not really believe that you have become a British subject, but I read about it in the papers! How dare you?* Mick replied with, *"I am an Australian. I grew up here! I am now nineteen years old, and I am staying here! By the way, I am going to Darwin soon!"*

Australians Set up at Nui Dat

During a day of August 1965, while speaking to General Bill DePuy, the Chief of Staff to Westmoreland, Australian Major General Ken Mackay said, *"Just put a ring around Phuoc Tuy Province!*[53]*."*

Mackay was in conference with the American commanders about where to deploy the First Australian Task Force (1ATF) which had been formed to defend a chosen South Vietnamese province. The result of the US experiment of having the Australians under direct command had clearly not worked and the Australians were now going to get their own area of operations. The decision to approve the setting up of the Australian Base Camp at Nui Dat was approved by Lieutenant General John Wilton, Australia's Chief of the General Staff and Brigadier David Jackson, the designated commander of 1ATF. Wilton approved Phuoc Tuy because it met his strict criteria.

Try to imagine Phuoc Tuy Province as a rectangle measuring thirty kilometres from north to south and sixty kilometres from the east to the west. It has a boundary of the South China Sea to the south plus the Rung Sat marshes and Saigon River to the west. It is bordered by Binh Thuan Province in the east and Long Kanh Province to the north.

In 1966, Phuoc Tuy Province contained almost one hundred and three thousand people who were populating more than thirty villages and one hundred hamlets. The religion of the people appeared to be that two-thirds of the people were of the Buddhist faith, while up to one third of them followed the Catholic Church. These people lived in a

---

[53] Ham, 2007.

province which had mountains, jungle, grasslands, and swamps[54].

In the north-east corner, are the Nui Thi Vai and the Nui Toc Tien Hills, while to the west of Nui Dat. The Long Hai Range is between the province and the South China Sea to the east. It was stated by an Australian Army Officer, "Phuoc Tuy offers the perfect terrain for guerrilla warfare. It has a long coastline with complex areas of mangrove swamps, isolated ranges of very rugged mountains and a large area of uninhabited jungle containing all of the most loathsome combinations of thorny bamboos, poisonous snakes, insects, malaria, dense underbrush, swamps, and rugged ground conditions that the most resolute guerrilla warfare expert could ask for.[55]"

When asked about the strategic value of Phuoc Tuy Province, the former chief of propaganda of the Liberation Front, called Nguyen Gia Ho stated, "We saw the province as very important strategically, because Vung Tau is at the mouth of the Saigon River and is connected by road to Saigon. Phuoc Tuy was one of four fronts to Ho Chi Minh City."

The national war of independence as practiced in Phuoc Tuy Province meant that the Viet Minh completely overran the province, and it became one of the major Viet Minh bases of the south of Vietnam. This in turn resulted in up to seventy percent of the population of the province either being active serving members of the Viet Minh and later on, the Vietcong, or else they were sympathisers. So it was that only the provincial capital city of Ba Ria had any link with

---

[54] Ham, 2007.
[55] Ham, 2007.

the South Vietnamese Government at Saigon. In every other part of Phuoc Tuy Province, the Vietcong (American slang meaning Vietnamese communist) were in full control and unopposed.

People of the Catholic religion were also in Phuoc Tuy. These were Catholic refugees from the north of Vietnam who built heavily fortified villages like Binh Gia, replacing the Buddhist pagoda with a small Catholic Church. That in itself caused some resentment between the Catholics and Buddhists. Some of these refugees from the north were no doubt the very landowners and mandarins who caused so much misery which in itself was a major cause of revolution. It was in this environment that the men of 1RAR set up the new Base Camp of 1ATF. The soldiers put in minefields around the perimeter, barbed wire entanglements trenches and gun/mortar positions.

After some time, the last remaining men of 1RAR returned to Australia, and were replaced by the two battalions and their supporting units. The two battalions well trained with almost half of them being National Servicemen. These men were about twenty years old and were chosen by a raffle. So it was that the defoliation of Nui Dat began immediately, using ground spraying teams. These men defoliated five square kilometres of the Nui Dat area and the thirteen-kilometre perimeter.

The old and tall rubber trees were left untouched, except in the area around the perimeter, where they were cleared in order to have long and clear areas of fire around the perimeter. The shade provided by these rubber trees was most welcome as the tents of the soldiers were under them.

Thickly forested regions of Phuoc Tuy including the Rung Sat swamps and farms considered to be controlled by the Vietcong, were regularly sprayed by defoliants including "Agent Orange" using aircraft. This was both an inhumane and unsuccessful strategy which only destroyed enough food to feed 245,000 Vietnamese people for a year resulting in a propaganda gift to the Vietcong[56].

Given that defoliation did not uncover the enemy, who kept on fighting from jungle, caves and tunnels, the whole defoliation programme must be considered a failure. Given also, that birth defects and other health problems associated with defoliants can be directly blamed upon *"Agent Orange,"* it stands to reason that the allies in the Second Indochina War who sprayed it upon villages and farms can in fact be said to be, "Guilty of War Crimes![57]"

The First Australian Task Force

The 5th Battalion Royal Australian Regiment was created at Holsworthy Barracks on the 1st of March 1965. It was made up of the former 1RAR Veterans who had returned to Australia and who were now the NCOs and, in some cases, officers training the new battalion.

Although the area of the 1ATF Base Camp had already been set-up by 1RAR, that battalion was about to leave for return to Australia, being replaced by the newly arrived First Australian Task Force. 1ATF at the time comprised by 5RAR and 6RAR plus supporting units. Over

---

[56] Ham, 2007
Chemical attack involving "Agent Orange" and other chemicals were used against the Vietnamese by allied units who sprayed it upon farms, villages, and jungle without any regard for how it affected the Vietnamese people.

time, 1ATF would be expanded to three battalions plus supporting units.

The moment the Nui Dat area had been cleared and secured; the task Force began aggressive patrolling of the Phuoc Tuy Province. The reasons behind having these patrols were to undermine Vietcong (VC) and North Vietnamese Army (NVA) operations in the area. The objective was to seek out and close with the enemy and to kill him. Usually this meant engaging the enemy in small contacts and limiting his supplies and re-supplies.

Northern Territory

Mick's new job in the Territory was across the harbour from Darwin at a place called Mandorah. The job was the building of the studio and transmitter as well as other buildings for Radio Australia. By ferry, the journey from Darwin to Mandorah took just twenty minutes, but by land, the trip was a three hour or longer slog, because people had to travel right around the bays of the Darwin harbour.

Even now, this journey involves a trip of over 98 km from the turn-off linking the Stuart Highway to the roads around the bays of Darwin Harbour and things were a lot worse for travellers then. Mick's new employer was Luigi Campeirrie, who provided both accommodation and meals in the Mandorah construction site. The meals were very good. They were typical Italian cooked meals which were greatly enjoyed by all members of the construction gang. This gave Mick a great respect for people of different ethnic backgrounds to his own. Over time, he greatly appreciated the efforts of his Italian and Creek co-workers, and he understood their ways of life.

Luigi spoke to Mick. He said, *"Mick, I need you to go to Rum Jungle for a few weeks; there is some carpentry I want you to do in order to complete my maintenance contract with Rio Tinto who operate the uranium mine there. I want you to take the three-ton truck from here and drive it Batchelor, the residential part of the Rum Jungle mine. Take both Raymond and Peter with you. They shall both assist you to carry out the tasks that I have given you. I also need you to write reports on the situation with the maintenance at Rum Jungle that we are responsible for!"*

So Mick gathered both Ray and Peter, obtained the truck, fuelled it, and set off for Batchelor. Upon their arrival, the men were delighted to discover that all meals were provided again, something that they were now accustomed to.

The maintenance proved to be a mixed bag of jobs, ranging from the installation of new timber slats in the uranium treatment ponds though to the hanging of new doors in various buildings. As the work was so varied and interesting, time passed quickly until they were due to return to Mandorah and the job on Radio Australia. Mick and Raymond became good friends and they both decided that the constant drinking which formed the main activity of many of their colleagues was not for them. Instead, they would go out and hunt wild pigs, crocodiles and also prospect for uranium, gold, and opals.

The workers on the Mandorah construction site were of many different ethnic origins, but everyone got on well together. Some of the men succumbed to alcohol poisoning due to them excessively consuming self-brewed beer made from ingredients with a very high sugar content before fermentation. The drinking of excessive amounts of alcohol can quickly lead to dehydration. In a hot and humid place such as Darwin that can quickly lead to heat exhaustion. For these reasons, the only substances that Mick and Raymond would drink were water, tea, and commercial beer.

That proved to be a saving grace for them because it meant that other than having some beer on alternate Fridays, they did not spend money on alcohol at all. Mick would bank as much money as he thought it was prudent to do so and soon had enough money to purchase a Landrover four-wheel drive using his saved money.

The work on the studio building of Radio Australia was progressing at good pace, with the footings, the floor slab and lower brick walls now completed. The construction gang was called upon to construct the second floor level, known as the first floor in Australia and the second level in the USA. In order to do that, Mick and his co-workers put into place, the adjustable height props and jacks that were to hold the temporary beams and sections of timber which supported the wet concrete floor until it was cured and could support its own weight.

The upper floor, (called suspended concrete floor) was mainly supported by the use of prefabricated concrete beams which were joined together using bolts nuts and washers. Mick fund that his abilities in electric arc welding and carpentry were in constant demand so that various sections of trench mesh and reinforcing fabric were joined. Now that things were finally ready for it, the entire upper floor level was poured as a monolithic pour. Mick and Raymond proceeded to use vibrators to get any air bubbles out of the wet concrete so that it would become a very dense and solid mass.

While the floor of the upper level cured, other work continued, such as the fitting of the steel door and window attachments to the brickwork of the lower level walls. Meanwhile, Luigi arrived and inspected the work before he left to negotiate the next project for his building company. Then came the fitting of the actual doors and windows onto the attachments that had been installed earlier. Seven days later, the foreman was satisfied that the curing of the upper level was now at the point where the supporting structure beneath it could be removed, so that was done.

The meal on that night was ravioli. For the first time in his life, Mick tasted a wine called Tarrango. Some of the construction workers said that it was an Italian wine, while others said that it was of Spanish origin. He liked the way that this red wine complimented the pasta meal, and he made a mental note of it.

As the meal progressed, the workers all discussed the progress of the building of Radio Australia as it was apparent that things were close to completion. Fresco, the foreman said, *"Gentlemen, this job is getting close to completion and although we still need to do a small number of things like the installation of some items, we are going into the phase of cleaning up and getting ready for the hand-over of the buildings to Radio Australia.*

We should have things ready for the brick layers to lay the final bricks by late tomorrow afternoon. After that, we install the attachments for the windows and doors on the second level, followed by installation of the doors and windows themselves. That will mean that the buildings are at the Lock-up stage by tomorrow afternoon. That that the only things still needing to be done is the installation of electrical wiring and plumbing! Those of you who wish to

The Full Circle for Mick

remain with this company, see me after the finish of the "End of contract party which will be held on the second floor of the Victoria Hotal in Smith Street Darwin.

All of you and your guests are invited and there is no need to bring your money, as everything is already paid for by Luigi. Luigi is very happy with our work and the entire project has been completed two months ahead of schedule. For those reasons, Luigi has authorised the payment to each of us of an extra one hundred dollars."

That was like music to the ears of Raymond and Mick, who were both looking forward to the "End of Contract Party." Early in the following afternoon, they both had showers and got cleaned up in general. After that, they and other construction workers went to the wharf at Mandurah and awaited the arrival of the ferry to Darwin.

After boarding the ferry, there was a 20 minute long voyage before the ferry coasted in to its berth on the Darwin wharf. Soon after, Mick and his co-workers made their way to Smith Street and the Victoria Hotel. Arriving at the Victoria Hotel, Mick and his workmates were ushered to the upper level of the hotel, which had been booked for them by Luigi. Mick and Raymond, along with Colliin and Dean, decided to use tables on the balcony overlooking Smith Street. Mick obtained the first jug of beer, and he placed it on the table, after pouring beer into the glasses for his workmates. As time progressed, more of the workforce on the studio and transmitter of Radio Australia arrived. Some of them, had their wives accompanying them.

A very enjoyable time was had by everyone and soon, Luigi arrived with his wife and eldest son, Mario. Mario was the manager of his father's building company, and he was as popular as his father, for they both had the same values and respect for their workers.

As the evening went on and became night, one by one, the married workers and the older ones left the Victoria Hotel until there were only ten young men left. All of them were single and aged from eighteen through to twenty-two years. The time was now 11pm or 23:00 hours of Australian Central Standard Time. All of the young men were drunk, as they had consumed vast amounts of beer.

As the night progressed, suggestions were made to the rest of the group by some of its members. As the night wore on, these suggestions became sillier all of the time. Next, someone made the suggestion, *"How about in the morning, all of us go to Larrakeyah Barracks and join the Australian Army on the condition that we go to Vietnam and get to kill the new enemies of Australia?"* Perhaps it was because they were drunk, that the silly suggestion drew the response of, *"Fuck, that sounds like a fucking good idea!"*

Australian Army

Mick and Raymond were the only ones from the group of the night before to arrive at the Recruiting Office of the Australian Army. That did not surprise Mick for he already knew that what men say and what they actually mean can be two very different things. Colin arrived there ten minutes later, and so, the three young men went in to see the Recruiting Officer. It was now Monday, the 10th of January 1967. After they had been given chairs to sit on, an army officer walked into the office. He said, *"Welcome Gentlemen, I am Captain Smothers, how can I help you?"*

Mick answered for the trio, *"Sir, we would like to join the Australian Army on condition that we get sent to*

The Full Circle for Mick

either an infantry unit or else, a Special Forces unit and serve in Vietnam and kill the fucking enemies of Australia!" Captain Ian Smothers smiled at this and said, *"I shall interview each of you individually and take it from there, as there is a lot to be c*

overed, and I am very pleased to have three volunteers for active service!

First, I need to know whom I am addressing. So, all of you are to write your first and surnames on the paper provided and then pin the paper onto your shirts. That was done, and the three men had their names on their shirts. Ian said, *"Let's start with you, Mick!"* And so, the interview between Mick and the Recruiting Officer was underway.

Captain Smothers took Mick through the "Oath of Allegiance" and asked, *"Michael Kramer, do you swear by almighty God that you will faithfully serve Queen Elizabeth the Second, her Heirs and Successors and Uphold the Laws and Constitution of Australia?"* Mick answered, *"I do!"* Ian responded with *"Congratulations Mick, you are now aa member of the Australian Army!"* Ian now produced forms that had to be filled out and signed by Mick. The recruiting Officer's next action was to ask Mick, *"Michael, I now have to sight your proof of age. A birth certificate would be great, but in its absence, I can also accept you Australian Naturalisation Certificate, if you happen to have it on you!"* So, Mick showed him his Australian Naturalisation Certificate. Ian looked at it and said, *"My boy, there is something wrong here; the date on the back of the Naturalisation Certificate says that you were born on the 1st of March 1947; that means that you are one year too young to do things in your own right and that therefore, you must* have the signatures of your parents giving you permission to join the army!"

Mick could not believe what he was hearing, and he said, *"You have to be pulling my fucking leg! Even by official reckoning, I am now twenty years old, and the Government of this country is conscripting blokes who are twenty years old, but who do not want to serve the country! Are you for fucking real? Are you really turning away a volunteer because of this bureaucratic bullshit?"*

Ian replied, *"It does not matter what I think, I must apply the law, but let us see what sort of initiative you have. If you are really serious about this, you will quickly find a way of doing this!"* To that, Mick replied, *"Can you let me have a black ballpoint pen?"*

Captain Ian Smothers handed Mick the black ballpoint pen. Mick then proceeded to alter the of birth shown on his naturalisation certificate from the 1st of March 1947 to the 1st of March 1946 by simply taking the black pen and altering the 7 of 1947 into a 6. So his date of birth now read as the 1st of March 1946. Ian Smothers said, *"Brilliant initiative shown Mick, welcome to the Australian Army! Tomorrow, you shall travel to Wagga Wagga for basic training. That will be followed by Infantry Corps Training at Infantry Centre, Blamey Barracks at Ingleburn NSW."*

Infantry Corps Training

After he had completed the Basic Training at Wagga Wagga, Mick was taken to Infantry Centre at Ingleburn. It was now that he learned minor infantry tactics on a section and platoon level. Also, he learned radio voice procedure, including the phonetic alphabet.

The Full Circle for Mick

Mick, Collin, and Raymond got out of the buses which had taken them to the Infantry Centre at Ingleburn. They were spoken to by sergeant Rodger Thorpe. He said, *"Welcome to Infantry Centre, Ingleburn! Unfortunately, your bus has arrived late, and your first lessons are already in progress in that classroom over there. Get yourselves to it now and learn what you can."* As the three men went into the classroom, they found a lesson using the phonetic alphabet was in progress.

AN/PRC 25 Radio

Corporal Alfred Burgess was giving the lesson. He said, *"You three late-comers quickly go to that table and get your pens and notebooks. You shall now learn the phonetic alphabet and correct radio voice procedures. Be sure to copy down all of the stuff written on the black boards because you have to know all of this, and your lives may well depend upon how well you remember all of this! All of you will be tested in this and anyone found to not be "Up to speed in any area, will be 'Back-squadded!' So make sure that you learn the phonetic alphabet by rote!"*

Mick at the closest blackboard and saw the alphabet he was expected to learn: A-Alpha; B-Bravo; C-Charlie; D-Delta; E-Echo; F-Foxtrot; G-Golf; H-Hotel; I-India; J-Juliet; K-Kilo; L-Lima; M-Mike; N-November; O-Oscar; P-Papa; Q-Quebec; R-Romeo; S-Sierra; T-Tango; U-Uniform; V-Victor; W-Whiskey; X-Xray; Y-Yankee; Z-Zulu. He decided to learn everything by rote so that all would be second nature to him.

Corporal Burgess now said, *"Gentlemen, as of now, you shall all complete daily sessions in the use of our portable radio sets. These are the AN/PRC25 sets. In the coming lessons we shall concentrate on coding and decoding of messages, and everyone one of you shall have at least eight hours of experience using the radios. You will learn how to adjust frequencies, and you will learn various call-signs and how to use them. All of you must now practice the voice procedures. Tomorrow afternoon, you shall learn minor infantry tactics and contact drills. Make sure that you apply yourselves well to all of these, because your lives will depend on how well you carry out the drills and how well you communicate with other Allied Units!"*

He then said, *"Gentlemen, we start the voice procedure for getting in touch with our headquarters now."* He then nodded towards where an AN/PRC25 and operator had set up in the class room. The radio operator said loudly, *"Zero Alpha Delta Zero Alpha, this is this is Alpha Delta Two, a message for you, over."*

Corporal Burgess again spoke. He said, *"Make sure that you know that HQ is always Alpha Delta Zero Alpha and that the sub-unit that you could be a part of will have its own identifying call sign. It is critical that correct voice procedure in maintained and that the correct call signs are used at all times! Now then, when ending a message, we say (call sign e.g. Alpha Delta Two) "Rodger (meaning understood) – out."*

M72 LAW

That was followed by the members of the training platoon travelling to the rifle ranges and being introduced to the M72 rocket launcher, the GPMG M60 Machine Gun and the M79 Grenade launcher. Again, the soldiers were instructed by Corporal Burgess.

He said, *"Gentlemen, this is the M72 LAW. LAW stands for Light Anti-armour Weapon, and it replaced the M20A1 "Super Bazooka" which was used previously! It is role is short range enemy tank destroyer. Its secondary role is for use as an anti-bunker weapon. It can be fired from any rifle or machine gun position. This is a single shot weapon which cannot be reloaded!*

Therefore, upon using it, we must destroy what is left so that the Noggies cannot convert it into something to use against us! After that we bury what is left of it!" That was followed by all soldiers taking their turns in firing the weapon at various targets.

M79 Grenade Launcher

When Mick and the rest of the soldiers entered the classroom, they saw three M79 Grenade launchers and many posters about these weapons hanged up on the walls. Again, the lesson about the weapons was given by Corporal Burgess. He called the class to attention and marked the role book. He said, *"Gentlemen, it is time for you to get to know a little lady whom we call "The equaliser!" She is the M79 Grenade Laucher, and she replaces the 2 inch mortar that was used previously! She has a wooden stock and aluminium rifled barrel. She is accurate and her range is up 375 metres. She has a fixed foresight and folding rear sight. She is single shot and fires a 40 x 46 mm grenade. The grenades that can be fired, include High Explosive, flechette and cannister. We are going back to the rifle range today to give you all practice in the use of this weapon!"*

GPMG M60

When Mick and the others went into the class room on the following morning, they found that four (4) M60 machine guns were set upon tables. As usual, Corporal Burgess was their instructor. He said, *"Welcome gentlemen to the class on the use of the GPMG M60 Machine Gun"* He then went to where one of the machine guns was set upon a table.

He said, *"All of you, organise yourselves into groups of seven soldiers ad go to one of the M60s you see in front of you. This weapon provides the automatic firepower for Australian Infantry Sections now! It is critical that all of you know how to use and maintain this weapon, as your very lives will depend upon its successful use. Before the main lesson begins, we shall start with the history of this weapon!*

The M60 is an American redesign of the German MG 42, which had a nickname of 'Spandau'. It was a very formidable weapon of extreme reliability with an extremely high rate of fire. It had a cyclic rate of fire of between 1,200 to 1,500 rounds per minute. So much for the original design! The American designers decided to replace the Browing light machine gun with the now "Americanised MG 42", which they called M60. The reality is that the M60 is a far inferior weapon to the original German MG 42, and it only has a cyclic rate of fire of 600 rounds per minute!

One bad characteristic that it has is that the gas plug looks as if it must be inserted in a certain way. However do not be misled, because what appears to be the correct way is in fact wrong. If the gas plug is inserted the wrong way, the machine gun will only fire single shots!

You must all become proficient in the feeding, chambering, locking, firing, unlocking, extraction and cocking of the M60! Drills which you must all learn by heart include the repair of sluggish performance, clearance of

The Full Circle for Mick

stoppages, action to take upon misfire and/or cook-off of the gun! All of you must know how to strip and re-assemble the machine gun. We are going to the rifle ranges every day for the next few weeks. During that time you will all be tested to make sure that you are proficient in the use of all weapons. We shall then have that followed by even more use of the rifle range activities, but for completing exercises in 'Fire and Movement' using live ammunition and other minor infantry tactics!

You are all required to know the hand signals shown in your soldiers' Vietnam handbooks." Three weeks later, Mick, Raymond and Collin had all completed their Infantry Corps Training and they found themselves in the 'Re-Inforcement Wing' of the Infantry Centre, waiting for posting to an infantry battalion. Then came the call for more Australian soldiers to complete their training at JTC (Jungle Training Centre) at Canungra, in Queensland.

The call was answered by, Mick, Wally, Raymond, and Collin who all were all sent Jungle Training Centre at Canungra in Queensland. Six weeks later, all of these young men returned to the Re-inforcement wing at Infantry Centre at Ingleburn.

A Posting to 1RAR?

Now that Infantry Corps Training was completed, Mick and his friends were eager to get to their various battalions and to become 'Real Soldiers.' Meanwhile, Mick and met Carolyn and they formed an ideal couple. They were both passionate about each, and a lot of kissing and going out followed.

Michael was ordered to report to the Adjutant of Re-inforcement Wing and did so. As he entered the adjutant's office, Mickk saluted, and Lt. Sommers returned the salute. He said, *"Kramer, there is a posting to 1RAR at Holsworthy available. Get yourself to that unit and your paperwork will follow in due course!"*

Arriving at the part of the Holsworthy base where 1RAR was, Mick asked for directions to the 1RAR Orderly Room. Getting to the Orderly Room, Mick was asked for his paperwork. He said, *"The Orderly Room at Re-inforcement Wing said that they will send it to you!"* that prompted a phone call from the 1RAR Orderly Room to the one at the re-inforcement Wing of Infantry Centre.

Next, he and some other new members of 1RAR were taken to the hall, where they were spoken to by the RSM. He said, *"Welcome gentlemen to the only battalion in the Australian Army, the First Battalion, Royal Australian Regiment! This unit is the very best there is and do not you ever forget that!"*

He then called the roll and when he read out the name Michael Kramer, after that, he said, *"Kramer, this is Lt. Jenkins, and he shall be your Platoon Leder. You are being sent back to Infantry Centre for training in the care of and use of Mortars!* So, Mick returned to Infantry Centre and looked forward to his new training.

The Mortarman's Course.

After arriving at the Infantry Centre at Ingleburn NSW, Mick found the mortarman's course to be interesting and challenging. He was again, taught navigation, map reading and the calculations of mortar trajectories. He particularly enjoyed plotting the deliverance of the fired shots known as 'Delivery of ordnance of ... rounds upon grid reference ... as required. After the third week of this new training, he developed glandular fever and his temperature rose alarmingly.

He was admitted to the Second Field Hospital at the Ingleburn base. He was treated and in time, his temperature returned to normal. By the time he was fully recovered and fit for duty, he found that 1RAR had sailed to Vietnam and he was placed on the unallotted list. Upon discharge from base hospital at the Infantry Centre at Ingleburn, Mick returned to his familiar environment at the Re-inforcement Wing of the Infantry Centre. As he was going into the tent forming the sleeping quarters, Collin Smith said, *"Welcome back, Mick it is good to see you again!"* The young men resumed waiting for a call to an infantry battalion.

Telling the Storey from the Other Side

Following the call of the Vietnamese "Fatherland" to do everything possible to ensure victory against the invading Americans and their allies, a huge amount of young people went to southern Vietnam to take on the invaders of their homeland there. During the war of resistance against the imperialist aggressors, the territories of Ba Ria and the Province of Long Khanh suffered great destruction because they were situated at the northern gateway to Saigon. There, the foreign enemies concentrated all of their power to establish an extremely strong defensive line as a shield to defend the city.

Among the heroic groups to answer the call to liberate the Fatherland was 2nd Infantry Battalion (Group 211 of the 9th Regiment of the 304B division). Upon reaching the area of operational responsibility in the Ba Ria and Long

Kanh, the unit's title was changed to D440 Battalion. The soldiers of the D440 Battalion grew up in many areas of Vietnam, but the majority were from the Thai Binh region. They now became the soldiers of Ba Ria – Long Kanh and they were very closely attached to that land[58].

Areas of Responsibility for D445 and D440

About two-hundred years ago, the scholar Trinh Hoai Duc wrote, "Ba Ria is a famous region … This land has its back to the mountains and faces the sea … There are many important passes that are difficult to access … no different to the national capital of our princes[59] …"

Here Is a well-developed road system in the Ba Ria – Vung Tau region and Route 15 (now renamed to Route 51) connects the city of Vung Tau to the cities of Bien Hoa and Ho Chi Minh City (Saigon). The town of Ba Ria is located centrally between the Province of Ba Ria -Vung Tau (formerly Phuoc Tuy Province) and the coastal area of Eastern Nam Bo at eighty-seven kilometres from Ho Chi Minh City to the north-west. Bien Hoa is located seventy-five kilometres to the north-west and Xuan Loc is fifty-five kilometres to the north.

The Xuyen Moc district Is also In this province. Some other paces within it are: - Tan Thanh, Hoa Long village, Long Dien, Dat Do. These areas were adjacent to the resistance base areas and were therefore important to the Revolution.

Establishing D440 Battalion

---

[59] Chamberlain, 2013.

The Full Circle for Mick

On the 9th of July 1967, the commander of the 2nd Infantry Battalion, Colonel Luong Van Tinh held an "O" Group with his officers. Present were, the Political Officer, Nguyen Huu Thi, the Battalion second in command, Tur Nhur, the assistant second in command, Nguyen Hong Chau and Nguyen Van Quang who was Deputy Political Officer. Other officers were also present. Colonel Luong Van Tinh spoke to his assembled officers.

He said, *"Gentlemen, this unit has been renamed as the D440 Battalion. As of the next morning, we are all moving down south to the Ba Ria-Long Kanh area. This has been made necessary by the devastating defeat suffered by Ba Ria's own D445 Battalion which has suffered immense casualties at the hands of the American lackeys – the Australian mercenaries who have proved to be tough jungle fighting experts.*

It Is a pity that we must fight them but fight them we must. Our D440 Battalion shall have the following sub-units: - 5th Infantry Company commanded by Comrade Nguyen Van Be Gio and Comrade Truong Quang Ngo who is Political Officer.

- *6th Infantry Company commanded by Comrade Lam Buu and Comrade Phung Nhu'Y the Political Officer.*
- *9th Infantry Company commanded by Comrade Nguyen Hung Tam and his political officer, Vo Van Nhan.*
- *8th Fire support company commanded by Comrade Ba Kim and his political officer Comrade Hai Rau.*
- *Reconnaissance Platoon Commanded by Comrade Tu Quy and his political officer Comrade Dinh Van Rang.*

- *Communications platoon commanded by Comrade Thanh and his political officer Comrade Thao.*

Now, regarding higher leadership and direction, the following are appointed: Comrade Le Dinh Nhon will be secretary of the Province committee. Comrade Dang Huu Thuan will be commander of the Province Unit. Comrade Dang Van Chuong will be political officer and deputy commander of the province unit; Comrade Ba Can will be deputy commander of the Province Unit, and he shall be directly responsible for leadership and guidance of all unit activities. Gentlemen, I will now go on to outline additional information which you must all communicate to your soldiers. Using the attention and assistance of the Provincial Committee, we, and the people of Ba Ria-Long Kanh shall have good formal training and we will be equipped with good weapons.

You must both instruct and inspire you men so that the whole Battalion is determined to win this great struggle for freedom of our country. In order to do so, all must quickly become familiar with the terrain, weather, and climate. We must make use of our basic training and skills, always applying them in practice during combat and other tasks!"

And so, the newly named D440 Battalion moved into the Long Khan and Ba Ria provinces (Ba Ria Province was formerly Phuoc Tuy Province). While the battalion was preparing itself for its first contacts with the foreign and their puppet ally aggressors, it was reported that two intelligence companies of the 48th Task Force of the ARVN (Army of Republic of Vietnam or South Vietnamese Army) had gone deeply into the Doi Dau area. In reaction to this news,

Colonel Luong Van Trinh called for an "O" group to take place.

Addressing his assembled officers, he said, *"Gentlemen, I have an urgent task for you! The enemy puppet army is present in our area of operations here in Long Kanh Province and I want these traitors to be taught a lesson that the American invaders will not forget! I am ordering the deployment of two platoons and two reconnaissance sections led by Comrade Sau Ho the second in command and by comrade Tu Quy the commander of the Battalion's reconnaissance platoon. Your orders are to find and ambush the enemy and to wipe out as many of the ARVN 48th Task Force traitors as you can".*

At 05:00 hours of the 25th of September 1967, the entire enemy force was trapped in the ambush site and lost many of their soldiers after only 15 minutes of combat with the men of D440 Vietcong Battalion. The few survivors fled back to the town of Long Kahn. With the assistance of the Party leadership and Vietcong secret agents, in Long Khanh-Dinh Quan the D440 Battalion conducted some counter-sweep battles, destroying strategic hamlets on route 2 in the areas of Cam Duong, May Tao and Rung La.

They attacked and reduced the strength of the enemy and consolidated their own base areas. Most importantly, the entire battalion had fought with skill and its soldiers had gained a clear understanding of the enemy soldiers' tricks on the battlefield. In the summer and autumn of 1967, the Vietnamese Patriot Forces on the Eastern Region fought hundreds of actions with the foreign aggressors. These included two at divisional level and two more at regimental level. These resulted in heavy casualties being inflicted upon the foreign enemies. Two American infantry battalions were removed from the fighting.

An American artillery battalion was also wiped out. Other successes were the removal of a puppet (South Vietnamese or ARVN) battalion and two puppet (South Vietnamese or ARVN) armoured companies.

On the 12th of May 1967, the 724 the Regiment launched an artillery attack upon The American Air Base at Bien Hoa. That action resulted in the destruction of one-hundred-and-fifty aircraft of various types and well as the killing or wounding of many enemies.

So that the build-up of our strength would continue a resolution was passed by the Party's committee and regional committees to s and to *"Strongly advance during the winter spring of 1967-1968 and develop the capacity for comprehensive attacks without interruption across all battlefields seize decisive victories!"*

The resolution also said, *"By seizing our military and political victories across all battlefields, our troops will be fired with enthusiasm, and they will be motivated to rush forward and defeat the invading American aggressors and their lackeys."* Our operational motto was: *"Strike at the Americans, overthrow the puppets and put political power back into the hands of Vietnamese people"*

The task of political education and ideological leadership was seen as one of the critical aims of the programme to prepare for the General Offensive and General Uprising of Tet Mâu Thân 1968. A large phase of political action was organised among all the armed forces with the aim of ensuring a thorough understanding of the resolutions of the Politburo so that every cadre and soldier in the units was clearly aware of the historical opportunity, the responsibilities, and the glorious mission that the Party had given to the armed forces.

It was known and understood that the Eastern Region was the primary battleground, with Saigon-Gia Dinh as the decisive battlefield. In particular, each of our patriot soldiers had the spirit of "I shall face death so that my Fatherland may live!" There was a determination to, "Win Decisive Victories" in particular among the sapper units, special task group and assault forces[60].

In October 1967, on the actual battlefield, the Ba Ria-Long Kanh Province Unit decided to establish an Engineer Company – by withdrawing forty soldiers from 440 Battalion's 8th Company and creating two platoons. The company commander was comrade Nguyen Van Tan and political officer was Comrade Le Thong Thaut. The platoon and section level cadre were comrades that each experienced the battlefield and had technical knowledge and core engineer skills.

The key weapons equipping the company were anti-tank mines that the company had produced itself. These types of mines that the unit created from unexploded enemy bombs and shells. They were collected and, having been sawn open, the explosives were removed, divided up and affixed into sheet iron or thin steel frameworks – with either convex or concave shapes[61].

As was stated by the Company's commander, Nguyen Van Tan to his men, *"The primary task of this*

---

[60] Chamberlain, 2013.

[61] Chamberlain, 2013.

company is to use its technical engineering skills to create a tight belt around the Suoi Ram base (Base of the American 11th Armoured Brigade with the aim of limiting to the maximum the brigade's attacks and relief operations on the province's battlefields. Our tactics are to ambush and interdict every section of Route 2. We will also ambush the intersections around our bases at Bao Binh, Cam My, Binh Ba, Suoi Nghe and other places as necessary!"

The Political Officer of the Company, Comrade Le Thong Thaut now stepped up to the lectern where the company commander had been speaking. He said, *"Comrades, we shall be mainly deploying the mines that we have made from the unexploded bombs and shells of the enemy to all favourable ambush sites and heavy traffic routes that are in constant use by the enemy. We shall destroy the enemy tanks, armoured vehicles and other vehicles and neutralise their firepower once our mines have detonated and blown the fucking invaders to hell!"*

The Tet Mau Than Offensive and General Uprising of 1968

Comrade Nguyen Van Tan, the company's commander again stepped up to the lectern in order to again address his men. He said, *"Gentlemen, together with the whole COSVN area, the Revolutionary movement in Ba-Ria-Long Khanh province is experiencing difficulties and new developments which we must overcome!*

Once we achieve this, the real strength of the revolution shall be substantially developed. Through the awesome reality of combat, 440 Battalion ... together with our brothers from 445 Battalion, will progressively increase our tactical standards and so become the "Main-Force Fist" of the province with more than sufficient strength to provide and complete all tasks and requirements of the revolution."

That was followed by a short break in proceedings while a messenger came and asked to confer with him. He said, *"Excuse me Ladies and Gentlemen, some news, and messages of some importance have arrived. Please remain seated where you are until I return with this new information."* With that said, he walked away with the messenger. About a half hour passed and he returned the lectern and spoke to his audience.

He said, *"Comrades, I have been told that I am to develop plans and tasks for the General Offensive and General Uprising in the local Ba Ria-Long Khanh areas as well as co-ordinating the attack upon Saigon. The Ba Ria-Long Khanh Province Committee has directed us to mobilise the whole of the people and military of the province for extraordinary efforts and the highest determination to fulfil the mission of the simultaneous General Offensive and General Uprising. This is to be accomplished using a strong three point attack. The method of attack is to use co-ordinated strikes, both internal and external. These are to be launched simultaneously; we shall concentrate on key targets. We will attack decisively and make a strong impact on the enemy throughout the province. The centres of gravity for the attack are the towns of Ba Ria, Long Khanh and other places as we can attack the invaders and their puppets. We launch the simultaneous attacks with the H-hour being the night of the 30th of Tet Mau Than (i.e., 31 of January 1968). The message that has just come in has stated, that the Headquarters of the Liberation Armed Forces of the South hereby orders all cadre and soldiers to perform the following:*

One: Rush forward with great courage and annihilate a very large number of American and their vassal allied troops and shatter the puppet (ARVN) military and the puppet authorities. Every cadre and soldier must fulfil their combat task. Every unit and each local area must decisively win and seize their targets.

Two: Exploit to the greatest extent our heroic revolutionary ideology and make every sacrifice while overcoming all hardships and difficulties. We are to fight continuously, explosively, and thoroughly. We must shatter every enemy counterattack and firmly maintain the revolutionary standpoint. These things shall be done, no matter what the situation may be! We will win and we shall also be determined to win continuous victories, and we shall win them all completely! Comrades, over to you now, are there any questions?"

Duc Tuong spoke and asked, *"Sir, you know that I am a loyal soldier and patriot of Vietnam. I will do whatever is necessary to drive the foreign invaders from our country. My question is: Is there another patriot force with whom we must co-ordinate our efforts? If so, what is this unit or units? And what do we have in the way of ammunition for our mortars and, what enemy units are we likely to be facing when we launch these attacks to reclaim our Fatherland?"*

The D440 Battalion commander again spoke. He said, *"Thank you for your question, Duc, I am sure that many here will have the same sorts of questions forming in their minds. In order to successfully launch the General Offensive of the Mau Than in the spring of 1968, the Ba Ria-Long Khanh armed forces have two battalions. These are us, the D440 Battalion, and the D445 Battalion. As well, the districts and the towns also have their own concentrated* companies and special operations units. The villages and small towns have "A" and "B" forces and people's guerrillas. The Province Unit has decided that we, the D440 Battalion shall the task of attacking and annihilating the enemy in Long Khanh. Apart from its current weapons and equipment, Province has provided our unit with an additional one-thousand-six-hundred 82 mm mortar rounds.

The situation of our forces compared to our enemies is as follows: the enemy (American) has three American brigades. These are: the 173 Airborne Brigade (Sky Soldiers), the 199th and the 314th, the 11th armoured Brigade at Suoi Ram (Long Khanh), the II field force Headquarters at Long Binh, and artillery bases at Gia Ray, Song Thao, Trang Bom, and Suoi Día etc. There is also a Thai Regiment at Long Thanh and Nhon Ttrach.

The puppet (ARVN) military has five Infantry battalions which are from the 18th infantry Division, forty-six regional force companies, five parachute and marine battalions, two artillery regiments, the first Task force of Australian and New Zealand vassals based in Ba Ria, an armoured regiment, seven combat support companies, two Ranger Battalions and thousands of Popular Forces, public security personnel, Police Field Force and People's Self-defence Force personnel. Additionally, their air force elements at the Tan Son Nhat and Bien Hoa airfields are ready to provide support.

In the Ba Ria-Long Khanh area, the enemy has many troops armed with modern weapons and equipment – as well as the tactical support of many arms and services such as artillery, tanks, and aircraft." A direct result of all of this was that the tasks of the patriots' armed forces were very difficult and complex. This led to the Ba Ria – Long Khanh

Province Committee confirming the basic tasks of the province's armed forces in the General Offensive and Uprising of Spring 1968. These were: to attack and wipe out enemy strength, co-ordinate with the uprising of the revolutionary masses and take control of the towns of Ba Ria and Long Khanh[62].

As well, the Province Committee decided to disband the Party Affairs Committee of Xuyen Moc District and re-establish the Xuyen Moc District Committee with the aim of strengthening the leadership of the Party elements within the armed forces under new guidelines. Comrade Sau Lun was appointed as secretary of the District Committee. Comrade Duong Van Dong became the deputy secretary, and Comrade Bay Thung was the commander of the District Unit.

The implementation of the order of higher authorities would now be implemented, in phase 1 – from 31 January until 25 February 1968, all cadre and soldiers of D440 Battalion urgently prepared to enter the fighting. They had stated, *"We have resolved to die so that our Fatherland may live."* Representing the Party Committee of the Battalion Headquarters, Comrade Luong Van Tinh, the Battalion commander expressed his determination to fight and read Uncle Ho's poem. (Ho Chi Minh was called Uncle Ho by his people)

"This spring is completely different to springs past,
The news of victories spreads happiness across our land,
The north and south compete to strike the American bandits,
forward! Our complete victory is certain!"

---

[62] Chamberlain, 2013.

The Full Circle for Mick

Meanwhile, the call of the COSVN Headquarters read: *"Comrades! The American bandits will be soundly defeated, the battle's bugle call for independence and freedom resounds! The Annamite chain has completely changed, Waves are boiling on the Mekong River, Comrades, be worthy of the heroic Vietnamese People, deserving of the Title 'Impregnable fortress of the Fatherland' and worthy of the stamp of the courageous and unsurpassable liberation armed forces. Our complete victory is certain."*

These were the main orders for the fighting and victory, urging all units into great battles with the momentum of spring. The Battalion Headquarters, the company and platoon cadre all exchanged views, and gathered around map models and made combat plans.

The soldiers used the time to clean their weapons, get additional ammunition magazines, arrange everything neatly and awaited the orders to deploy. Many took the time to write slogans like "Resolve to die so that the Fatherland may live[63]!"

On the 29th of January 1968, (known as the first day of Tet), the entire battalion moved from the Doi Dau base to the edge of jungle beside the "Rice-hulling Mill" base, adjacent to the target which had been selected. "The Rice-Hulling Mill Base" was in the area beside the edge of the jungle at Bao Vinh Village and it was the rear services base of the Ba Ria – Long Khanh Province. There were many rice-hulling mills concentrated here[64].

---

[63] Chamberlain, 2013.
[64] Chamberlain, 2013.

The D440 Battalion's commander, comrade Nguyen Van Tan, again spoke to his men. He said, *"We are deploying a new column which shall be responsible for the north of Long Khanh town, and it will be comprised of two companies, which shall be commanded directly Comrade Phan Thanh Ha, who is Chief of staff of the Battalion. 5th Company led by the company commander, Nguyen Van Be and Comrade Truong Quang Ngo the Political Officer. These have the task of attacking the communications centre. The 6th Company will be led by the company commander, Comrade Lam Buru and the Political Officer, Comrade Phung Nhu Y. This unit has the task of attacking the headquarters of the puppet (ARVN) 43rd Infantry Regiment at the Nho Market intersection.*

A reconnaissance section and an entire section from the 5th company led by comrade Luong Ngoc Can who is the deputy commander of the reconnaissance platoon has the task of attacking the offices of the village council." The Battalion's commander went on to say, *"We have covered the responsibilities of the first column, now we discuss the role and responsibilities of the Second Column! It will be responsible for the west of Long Khanh Town, and it will be directly led by Comrade Nguyen Hong Chau, who is the deputy commander of this battalion. It shall be comprised of the Ninth Infantry Company and will have comrade Nguyen Hung Tam as its commander and Comrade Hong Ky Nam as its Political Officer. The third column shall be led by Comrade Luong Van Tinh, that is, myself in the east and south of the town and will comprise all the firepower of the 8th company led by Comrade Ba Kim, the company commander, and his Political Officer, called Hai.*

This group shall establish two firing positions in Bao Dinh hamlet in order to shell the Hoang Dieu post, the Long

Khanh tactical airfield, the artillery sites, the armoured area, and the headquarters of the puppet (ARVN) 18th infantry division."

On the 28th and 29th of January 1968 (that is the 30th and the first day of Tet Mau Than) the whole of the south simultaneously launched the general Offensive and uprising. On the Ba Ria and Bien Hoa Front, the sound of the D440 Vietcong Battalion's attacking weaponry could be heard booming and resounding. The ammunition warehouse at Long Binh and the Bien Hoa Airbase were fiercely shelled.

In Ba Ria town, the soldiers of the Vietcong D445 Battalion and the Liberation forces' units opened fire in order to take control. In Ba Ria town, the soldiers of the Vietcong D445 Battalion and the Liberation forces' units opened fire in order to take control. Meanwhile, on the Long Khanh Town front, all of the enemy had received the warning order, and took the initiative to man their defences ready to engage the Vietnamese Patriots.

The reaction of the enemy was to oppose the patriots using eleven infantry battalions which were well-armed in order to set-up blocking positions and prevent our access into the town. Groups of enemies (ARVN) armoured vehicles of the 11th Armoured Regiment from the Suoi Ram Base were deployed to the town. They were on defensive patrols and so were lying in wait at all road intersections. Enemy artillery positions around the town fired salvos of shells into target areas where the puppets (ARVN) and their misguided foreign allies thought that Vietcong were sheltering. They thought that they could beat us in this way[65]!

---

[65] Chamberlain, 2013.

At 16:00 hours of the 2nd of February 1968, a fierce enemy artillery barrage struck the D440 Battalion. This in turn, resulted in the wounding of Comrade Nam Cur. He was the secretary of the Dinh Quan District and the commander of the group. He later died from the wounds he received during that shelling.

There was now a hatred building up of the enemy invaders and the traitors who were members of the ARVN supporting them. The entire battalion reformed and deployed that night from Bao Vinh, Suoi Chon and Tan Lap to areas close to Long Khanh Town. During the night, the enemy constantly fired illumination shells and that had the effect of turning darkness into daylight for much of the night.

In accordance with our plan of attack, the columns advanced until they were close to their targets. At 24:00 hours of 30/January/1968 (the second day of Tet), our soldiers simultaneously opened fire and attacked. The 9th Infantry company attacked the Offices of the Province chief and the 33rd Tactical Sub-Zone.

The 5th Infantry Company attacked the Offices of the Village Council and pursued the enemy in the Red Cross Street area. The 8th Fire support company shelled the Hoang Dieu post, the Long Khanh Tactical Airfield, and the headquarters of the puppet (ARVN) 18th Infantry Division.

The 12.7 mm anti-aircraft detachments fought against the enemy aircraft that flew in support of enemy units. After more than half-an-hour of decisive exchanges of fire, many enemy bunkers and other posts were either taken or destroyed. The good news was reported to the Battalion Headquarters. The 9th Company's attacking column was personally led by Comrade Nguyen Hong Chau, the Deputy

Battalion Commander. This resulted in the seizure of the Province Chief's Offices and the flag of the People's Liberation Army flying above the roof of the offices which had been captured.

That resulted in the enemy forces launching frenzied counterattacks. The 11th Armoured Regiment of the USA hurriedly deployed from its Suoi Ram Base to relieve Long Khanh, was blocked and attacked by our soldiers, resulting in many tanks and armoured vehicles being destroyed and set alight. Comrade Truong Dinh Vong attacked and set fire to three enemy tanks on his own. He was a member of the Muong minority and came from Ba Thuoc, Thanh Hoa.

Other acts of courage were Comrade Cuong of the 5th Company, leaping upon an enemy tank and then using a grenade and satchel charge to destroy it. Luong Ngoc Can who be deputy commander of the Reconnaissance Platoon and Hoang Ngoc Man both heroically gave up their lives while they were blocking a column of enemy tanks on Red Cross Street.

According to information from technical sources, in the first wave of the General Offensive and General Uprising on Long Khanh Town Front, more than one hundred enemy were wiped out. Three artillery bases were destroyed, and twelve tanks and armoured vehicles were set on fire. To the west of Long Khanh Town, our soldiers were able to break through the enemy's defences in the bank of the dyke.

The battle developed very fiercely because the enemy had mobilised their defences as we made a breakthrough. That resulted in the enemy artillery firing quickly into our attacking formations. Meanwhile, columns of tanks with blue lights on top of them, appeared before the fighting trenches. This was a surprising situation, and our attacking formations were halted. The enemy tanks then attacked fiercely into our ranks. Many our troops became casualties. We suffered 60 comrades killed. With an unmatched courageous spirit, the troops resolved to hold their positions, wait until the enemy tanks were close – and then fire their weapons to wipe them out. The number of B40s and B41s gradually declined. To keep our forces intact, the unit commander gave the order to withdraw from the town.

At 05:00 hours of the 3rd of February 1968, the battalion's attacking columns were ordered to withdraw from the town and return to our rear areas and consolidate our forces, and to await orders. Only the 9th section of the 9th Infantry company led by Comrade Ngoc (the section commander) was still trapped in the town. The whole section resolutely held on and fought until 08:00 hours on 03/February/.1968 – and all of its personnel fought to their last round of ammunition, and all were killed. In another area, the Province Engineer Company was asked to blockade the Suoi Ram base with the aim of preventing the enemy tanks from moving along route 2 and providing support for Long Khanh or Ba Ria when attacked by our forces.

However, as with other local units, as they were late in receiving their order to deploy, they lost their opportunity. The company was not in time to attack the first vehicle that deployed and were only able to attack the second group of the enemies deploying vehicles. The total number of enemy tanks that were destroyed in this battle numbered ten. (Seven moving north to Long Khanh and three moving south to Ba Ria.)

The unit's exploits have the effect of limiting the mutual assistance between enemy elements, reducing their violent impact on the two principal battlefields, and contributing to the Tet Mau Than victory of our provinces' armed forces. Following this battle, the Military Region commended the company with the title of "Steel Belt Unit" and many comrades were awarded the military exploits Medal III Class. D440 continued operating against the invaders and their puppet ARVN allies. The battalion had tested the enemy and now knew the way the foreign invaders liked to do things. In June 1969, we would face the Australians in the Battle of Binh Ba[66].

1RAR Goes to Vietnam for its 2nd Tour of Duty

The advance party of 1RAR left for Vietnam on the 17th of February 1968 from Sydney's Mascot Airport by Qantas passenger jet. The aircraft refuelled at both Darwin and Singapore. The main body of the battalion of left on board the HMAS Sydney fourteen days later. While the ship travelled towards Vietnam, the soldiers carried out foot and rifle drills and shot at targets floating in the water. Arriving at a point three miles off the coast near Vung Tau, the soldiers were transferred to landing craft. When they finally set foot upon Vietnam, they went through the same reactions as were experienced by the soldiers of the unit when they landed in Vietnam for the "First Tour of Duty in 1965."

Once they were on the ground at Vung Tau, the soldiers boarded trucks and travelled to the 1ATF (First Australian Task Force) Base at Nui Dat. Arriving at the former 7RAR lines at Nui Dat, the soldiers were briefed about operational procedures. A first lieutenant who was a

---

[66] Chamberlain, 2013.

member of the advance party, addressed the incoming soldiers. He said, *"G'Day Blokes, there are some things that you should know. Firstly, it is of critical importance that each of you take your anti-malaria suppressant pills when they are issued to you. You will be given the pills by your section commanding corporals and they shall watch you take them.*

If anyone refuses to take his medication, he will be committing an offence and will find himself on an A4. (Charge Sheet) Something else that you should know is that we are required to inform the South Vietnamese Army Units (ARVN) of where we are and when we are doing. As far as I am concerned, that is all bunkum, and we should not do it because the Slopeheads making up the AVRN cannot be trusted. All too often, the members of the ARVN turn out to be the enemy! However, orders are orders! We have been given an ARVN liaison officer who accompanies us on operations! I consider that to be a compromise of our security, and I would be far happier if we could operate entirely without having the Noggies with us at any time! The problem is that I must also obey orders, and they say that we must have these Noggie spies with us!

Anyway, it turns out that the ARVN Liaison officer is in fact a sergeant. According to the 7RAR people with whom I have been discussed this problem, the ARVN people cannot be trusted, so keep a close watch on this turkey, because of the high likelihood that he is in fact a Noggie spy! According to the 7RAR blokes, he will take a chopper out of the area if he thinks that enemy action is likely! So, we can keep him around to use as a forecasting tool to warn us of probable enemy attacks upon us!

Make sure that you have clean dry socks in your kit and go to the 'Q' Store and replace your twenty round 7.62 or 5,56 mm magazines with thirty round magazines. With reference to ammunition, everyone shall carry a minimum of 210 rounds of either 7.62 or 5.56 mm ammunition. I want all of you other than the M60 gunner to have a minimum of seven fully loaded 30 round magazines on you at all times!

You will be eating one-man ration packs, and you must make sure that all of you have at least four full water bottles of one quart capacity. That is critical for your health and effectiveness. All of you must now go to the 'Q' Store and obtain water purification kits. Your lives could depend upon that. Also, every man must carry at least one shell dressing in case someone is wounded. Are there any questions?"

Things remained quiet, so he assumed that everybody knew what was expected. Suddenly a soldier asked, *"Sir, how do we know whom to shoot?"* He was answered with, *"Good question private! If we are near villages or built-up areas, we will not shoot without first being shot at! If, on the other hand, we are we are operating in a 'Free Fire Zone,' then you can safely assume that everyone you see is an enemy and shoot the bastard on sight before he can shoot you! Our job here is not to die for our country, our job is to make the enemy die for his country!"*

He went on speaking and informing the soldiers what was happening and what was expected of them. He began and explained such things as R and R[67] and also R and C[68] leave and when the soldiers could look forward to it. Because the Australian soldiers were about to enter an 'Air Mobile War' he explained the training requirements for it. He said, *"Gentlemen, we will go into battle as passengers on board the American 'Iroquois" helicopters. Sometimes the choppers will be from the US Army, and at other times they will be supplied and flown by 9 Squadron of the RAAF[69].*

You will find that they have a crew of four men, consisting of a pilot, a co-pilot, and two door gunners manning the left and right hand sides of the aircraft! While these machines are on the ground, they are vulnerable and that is why you shall all learn the drills of getting into and out of the choppers very quickly! Our lives may depend upon how fast we can all get into and out of these machines. Because of that, we will begin training in order it get down our times for the activities of enplaning and deplaning!"

"Operation Pegasus" – 24th of April to 1st of May 1968

The battalion became involved with Operation Pegasus which was the first fully tactical and war-like operation of 1RAR during its 2nd Tour of Duty. The battalion practised airmobile assaults from real helicopters. It was a good opportunity to practice them with realism rather than using models and the imagination of soldiers. It also provided soldiers with a chance to become familiar with the surrounding terrain and supporting units or their elements. As well, it allowed the men to refine their operating began

---

[67] R & R leave was Rest and Recreation leave lasting for 5 days. It involved free air travel from Vietnam to places such as Bangkok, Honolulu, Sydney, and Taipei.
[68] R & C leave was similar, but it was only taken within south Vietnam.
[69] Royal Australia Air Force.

procedures which were made necessary because some faults were discovered and had to be rectified before the major operations against the enemy began.

Operation Blaxland

Operation Blaxland was the first major operation against the enemy by the First Battalion Royal Australian Regiment (1RAR). It started soon after the battalion had arrived in Vietnam and was meant to locate and destroy Viet Cong and NVA (North Vietnamese Army) camps in the Nui Dinh Hills. Alpha Company achieved its first enemy kill when two enemy were sighted at an estimated range of one-hundred-and-thirty metres.

A soldier of Alpha Company shouted, *"Look over there at about one-hundred-and-thirty-metres, there are two Noggies!"* Having said that, he opened fire and made the battalion's first kill of its 2nd Tour of Duty. The other enemy escaped. The battalion was kept busy during this operation, which resulted in several enemy camps being found and destroyed. The Nui Dinh Hills area was known "To be thick" with anti-personnel mines which the Vietnamese patriots had lifted out of an Australian laid minefield that was not covered by fire. The likelihood of stepping on an anti-personnel mine played on the minds of many Australian soldiers and caused some stress. Aggressive patrolling by the Australians also resulted in the discovery of several enemy caches and the operation was considered to be successful.

Operation Toan Thang 1 (3rd of May 1968 to the 6th of June 1968)

There are more books available which deal with the actions of allied forces at the battle of *Fire Support Bases Coral and Balmoral* available to the public. I have put the main points of this into a single chapter here, because the scope of this book is to look at the historical aspects of the Indochina Wars including the 2nd Indochina War. Therefore, I cannot devote too much space to a single battle. Those readers who wish to read a much more detailed account of Australia and New Zealand actions at Fire Support Bases "Balmoral' and 'Coral' can obtain McAulay, L, *The Battle of Coral,* Century Hutchinson, Sydney. Operation Toan Thang 1 is generally regarded as the defining operation of 1RAR, and it is celebrated as the battalion's most revered action[70].

The First Battle of 'Coral'

After arriving, the tired Australian and New Zealand soldiers began to settle in for the night. Thet cooked their evening meals from their ration packs, made cups of tea and generally relaxed after they had cleaned their weapons and ensured that each man had his full issue of ammunition. Over at 102 Artillery Battery, Gunner Greg Ayson was manning the number six gun of the battery. He heard noises which he did not like the sounds of! Worried about the noises, he went to his sergeant and informed him about them.

Upon meeting with Sergeant Max Franklin he said, *"Hey Max, I keep on hearing noises just out from number six gun, and I cannot identify them, but I do not fucking well like them!"* Sergeant Franklin replied, *"Just return to your post at number six gun and keep your wits about you! The*

---

[70] McAulay, 1989.

word from the Yanks is that the Noggies are coming to us. I hope not, but it could be what you have been hearing!"

At 19:25 hours, there were the sounds of a firefight and that was quickly followed by "B" Company reporting a contact with ten enemy soldiers who withdrew towards the south. At 19:41 hours Col Adamson of "A" Company reported the sighting of two red flares which appeared to be answered by others to the north. Then it began to rain, resulting in the soldiers gathering the rainwater which was coming off their one-man tent shelters. (called hutchies)

At the M60 machinegun position located between the artillery HQ and the mortars, Andy Forsdike and Kershaw needed to urinate and so they move forward several paces in order to do so. Suddenly, green tracer was seen to flash at them during the darkness from outside of the perimeter of the Fire support base. Two enemy soldiers were scouting on a reconnaissance when they were fired upon by a machine gun from Mortar Platoon. That resulted in the enemy returning fire and green tracer rounds were seen to be passing over Murtagh's area. It was unknown if the two enemies had been killed by Australian fire, and the incident was reported to battalion HQ by Lt. Jensen using a radio.

Meanwhile, back at Fire Support Base 'Coral,' that was also noticed. Jim Kearns who was the Battalion Intelligence Officer was on duty at the command post. He said, *"At about midnight, reports came in from the guns of red and green tracer being fired into the air. We discussed that and concluded that these were being used as markers for the advancing enemy and that it was showing them the way to the Australians!"* At 11:45 hours, a sentry manning an M60 machine gun saw a group of enemies crossing the cleared track in front of them.

He reported that and the gunners were not sure of what was happening, so they decided to check by asking the Artillery Command Centre if it was known who was moving about. With the enemy moving silently, they returned to an area from where enemy had originated from an hour beforehand. Quiet returned and that was followed by loud rustling in the long grass. In turn, that caused Forsdike to again use the field telephone to ask for permission to fire. The answer said, *"Hold your fire!"*

During the night, there were many intermittent contacts with small groups of enemy soldiers who appeared to be intent on bypassing the positions of "A" and "D" Companies. At 02:00 hours, Hammett was with his company in the triangular ambush position of the track junction. Suddenly, there was a burst of machinegun fire from a section of 10 platoon, which was facing north-west. Further along the track, 11 platoon caused several explosions followed by more firing.

Corporal Boyd was heavily involved in the action, and he spoke about it. He said, *We saw movement and because we had been experiencing enemy probing and activity for much of the night, I fired at what I thought was people moving. That resulted in answering fire from both enemy small arms and rocket propelled grenades (RPGs). The Noggies aim was good and resulted in Eleven Platoon having eleven casualties who required medevacs.* (Evacuation to Field Hospitals using helicopters)

The Full Circle for Mick

Perry Neil from 11 Platoon had completed his turn of sentry duty on the gun and was asleep when the firing began. He used two complete magazines of ammunition (60 rounds) and inserted the third magazine into his weapon. He later told me about it. He said, *"I began firing and I had used up two fully loaded magazines. Therefore, I was inserting the third one when I saw two Noggies moving out in the darkness.*

I called out to warn 'Hobs' on the machine gun that there were enemy to our left. I was about to give a more detailed direction when I saw the flash of an RPG exploding directly above him. Then I heard our platoon commander, Dick Utting, yelling out for us to continue firing. Next, someone said, "I am hit all over!" A short time later, I heard myself yelling in pain, after which I said to myself, *"What the fuck are you yelling about? Next, I stopped it and checked myself for wounds. I found that both legs and my right arm could not be moved."*

The result of the action left the platoon's strength lessened by forty percent. Four section had one Killed-In-Action (KIA) and another seven had been Wounded-In-Action (WIA). The only section member who was unhurt, was Private Thomas. Five Section had one KIA and Six Section had four of its members WIA. The two dead members of 1RAR were McNab and Sheppard. These men were the first members of the battalion to be killed on its 1968-1969 "Tour of Duty".

Meanwhile, at Fire Support Base 'Coral,' Hammett and his company now had the support of the 102 Battery of Artillery. The battery responded to its support task by firing guns 4,5, and 6 in support of "D" Company of 1RAR. It was decided to move the guns from the east to the north for that fire mission. Matt Cleland, commanding the 102 Battery Section consisting of guns 4,5 and 6 spoke to sergeant Max Franklin, the commander of number 6 gun.

He said, *Max, I think that we had better prepare and get going with cleaning up after the fire mission and prepare for the next one or a series of them! We have a lot to do, we must remove the packing and expended cases of the fired shells, and we must also prepare the new shells before we end up being swamped with work!"*

Now that the action was over, quiet returned to the ambush position of Hammett and "D" company of 1RAR at their ambush site at the track junction. It appeared to the men of 1RAR that the enemy had moved away from them. What was actually happening was that that the enemy soldiers were detouring around that position and were on their way to their real target which were the guns of the artillery in front of them. Due to "D" Company now having a more quiet time, a helicopter medevac was organised, and it was quickly provided by 9 Squadron RAAF. (Royal Australian Air Force) that resulted in a landing zone being selected in front of 10 Platoon. Captain Brian Altham and Corporal Mick Strong guided in the Hueys.

Hammett decided to send word of the details of the action to Battalion HQ at 03:10 hours and reported the helicopter medevac as being on the ground and having taken thee wounded to field hospitals. Only the wounded were taken resulting in the dead remaining on the ground until later flights could take them. Now that the Dust-off

The Full Circle for Mick

(medevac) had been completed, the helicopter gunships covering it flew back to their bases. Quite then returned to the 'Coral' area. Lt. Col. Bennett had been getting reports of movement activity outside of the 'Coral' position. Speaking about It, he said, *"I was getting the reports of movement, but it was not possible to do anything in the darkness of the night."*

At Jensen's mortar position, Corporal Bob Hickey went to lieutenant Jensen and spoke to him. He said, *"Sir, I have just come in from outside the Command Post and I have to report to you that I could see some shapes of people and that I could hear many Noggies gibbering away in Vietnamese about fifty metres away from us!"* Jensen went to his shell scape and together with an Australian soldier who was manning the radio, went around waking everyone up. Next, Jensen collapsed the small tent over the Command Post and tried to convince Kim Patterson that a large number of enemy soldiers was nearby. The time was 04:05 hours.

While they were located in front of HQ of 12 Field Regiment Royal Artillery, Andy Forsdike and his M60 team were still trying to identify who was to the left of them. Andy said, *"Everyone just fucking froze as a green flare went high into the sky! It was quickly followed by a red flare which also went high into the sky. Then all hell broke loose! The enemy who had crawled in suddenly stood up, not realising that they were so close to us. Next, everyone including the enemy went to ground as a heavy barrage of mortars and rockets came into the position."*

At the Command Post of 102 Battery, Bob Lowry was Duty Officer, and he heard the rockets flying overhead. As that was happening, he thought, *"Aw shit! Rockets!"* he then ordered, *"Stand to!"* To the left of him, in a fighting pit at the edge of an irrigation ditch, Ginger Orford was alone because Vic Page had gone to complete a turn as the sentry manning the machine gun. He walked fast towards the pits and encountered a warrant officer on the way. He said to him, *"Sir, I suggest that you get cover from view at the least because there are many Noggies coming this way and fast!"* The warrant officer replied in a disbelieving tone of voice. He said, *"I have trouble believing that, now settle down!"* Vic Page reacted by thinking, *"You arrogant fuckwit, you will settle down when you see what is coming!"*

At the number six gun position, Matt Cleland had emptied his pistol at the advancing enemy. He now spoke to Sergeant Max Franklin. He said, *"I am running to my tent to get my sub-machine gun. There are just too many Noggies to kill using a pistol!"* Next, he ran to his tent and returned with the sub-machine gun. As he was running past number five gun, Franklin grabbed him and said, *"Stay here, there is no-one at the number six gun anymore. The NVA have forced the gun crew out! Before leaving it, I took the time to remove the firing mechanism from the gun and it is now useless to the enemy!"*

The assaulting formations of enemy soldiers were close enough to stop the mortars from firing at them easily. That was quickly followed by them being so close that only small arms could be used. Later, Corporal Jock Whitton said, *"I asked for permission to fire the mortars straight up, but the enemy were advancing too fast! Over there* (he was pointing as he was speaking) *Lieutenant Jensen told his blokes to hold their ground, but there was nowhere else to go other than back to the positions of 102 Artillery Battery.*

There was a lot of ammunition in that area which we thought should not end up in enemy hands!"

The gun crews of 102 Battery were In danger of being overrun by enemy soldiers! Sergeant John Stephen went to his radio and asked for asked for assistance. He said, *"This is sergeant John Stephen of number four gun of 102 Battery! We are being overrun by North Vietnamese Army Soldiers; they are everywhere! My men are using small arms ammunition to save the guns and their own lives. I am asking for permission to use anti-personnel "Splintex" rounds, and I mean all six of them per gun! That is the only way that we have to stop this enemy assault!"*

I will now explain that each of the rounds called 'Flechette", contained 7200 arrow shaped darts. They were used as well as 'Splintex rounds. Permission was granted and the guns changed their settings to muzzle burst. They then used the "Splintex" rounds upon the enemy who were devasted! To the right and south-east of the guns, Les Tanter's Anti-tank Platoon awoke because of the noise, and he found his men were already standing-to. He said, *"Only fire at known targets! We cannot afford to waste ammunition by firing into the night!"* Some enemy soldiers came so close that they were engaged using 9 mm pistols. Being mindful that he only had eight rounds for each of his two 90 mm recoilless rifles, Tanter contacted Battalion HQ in order to obtain permission to use them. Permission was granted.

Tanter went to the left-hand gun manned by Corporal Dupille and Private Rich. Then Tanter was impressed to hear Dupille and Rich calling out the procedure for successfully using their weapon against the enemy. He could hear Dupille saying, *"Range is sixty metres, fire!"* Almost at once, RPGs and machineguns fired back. After the first wave of enemy soldiers had passed the 1RAR mortar position, Tony Jensen saw the enemy again assaulting the battalion's positions. He said, *"I saw a mass of enemy doing fire and movement across the Australian position, and I heard voices calling what I assumed to be orders. That was because the voices were followed by RPG fire!"*

` Some wounded mortar crews arrived at Jensen's position, and he said, *"Over there, you will find my sleeping scrape. It has already been hit by an RPG, so I doubt if the Noggies will bother with it again, because they believe it to be wiped out! So, get into that because it is the only cover from fire in this area!"* To the north-east was Col Adamson's "A" Company which had been bypassed by the enemy. Col was speaking to Neil Weeks, commander of three Platoon. Adamson said, *"Neil, it seems to me that the enemy are not running away from the attacks on Saigon, they are in fact here for the purpose of attacking us!"*

Neil Weeks stood up and saw the rockets, flares and tracer which showed that 'Coral' was under attack. He said, *"Sir, 'Coral' is under attack judging from the tracer and the sounds of battle coming from the Fire support Base. The information on the radio is incomplete, but it appears that Mortar Platoon has been overrun and at least one artillery gun is believed to have been captured by the enemy!"*

Meanwhile, "C" Company had been deployed southwards in order to secure the road to Tan Uyen so that a convoy could move along the road on the following day. Lorne Clarke the company medic said, *"We could hear the commotion distinctly. There were artillery and mortars as* well as small arms fire. We knew that there must have been contacts with the enemy, but we did not know anything about what was happening at 'Coral.'

From his battalion HQ in the rubber trees to the north-west of the battling mortar and guns, Lieutenant Colonel Jim Shelton (3RAR) switched his radio frequencies over to those of 1RAR and asked to speak to Phill Bennett. He said, *"G'Day Phill, it is Jim here, and I will be keeping a watching brief on the radio. It appears that we have a 'Show' on our hands!"* Although the enemy forces had overrun the mortar and some gun positions, they did not have things their own way. The surviving members of Mortar Platoon fought on. Jack Parr and Tony Jensen had been able to adjust the placement of the falling shells to within twenty metres of the 1RAR fighting pits. That, combined with the 'Splintex' rounds from Tanter's Anti-Tank Platoon and the 102 Battery were casing many casualties among the enemy soldiers. At 07:38 hours, the commanding officer of 1RAR Lt. Col. Phillip Bennett, was informing 1ATF of his intentions.

He said, *"Listen carefully, you lot, I am going to relocate all of my companies in defence of 102 battery! I was never comfortable with your mad idea of sending all of my rifle companies out on missions and leaving the Fire Support Base virtually unprotected. It is only due to the courage and adaptability of the Australian soldier that we do not have a major disaster here!"*

The Second Battle of 'Coral'

It was a dark night and the Australian soldiers on watch were sitting at their various gun pits. Rodger was speaking to David. He said, *"I do not want to see more Noggies, but I get the impression that if they come again, it shall be tonight!"* Perhaps he was prophetic, but soon after that, there was some movement outside of the perimeters of the Australians at 'Coral.'

During the day, there had been no indications of a night time attack, although there had been some isolated "Contacts" with small enemy sub-units. They would contact the Aussies and then run off and avoid further contacts. Unknown to the Australians the Vietnamese patriots had laid out thin nylon cord which was attached to trees at some points. All the enemy had to do, was to run forward while just feeling the cord, and they were thus guided to the Australian positions. As a result of that, the North Vietnamese Army units were running towards the Australians. The objective of the Vietnamese was to close with, and kill all foreign troops in country!

The increased enemy activity near the edges of the Fire Support Base resulted in the companies of 1RAR 'Standing-to' as of 19:07 hours. As the time progressed towards 20:00 hours, various Command Posts in and near Fire Support Base 'Coral' reported that there had been a series of light signals, flares and rockets streaking across the sky. The Australian soldiers had learned the meaning of these signals and therefore knew what the intentions of the enemy were! As well, it was known that the enemy was using runners to convey messages because they no radios.

By 21:00 hours, the listening posts and some units were involved in ambushing possible enemy areas of approach were brought back into the Fire Support Base. Tony Hammett saw them come in and he thought, *"They most certainly managed to come back in pretty fast!"* Like others present at 'Coral,' he had seen the streams of green tracer streaking across the night sky.

A large group of enemy soldiers gathered close to the Australian perimeter, They thought that by them being close to the Aussies, it would save them from the Australians calling artillery down upon themselves to wipe out the enemy! Time passed and the Vietnamese patriots were spread along a very long drainage ditch. They were either lying along it or crouching down resting or even having a cigarette if there was appropriate shelter from view. They waited with great patience while their leaders were busy with last minute matters which needed to be dealt with. Most of them looked forward to *"Close with, and kill the foreign enemies of Vietnam!"*

Meanwhile, at Fire Support Base 'Coral' things had died down and aggressive patrolling was now the main activity of the Australians. Word had spread throughout the battalion that Operations Toan Thang 1 and Toan Thang two were about to end and that the Australians would back at the Nui Dat base camp in time to meet the Prime Minister of Australia, John Gorton, who had arrived in Vietnam. Prime Minister Gorton was informed about the recent battles involving Australians and he wanted to meet some of the soldiers involved. The Prime Minister went to "C" Company and met with the 2IC on "C" Company, Lt. Jock Smith and the company CO called Major 'Digger'' Campbell.

Digger spoke to Jock. He said, *"Jock, one of your corporals has so many others talking about him, that his fame has reached the ears of the Prime Minister who wants to meet him! I know that Corporal Brian Broderick is considered to be one of the best section commanders of the battalion, but please make sure that he observes protocol and is polite when he speaks to Mr. Gorton!"*

Jock answered with, *"Sir, as you already know, Corporal Brian Broderick is always dependable and arguably the best NCO in the battalion. However, he tells it like it really is, and he pulls no punches. So, are you sure that you want to have him speaking to the PM? After all, you may not like the result!"* Digger Campbel answered with, *"Just do it Jock!"*

The visit of Mr. Gorton proceeded, and he was introduced to Corporal Brian Broderick and the conversation between them began. John Gorton said, *"G'Day, Corporal, how are you going?"* Brian Broderick answered, *"Good sir, how are you going?"* The Australian Prime Minister answered, *"I am OK! Have you and your men got any worries?"*

Brian immediately answered, *"Yes, how about you get us some new machineguns?"* The Prime Minister of Australia now asked, *"What is wrong with them?"* Brian said bluntly, *"The M60 machineguns that we are using are no good!"* A nearby senior officer decided to jump into the conversation. He yelled, *"What on earth are you talking about Corporal? The M60 is based upon the best machinegun ever made, the German Spandau!"*

Brian took it all in his stride and said, *"Sir, it may be based upon the best machinegun ever made and that could be the German Spandau, but what we are using are old and worn-out weapons! When I was going through infantry corps training in 1961, I scratched my initials upon the feed cover of the M60 I was using, and I am telling you that this is the very same M60! I had twenty-three stoppages on this useless piece of shit yesterday[71]!"*

---

[71] McAulay, 1989.

Operation Elwood - The Buddhist Monk

By now Mick Kramer, Wally Heffy and Colin Smith had been sent from the reinforcement wing of the Infantry Centre at Ingleburn to replace casualties suffered by 1RAR. Mick noticed a pagoda between the villages of La Van and Vinn Thanh, then, at 11:45 hours while the company was resting, he decided to check it out. Both of the villages lie to the west of Xuyen Moc. Inside the pagoda, Mick found an old Buddhist Monk.

He decided to try to speak to him using a mixture of English and French. So, Mick began speaking to the old man and he was surprised to hear him say in perfect English, *"My name is Hao An Dung and that was also the name of my father, who stopped being a monk and then he married my mother. My name of Hao An Dung means Good Peaceful Hero. My father had that name before me while he was a Buddhist Monk. Now please, tell me of yourself, Australian soldier!"*

Mick Kramer replied, *"My name is Michael Georg Kramer, and I was born in Germany in 1947."* Hao answered, *"Are you related to a German engineer called Fritz Kramer?* Mick replied, *"Yes, he was my grandfather, he was working on building the railway line from Tsingtao to Jinan, the capital of Shandong Province in China. How do you know of him?"*

The old monk replied, *"My father was working on that very same railway during 1904 when he and the coolies whom he was preaching to were attacked by a German general called von Trotha! My father told me that you grandfather took action which resulted in him, and the workers being rested, while General von Trotha was issued with a demand for the payment of damages to the progress of the work being carried out by your grandfather's employer!"*

Mick could not help but to be impressed by the old man's command of the English language. So, he said, *"Your mastery of the English Language is very impressive, how did you earn to speak it so well?"* Hao replied, *"I learned my English when I was studying at Oxford, England."*

Mick was really liking the old man and decided to ask him about Buddhism. He said, *"Hao, can you tell me about Buddhism?"* The old monk replied, *"Yes, think of you mind and your body as being two separate entities. Your body will decay after death, but your mind will still exist! You should also remember that every action you carry out will affect your karma. The relationship between some-ones actions and reactions which may cause suffering or joy to other people is known as 'The Law of Karma.' Understanding of karma is the basis of the Buddhist faith.*

When you die, your mind shall leave your body and enter an intermediate state. That can be a dreamlike state during which you can experience many different visions arising from things that you have done during your life. These visions may be pleasant or terrifying depending upon your karma. We cannot choose our rebirth, but we are reborn according to our karma. If we have good karma, we are reborn as a human, but if we have bad karma, we are reborn in a lower state such as an animal or worse!"

The old monk continued, *"With reference to your grandfather, Fritz Kramer, it saddens me that the descendants of that fine man can be so misguided as to be in the service of the of the bullying American aggressors! That* is very bad for your karma, you know! But that is not the end of the world, because you can make up for it!"

Mick thought about this for some time and then asked Hao for advice. He asked, *"Hao, if I was to qualify as an engineer like my grandfather before me and then return to this country after the war with the aim of helping to rebuild it, would that help to fix my karma?"* Hao replied, *"Yes, it would, but please tell me what are you doing in league with the bullying Americans?"*

Mick answered, *"We are Australians and not the bloody Yanks! As to why we are here, ask the Australian Government! I personally think that successive Australian Governments have no guts, and they are looking for a protector; hence the Yanks can get the Aussie Government to do whatever they want. After I return to Australia, I promise you that I shall do everything that I can to qualify as an engineer and then return here and help your people out."* After that, both men went their separate ways, and Mick did in fact qualify as an engineer some years afterwards.

Operation Platypus

This was a joint operation involving both 1RAR and 3RAR. "D" Company secured the area for Fire Support Base 'Gladstone' and was supported by Three Cavalry Regiment. The objective was to disrupt the activities of enemy units, including D445.

Mick had just taken a turn at being the forward scout. He noted that some trees were felled, but in such a way as to not interrupt the jungle's canopy and that the trees were cut off at ground level. Also, he noticed that there was no sign of small branches and twigs. It appeared to him that 9

Platoon, "C" Company of 1RAR was walking straight into an enemy base camp. Accordingly, Mick turned to the 2nd scout by using hand signals, he said, *"Officer to me."* That was passed along the line and resulted in Lt. Jacket approaching Mick.

Jacket quietly said, *"What is the problem Mick?"* Mick replied, *"Sir, we are going straight into an enemy base camp area! Back at the fire trail, there was a tree which had been cut through in such a way as to make the top two thirds of it snap. Then the Noggies dragged the fallen top of the tree until the tip of It was pointing this way. On top of that, look over there, you can see how the Noggies have carefully selected large trees to cut in such a way as to not interrupt the canopy which would make the Noggies open to attack by the Yank Air Force! There is bound to be a major enemy bunker system very close by!"*

That information was relayed to company HQ and as a result a company attack was launched upon the enemy base camp successfully without Australian casualties. Some members of "D" Company were travelling inside an M113[72] when it ran over an enemy command detonated 500 pound bomb. That resulted in everyone in the M133 being killed. Overall, the operation was considered to be successful because many enemy soldiers had been killed and their major base camps overrun.

Arriving back at Nui Dat, the men looked forward to having their meals cooked for them by army cooks instead of using one-man ration packs. For the few days spent back at the base camp, the men had to work during the day at building or improving defences. They were allowed to have

---

[72] Armoured Personnel Carrier.

two cans of beer per man, perhaps, during the time that they were at the base camp.

Meanwhile, back in Sydney, Mick's fiancée, Carolyn, was working as a telephonist at the Sydney GPO. She was putting letters to Mick into the *'Special Forces – Vietnam'* mailbox at the Sydney GPO when she was violently pushed into the mailbox by a male attacker. He had attacked her from behind and he said, *"I hope that the bastard gets killed over there!"*

The next operation was Operation Nowra. The operation involved the defence of Baria, Dat do and Long Dien. The enemy tried to occupy these places but were prevented from doing so by the Australian Army! After that came Operation Hawkesbury during which yet another enemy bunker system was located and destroyed.

Operation Windsor

Again, both 1RAR and 3RAR were acting together in a joint operation. Seven Platoon had the lead, and the forward scout was becoming increasingly nervous because he noted that many trees were felled without interrupting the overhead canopy. Mick in nine platoon was noticing the increase in felled trees and Mick sent a message to the acting company commander Jock Smith about his concerns. At this point I should explain that the enemy base camps were constructed in the shape of a horseshoe. By now it was almost too late to rectify the situation. The company was now in the open end of the horseshoe shaped enemy base camp. If a unit got as far as the closed end of the horseshoe, it would have enemies on all sides of it and face total annihilation!

As the forward scout and his section commander moved closer towards the enemy camp, the Noggies opened fire upon the Australians and killed two of them them, while wounding another man. Peter Fustai from seven platoon rescued the wounded man and returned him to safety. He followed that up with attempting to find his section commander and the forward scout.

Then he was told, *"Fustai, return to your post and let's have no more attempted heroics from you today!"* Peter was awarded the Australian Military Medal for his actions. Operation Windsor had been successful in that it resulted in enemy bases being destroyed and enemy soldiers being killed.

Operation Capital

Between the 28th of October 1968 and the 29th of November 1968, Operation Capital was put into place. It was a costly operation for 1RAR in that "A" company lost a platoon commander and a section commander KIA. During the operation, it appeared that the enemy was avoiding contact with Australian units as much as possible, other than the action in which the two members of "A" Company were killed.

No matter what some may think or say about it, the war in Vietnam was little more than an attempt of the Americans to continue with the attempt by France to keep the people of Indochina *"In their place and enslaved"* That attitude was quickly discovered by the Australian soldiers who often talked against the war during private discussions among themselves. Very often, the Australians would say to each other, *"We have been lied to by the governments Australia, Britain, France, and the fucking USA! These* people are not a threat to Australia or any other country on earth! None of us should be here! By being here, all that is being done is to continue with the subjugation of a sovereign nation and compelling its people to buy US manufactured arms!"

Operation Goodwood One

On the 3rd of December 1968, 1RAR was on the tarmac of Kangaroo Pad, waiting to emplane on the choppers for the start of Operation Goodwood One. The operation was to run from the 3rd of December 1968 through to the 1st of January 1969. Yet again, this was to be conducted in conjunction with the ARVN forces and again, Sergeant Van Tung was to be the liaison. Many of the members of 1RAR were against having the AVRN sergeant along because they thought that he was an enemy agent, and they openly said so.

Mick Kramer, Wally Heffy, Colin Smith, and others complained to the 2IC of "C" Company about the inclusion of this man. He sympathised with them, but he said, *"We have orders to use this man, so we shall! I know that this pick will bug out on any available chopper if he thinks that large units of enemy are nearby! Therefore we will keep him around as a warning. When he catches a chopper out of where we are, that will warn us that something is wrong!"*

Soon afterwards the battalion was on board the choppers on the way to Fire Support Base Dyke. Upon arrival there, Support Company and Battalion HQ occupied the Fire Support Base. That allowed the rifle companies to begin aggressive patrolling. Mick had been very suspicious of ARVN Sergeant Van Tung for a long time and inquired as to his where-abouts. He was told, *"The Noggie ARVN Bloke just caught a chopper out of here!"* armed with that knowledge, Mick returned to his section and told the rest of the men that the ARVN sergeant had left in a chopper.

Nine platoon was placed into an ambush position at the junction of three trails which were all in heavy use. When the ambush was sprung, three enemy soldiers were killed and an unknown number of them were wounded, the enemy dead were all wearing proper uniforms, and they had pith helmets. Included among them was officer and that aroused the interest of Australian Army Intelligence. Further patrolling found caches of rice and ammunition and resulted in three enemy bunker systems being destroyed. That was followed by more contacts with the enemy. On the 25th of December, Nine Platon was conducting a platoon sized ambush at the junction of three well-used tracks and a fast running creek. After the men had carefully measured the distance from the hill to the track junction at the creek, ranging pegs were installed. These had the distance from the small hill to the creek marked upon discs which were on top of the ranging pegs. After that, the platoon occupied the high ground and laid the ambush. To know the exact ranges were a great help to the Australian soldiers.

The Nine section radio operator called Tony Boyle went around the section telling the men that there was officially a truce in progress. None of the Australian soldiers believed that for even a moment. They typically said, *"How could the Noggies know of a truce being progress? They have very little to nothing in the way of radio equipment! We shall stay alert and if Noggies come, we simply must wipe them out before they do it to us!"* Soon afterwards, Brod felt a pull on his hand. That was caused by a thin cord running from the Nine Section M60 machinegun to his hand. The M60 was being manned by Mick.

The Full Circle for Mick

Brian spoke. He said, *"Mick, leave the machine gun to me and get yourself into position among the other blokes! You have an M79, and I want you to use it against the Noggies loaded with 'Flechette' Ammunition! The orders have come down the line, we are not taking prisoners this time!"*

Soon after, assistance was called in from the mortars. The answer from the mortars was, *"Affirmative, commencing to lay fire on grid reference 148136. The fire mission shall be three rounds fired by battery! Commencing fire, out!"* The 1RAR Mortar platoon had been completely replaced and fired upon the enemy with devastating results. The enemy suffered eight dead and an unknown number of wounded. About two hours later, Brian Broderick got Nine Section together and spoke to the Australian soldiers. He said, *"Blokes, there is a small body of enemy coming this way along the creek! We shall take on these fuckers! See to it that the 'claymore mines are set out facing the creek! Mick how many rounds of 'flechette, do you still have for the M79?"*

Mick replied, *"Brod, I have four rounds of that stuff left!"* Brian responded with, *"Good, if you get the chance to do so, use them upon the Noggies! Use as many claymores as you want and whatever else takes your fancy."* So, Nine Section sprang the ambush using the claymore mines, the section's M60 machinegun and automatic weapons of the scout group and the rifle group, as well as M72 rocket launchers and M79 grenade launchers. That resulted in twelve enemy KIA.

That was followed by more aggressive patrolling and the placement of ambushes of tracks and waterways used by the enemy. There was the assault upon, and the clearing of enemy camps as well as locating and destroying of food caches and ammunition. A 'Standing Patrol had been put into place at the junction of three tracks and the fast-flowing creek.

The M60 machinegun from Support Company was deployed to help out Nine Section and it was commanded by a corporal who simply knew nothing about anything! He was so inept that he placed the machine gun centrally, so that it was surrounded by Australian soldiers and could not be used without hitting Australians. The Australian members of Nine Section noticed that, and they were alarmed by the action of the corporal who was effectively making the M60 useless because of its siting among the Aussie soldiers.

Mick had been ordered to cover the track which was going to the north of him. He did so and was uneasy because of the fact that the M60 machinegun was located centrally, directly behind him and if it fired, it would have wounded or killed himself and other Australian soldiers.

He was looking northwards and saw two enemy soldiers silently approaching the Australian position with their weapons in their hands. The M60 was immediately behind Mick, where it was useless. Mick turned to the corporal in charge of the machinegun and said, *"Fucking Noggies! Hurry up and get that fucking gun up here and help to wipe those Noggies out!"* The machinegun crew from Support Company did not move and so, Mick engaged the enemy on his own, resulting in one enemy WIA.

Meanwhile that enemy's companion, had gone to the left of his companion and he opened fire upon Mick with an RPG. Mick had wisely chosen to get behind a large ant hill and that was all that saved him from the blast of the rocket.

The remaining enemy then ran away from the area, leaving Mick free to concentrate on the matters at hand.

Mick yelled at the corporal from Support Company, *"You fucking stupid dickhead, why did you not bring up the M60 when I wanted that done?"* The corporal from Support Company said, *"We would have opened up on the Noggies, but you beat us to it and either killed them or drove them off!"* By now, Mick was furious. He said, *"You fucking useless prick, if you had fired upon the Noggies, you would have killed me and not them because you placed all of us directly into the path of the machinegun fire! Now, fuck off you useless prick, go back to Support Company and when you get there, you can keep the other useless pricks from that useless unit company! Now just fuck off!"*

Soon, he was relieved and returned to the platoon area. Soon after, Nine Section with Brian Broderick in command, placed a section ambush upon a well-used track. Brian chose an area which was well elevated and above most of the surrounding areas.

Operation Goodwood Two

The operation ran from the 13th of January 1969 to the 27th of January 1969. The soldiers of 1RAR were waiting to board the Iroquois helicopters at 'Kangaroo Pad' to take them into the 'Areas of operations' of the follow-up operation to 'Goodwood One'. The new operation was Called 'Goodwood Two' and it was conducted in similar areas to 'Goodwood One.' The main difference was that "C" Company found itself operating in the open fields of rice paddies. Overall, it was considered to be a successful operation, but not everything was as it appeared to be!

Nine Platoon had been without an officer in command of it for several weeks. During the interim, it was commanded by the platoon sergeant Bluey Burdett. At last, an "O: Group was held during which the section commanders were given information to pass on to the section rank and file members. Having called the members of Nine Platoon together, corporal Brian Whyte spoke.

He said, *"OK, Blokes! We are getting a new officer. The information about him is incomplete, but here goes! His name is either Hall as in what the scouts use, or else it is Whore as in slut! I was informed that he is very unsure of himself and that he will need us to give him the necessary confidence to do what he has been trained for!"* 2nd Lieutenant Hall joined the company just before it boarded the helicopters that were transporting it to action in 'Operation Goodwood 2'.

He was a likeable young man but he no confidence. The three section commanding corporals of Brian Broderick, Brian Payne and Brian Whyte held a discussion about the new officer and it was decided by them to give him the confidence that he was lacking. Brian Broderick began the conversation.

He said, *"Blokes, I think that we have to do something to make sure that this new officer gets all of the confidence that he needs, otherwise we are all in danger! I have looked at the areas we will be covering, and this is a map of that area! Have a look at this! We will be operating in the area of these rice paddies and that wide river. According to my calculations, we should be about here,* (He said that as he was pointing to an area marked on the map) *on the 10th day!*

Here at this bend In the river, would be an Ideal place for the platoon to 'harbour-up for the night. We will wait until it is completely dark and then wake up our blokes from their sleep. We must tell our blokes that there is a large sampan with several Noggies on board it in the middle of the river. I will throw several grenades into the river and then call for artillery or mortar back-up on the section radio. How does that sound to you, Whitey?" Brian Whyte replied, *"Fucking sounds good to me Brod! I think that your plan is a master-stroke! By asking for artillery or mortar support to wipe out an enemy sampan on the river, it will lend credence to us saying that we have engaged and sunk an enemy sampan! The result of that should be that Lt. Hall will then have something to brag about in the officer's Mess and that could fix his problem of having no confidence!"*

So, Nine Platoon found some caches of rice and destroyed them, soon after, some caches of enemy ammunition were discovered and destroyed. On the 10th day of 'Operation Goodwood 2' Nine platoon was deployed along the banks of the river and Seven Section was providing a rear-guard in case of enemy attack form the rear.

Night quickly fell into place and other than those who were on duty manning the guns on sentry duty, the platoon members were asleep. The section commanders went to their men and woke them up, saying, *"Stand-to, Brod has seen enemy in a boat on the river! We are going to ambush the river and sink the bloody boat! We fire into the river as soon as Brod throws his grenades!"*

Suddenly, there was the sound of Brod throwing his grenades and small arms fire, That was followed by the section radioing for artillery or mortar support to fire upon the river. That resulted in a fire mission and when it was over

Australian soldiers were seen to be helping themselves to fish which were floating belly-up in the river. In February 1969, 1RAR was rotated back to Australia.

Mick Sent to D & E Platoon Nui Dat

Colin Smith, Wally Heffy and Mick Kramer extended their period of service in Vietnam until the 2nd of September 1969. As soon as they had done so, they were transferred to HQ company 1ATF and they found themselves in D&E Platoon. Their first action as part of that new unit was to man the defences and bunker systems defending the Australian Base at Nui Dat.

So, on Mick's birthday of the 1st of March, the men were manning a bunker close to 'Kangaroo Pad' which was the helicopter emplaning and deplaning strip for airborne operations. The darkness of night had blackened the sky and there was no visibility. Suddenly, there were many explosions, and an intense fire-fight developed.

Then, there was the sound of the Iroquois Medevac Helicopters flying in to aid the wounded from 5RAR which had relieved 1RAR. The following day, at 11:200 hours, there was a company parade of HQ Coy, 1ATF.

The Australian soldiers were told, *"Sub-units of 5RAR had become disorganised and as a result, they had strayed into a minefield which was the responsibility of the local AVRN unit."* Many Australian soldiers were disgusted by that and they openly said, *"Fucking AVRN, they are in league with the enemy! We should attack the bastards and wipe them out!"*

Later in March, 1ATF was again involved in operations in the Long Bihn area of southern Vietnam. As usual, Mick, Wally Heffy, Collin Smith, and Tony Boyle were serving together with Leo Low. They had just heard that their friend, who had been transferred to 9RAR was killed during a contact with enemy soldiers. So, once again, the men discussed the stupidity of war and how immoral it was for Australian to be involved in the continued attempts of the USA to ignore the rulings of the Geneva convention on Indochina!

In 1969, there was a rising tide of resentment against Americans because Richard Nixon was soon to become the President, and he was under the illusion that would give him the power he needed to do things in Asia in the way he wanted. Again, he was both mistaken and very disappointed that he could not have his way.

Meanwhile, Mick and his friends noticed that there were groupings of two and three small army tanks scattered around Long Bihn. The Australians asked each other about them, but no-one knew what they were at the time. Mick found out about them after he returned to Australia and spoke to a French Foreign Legion Vietnam Veteran years later.

Speaking to Kurt Sommers at the Gerogery Hotel in 1987, Mick described those small tanks (armoured vehicles). Kurt said, *"At Long Bihn, those little tanks were Japan-man tanks. They were knocked out of action by the Viet Mihn during WW2. We, of the French Foreign Legion, would use those tanks as target practice for our Bazookas!"*

The 2nd Indochina War - Peoples' Attitudes

In 1969, Richard Nixon became the President of the United States of America and in due course, he and his main advisor Henry Kissinger were discussing the progress of the war in Vietnam. Nixon said to Kissinger, *"Henry, the Vietnamese Patriots have run out of stream in their Tet offensive against the 'Republic of Vietnam'* (What many people still call South Vietnam).

We currently have a mess of trouble brewing for this US Administration which has been almost jointly caused by our much higher than expected causality rates, the press running stories which are seen by the public as being against our presence in Vietnam, and the success of the agents of North Vietnam in convincing many of the members of our great society that we must get the fucking hell out of Asia, because what happens there should only be the business of the Asians.

There continues to be held, mass demonstrations against the war, not against the Communist Government of North Vietnam and no-one gives a fuck about what happens to the South Vietnamese people, government, or businesses. The American People have gone from having a luke-warm approval for the Vietnam War to outright hostility against it. Not only that, but our allies in Australia are getting even worse views of the Vietnam War from the Australian Population which is currently very anti-war.

All over the world, America is being seen as a swaggering bully and that is helping the anti-American propaganda of China, USSR, North Korea, and North Vietnam." (What he called North Vietnam is in fact called the Democratic Republic of Vietnam by the Vietnamese people and their leaders.)

Kissinger replied with, *"Richard you worry too much. I think that in order to get us out of this mess, you should announce some policy changes. You should announce a strand of policies which will involve the phased withdrawal of all US forces from Vietnam. You will have to bolster the position of the Republic of Vietnam (RVN or South Vietnam) by expanding the RVN's forces and giving them more training and arms. You will have to progressively increase their combat responsibilities, and you could call that the 'Vietnamisation' of the War.*

At the same time, we must begin a process of 'Triangular Diplomacy' and recognise China which will mean that I will be constantly travelling to the Soviet Union and China trying to obtain discussions which could lead the redefinition of the Vietnam conflict and that could then allow us to increase international pressures upon Hanoi."

So it was that as the American forces withdrew, their arms and lavish base facilities were transferred across to the RVN. The forces of the South Vietnamese Government were with getting more resources, but this also created any severe maintenance, logistic and training problems.

Rightly or wrongly, the United States of America now widened the war by invading Cambodia jointly with American and Army Republic of Vietnam or ARVN troops in March 1970. The plan was to find and destroy the Popular Liberation Army Front (PLAF or Vietcong) and/or the combination of these with the bases used by the People's Army of Vietnam (PAVN, better known as NVA). That largely failed and a further invasion was carried out by the well-equipped but badly led ARVN forces into Laos. The ARVN Forces experienced major difficulties, experienced casualties, and withdrew in disarray. This appears to fit in with what is thought of the ARVN soldiers by both the Australian soldiers and their officers.

When asked what they thought the prospects were of the South Vietnamese successfully carrying on the fight against the Vietnamese Patriots, many Australians were negative. They would reply, *"The Noggies take over the war here? You bloody well have to be kidding me. If that happens, then it will make this war a total waste of time and many Aussies will have died for nothing!"*

Senior Australian officers were even more sceptical about the 'Vietnamisation' of the war and its prospects. That sort of view was evident even right at the top of the Australian ranks. The Australian Colonel Alan Stretton circulated his thoughts by writing. He wrote, *"Everyone realises the futility of the entire war and 'Vietnamisation' is simply a face-saving device."* The New Zealand Commander was thinking, *"Phuc Tuy cannot be secured if allied forces are withdrawn."*

Going along with the American withdrawal plans, the Australian Prime Minister, John Gorton made an announcement on the 22nd of April 1970. He said, *"At the moment the first Australian Task Force in Vietnam is made up of three battalions and their supporting units. Our allies, the Americans have announced that they are beginning the Vietnamisation of the war and that they will begin phased withdrawals of American Units from Vietnam. Accordingly, I hereby announce that when the battalion known as 8RAR has completed its one year 'Tour of Duty' in Vietnam and when it returns to Australia, it will not be replaced.*

American's policy of Vietnamisation allows us to reduce our presence in Vietnam to two battalions and their supporting units. As we still have another battalion active in Malaysia, it still means that we continue to have one third of Australia's fighting capability overseas at any given time."

So it was that 8RAR left Vietnam and returned to Australia, leaving 1ATF with two battalions and supporting units. After the next four months, the 'Vietnamisation' was started earnestly in Phuoc Tuy.

Large areas of the province were handed in terms of operational responsibility to the local units of the RVN (South Vietnam) forces including ARVN. Malcom Fraser had by now become Minister for Defence. About this he was reported to say, *"This development is the very objective of the whole enterprise – so that the South Vietnamese can maintain security on their own in certain areas and ultimately over the whole territory."*

The First Australian Task Force had proved itself to be highly mobile, well equipped, and efficient. The enemies it encountered during its operations justly considered themselves to be true patriots of their country and they simply wanted to put an end to domination of their own country by foreign outsiders.

The local forces of the RVN (Republic of Vietnam or South Vietnam) were recruited from the same communities that supplied the recruits for the National Liberation Front or NLF (also known as Vietcong). This in turn led to the situation where many units of the South Vietnamese Armed Forces were infiltrated by enemy agents.

The elite Australian Army Training Team (AATTV) was transferred to Phuoc Tuy to work with the RF companies in 1970. The Australians found that in the short time left before the Australian withdrawal, there was little they could do. When the Vietnamese units were given wider areas of responsibility to cover in 1971, they proved to be unwilling and unable to fill the gap left by the withdrawal of 1ATF.

The American advisory support to the local forces was disorganised. The end result was that Territorial force operations were launched without a target or even a general aim … The operations of the territorial forces were fragmented and futile.

The Australian Army felt that a complete Australian withdrawal was desirable with the departure of the Task Force (1ATF), but the conservative government of Australia thought that there were political advantages in keeping a small force in South Vietnam. On the 9th of December 1971, the government stated that Australian Army Assistance Group Vietnam would remain. It was made up mainly of AATTV members who conducted training in Phuoc Tuy.

A small group remained until after the election in December 1972 after which the incoming Labour Government under the leadership of Gough Whitlam withdrew all remaining Australian personnel.

Richard Nixon's War

Before his election, in 1964, Johnston used a line which promised peace but also had a policy of war. The very same tactic was used by Nixon. Nixon had as early as 1954 called for direction intervention by American Forces which were to be on the side of the French colonialists. Now that he was the United States' President, he assumed that he was fully in control of the situation, and he was determined to win the war.

However, as he entered the White House in 1969, he found that he was not able to reinforce the US Expeditionary Corps. The American public opinion about the Second Indochina War was demanding that the American soldiers were sent back to the USA. A major reason for this

The Full Circle for Mick

happening was that American losses in Vietnam had now reached completely unacceptable levels for the American people to tolerate any longer.

The expenditure on the Indochina War had now gone beyond US thirty billion dollars per year while at the same time, American social welfare and school developments were denied funding. As a result, opposition to the war increased and America woke up.

For the Nixon administration the key question to be worked out was how to both continue the war and win it, as well reducing the losses in American lives and expenditure to levels which were acceptable to the American public. Somehow that had to be done without renouncing the claimed right of the USA to impose restrictions and regulations upon the Vietnamese people and for the USA to save face. The solution of the Nixon Administration was to "Vietnamise" the war.

In order for this to occur, it was known that some requirements had to be met: The puppet army (South Vietnamese or Republic of Vietnam Army) had to be strengthened in terms of men and equipment to make it the main fighting force, capable of being the main protection of the Saigon Administration which had to be entirely had to be entirely committed to the interests of the Americans.

As well, Washington would gradually withdraw all US ground forces, while maintaining in Vietnam enough air power and artillery to effectively support the ARVN. That US presence would be maintained as long as it was necessary. Not only that, but it was decided to "Make life unbearable for the Vietnamese People through the continued use of massive air raids and the continual spraying of toxic chemicals. Thus, forcing the population to regroup in towns which were controlled by the Americans/or and their agents."

The Harvard professor called Samuel P. Huntington advocated the forced 'Urbanisation' of the Vietnamese population by turning these parts of South Vietnam which were not controlled by the US forces into deserts pockmarked by bomb craters, where no vegetation grew, where there were no birds and therefore where the revolutionary forces would not go.

It was thought that millions of Vietnamese would therefore be forced to seek the shelter of towns and that they would not be able to support themselves if they did not join the forces of the South Vietnamese Republic (RVN) or South Vietnamese police. (These men wore uniforms consisting of a white shirt, grey trousers and a grey peaked cap which had a large silver coloured badge on it. They were known to be armed with pistols of heavy calibre, and they had the reputation of being very cruel men.)

In the areas controlled by the Americans, programmes were put into place to intensify the so-called pacification by the use of incessant raids, the killing of activists and patriots. As well, a programme involving the imprisonment and deportation of hundreds of thousands of Vietnamese People was initiated. The South Vietnamese military forces and their police set about intimidating the people without respite and the use of terror was stepped up using forty-four thousand specialty trained pacification agents.

President Nixon applied this policy at the same time that he was forced to start withdrawing the American soldiers, just as the American casualties were becoming worse and the resistance to the Americans in the south was gaining the upper hand both using the political and the military methods.

As the US Presidential elections drew nearer, Nixon unleashed his version of total war. While the Democratic Republic of Vietnam (North Vietnam) was being sporadically bombed, the weight bombs dropped on Laos and South Vietnam passed the 1968 total and it reached 1,389,000 tons. (Statistics from US Departments of Defence and State.) Those figures do not include the use of artillery to shell the areas or the use of the spraying of defoliants and other poisonous chemicals.

The defoliants were sprayed upon several millions of hectares, and it can best be described as virtual biocide. According to the figure from the Americans themselves, between the years of 1965 to 1973, ten million Vietnamese people were forced to leave their villages and move to cities because of what the Americans and their allies had done.

The Expansion of Nixon's War

Nixon wanted the continued propping up of the unpopular and very corrupt Saigon regime and he wanted to be seen as doing something to lower the very high casualty rate of the Americans. His 'Vietnamisation' programme clearly meant prolonging the war in Vietnam. It also led to the expansion of the war to the point where it involved action by Americans or their allies against all of the countries making up Indochina (Cambodia, Laos, and Vietnam).

It seems that in his mind, Nixon's policy of 'Vietnamisation' would be easily achieved by turning the war over to the Indochinese People and setting things up in such a way that Asian people would be fighting other Asian people for the benefit Americans. This course of action would help to ensure that the USA continued to be dominant in Asia. By so doing it would only be the colour of the skin of casualties that would be different. The Americans intensified the bombing of whole regions of Laos which were controlled by Lao patriotic forces. They used up to six hundred sorties per day with many types of aircraft including B52s. the Laotians were aghast to find that many of their villages had their populations forcibly removed rehoused in refugee camps.

Fifty ARVN Battalions which were under the command of twelve thousand American advisors and provided with overwhelming US air support invaded and launched an attack upon the Plain of Jars – Xieng Khouang area. The fighting in this part of Laos lasted until February 1970.

It was then that the Lao forces, with aid from Vietnamese forces launched a major offensive and were successful in driving the enemy including the hated 'Americans' out of the region. Many rejoiced that the successful counter-offensive had killed so many American enemies. So it was that the tactic of the Americans of using specially trained mercenaries, many American advisers and large-scale air support was doomed to failure.

At a meeting held to discuss how to rectify the situation, an agent of the CIA put forward his ideas. He said, *"Sir, it seems to me that in order for our President to have his way here in Asia, we shall have to organise a coup d' ĕtat against the neutral government of Cambodia. In order to do this, we must get rid of King Norodom Sihanouk who is standing in our way. Once we get rid of him, we can install our own agents and puppets called Lon Nol and Sirik Matak."*

King Sihanouk was toppled, and the Lon Nol government ruled in his place in the face of stiff opposition from the people. In order to save their Lon Nol puppet government, the USA command launched an attack by the Saigon Government and American troops against Cambodia. Cambodia was invaded by seventy thousand foreign soldiers while the Americans and their South Vietnamese allies bombed cities and villages. The CIA led coup against King Norodom Sihanouk bought about unexpected consequences for Washington.

Many Laotian people joined with their Vietnamese brothers and engaged the common American enemy in combat. That was followed by the reaction of American and world opinion which forced Nixon to withdraw American ground forces after June.

Gerald Ford stated, "There will be a bloodbath in South East Asia when all American Forces leave." He knew that his intelligence services had prepared for just that and that all conditions for a Vietnamese civil war were in place[73].

On the 22nd of January 1975, One thousand and five hundred people who made up fifteen different organisations, and were from various areas around Saigon, went to Ân Quy Pagoda in order to celebrate the signing of the Paris Agreement.

---

[73] Vien, 2009.

These organisations circulated a petition which demanded that the USA immediately was to stop sending military aid to Saigon and the immediate resignation of the puppet South Vietnamese President Nguyen Van Thieu.

On the 7th of April 1975, General Võ Nguyen Giap, minister for Defence and General commander of the Vietnam People's Army, ordered, *"All fighting units are to fight faster and more boldly in order to take advantage of this hour and remove the enemy from the Fatherland of Vietnam!"* These things together resulted in the Americans and their puppet forces being defeated and the Americans leaving Vietnam. Saigon was renamed to Ho Chi Minh City. The Australians had left Vietnam long before that.

Coming Home

As the date rolled around to the 5th of September 1969, the friends of Mick, Collin, Raymond and Wally, experienced mounting excitement because they know that on the 5th of September 1969, they would board a QANTAS 707 at the Saigon Airport. At 10:00 hours, Vietnamese time, they all boarded the QANTAS 707. As they were entering, they all noticed that the aircraft had the logo of the City of Perth, Australia on the fuselage just over a window.

Mick had invited his friends to the wedding between Carolyn and Mick which was to take place at Saint Lukes Church in Liverpool on Saturday, the 13th of September 1969. Mick now said to his friends, *"Well, blokes, I need a volunteer to be my Best Man!"*

Wally Heffy volunteered for the job. Soon after that agreement, the aircraft took off, and after climbing for a time, some male civilian stewards came around the aircraft serving the seated soldiers with champagne, which had been supplied by QANTAS for the homeward bound soldiers. Wally now said, *"When I get home, the second bang will be the front door! I am going to root, eat, drink booze, and have a great time. How about you, Mick? What are you going to do?"* Mick replied, *"Yes, Walter, I shall also do those things but perhaps in a different order!"*

After hours in the air, the plane landed at Singapore Airport. All of the Australian soldiers got off the plane, walked to the departure lounge bar, and drank two large beers each before they reboarded the QANTAS jet. They had been on the ground for thirty minutes during which time the efficiency of the ground crews was such that the jet had taken on fresh supplies and even refuelled.

Once they had been seated and had their seat belts firmly on, QF 712 again took off to the sky, with the next scheduled stop being Darwin, Australia. After a long flight, QF 712 landed at Darwin Airport. However, this time refuelling and restocking did not go so smoothly. After the jet had been sitting on the tarmac for four hours, most of the returning Vietnam Veterans were becoming concerned at the time that the jet was being held on the tarmac.

Wally asked Mick to find out what was happening, and that resulted in Mick making a phone call to the Duty Officer at Larrakeyah Barracks. Mick said, *"Good evening, sir, this is Corporal Michael Kramer, and I am part of plane load of Vietnam Veterans returning to Australia! When we landed in Singapore, we were only on the ground for thirty minutes and the plane was refuelled and resupplied during that time!*

Now, here we are with the 707 jet landed at Darwin Airport and we have already been on the ground for four hours! That being the case, it makes us think that something is happening that we know nothing about or else we would have been back in the travelling to Sydney hours ago! So, sir, can you please tell me why we are still on the ground here in Darwin?"

The Duty Officer at Larrakeyah Barracks was Lt. Chalmers. He listened to what Mick was telling him and then he spoke. He said, *"Nice to talk to you Corporal. With regards to your question about why you Vietnam Veterans are being held on the tarmac; the answer appears to be that you returning Vietnam Veterans are an embarrassment to the ruling Liberal/country Party Coalition Government of the Commonwealth of Australia!*

Those disgusting politicians have issued a decree saying that your flight cannot land in Sydney because the jet will wake people from their sleep. So Sydney Airport will be under curfew. You shall find it difficult to call a taxi because the taxi drivers will assume that someone is pulling their legs because they know that the airport is shut during the curfew hours. According to a memo about this, you should be in the air again in about half an hour from now.

This has been done mainly in order to prevent a clash between returning Vietnam Veterans and the unwashed hairy protesters who are likely to be at the Airport demonstrating about the war! All the same, when you finally land at Mascot Airport, it will be about 02:00 hours. Corporal, tell your mates that you will be in the air again in about a half hour and that it will be about 2 am in Sydney when you land! Good luck Corporal, I wish you and your friends well!"

Mick now returned to the departure lounge, and he spoke his mind! He said, *"To those of you who are wondering why we are still on the ground, the Duty Officer at Larrakeyah Barracks, Darwin just told me that it is because the ruling Liberal/Country Coalition Government of Australia considers returning Vietnam Veterans to be an embarrassment! We should be boarding the jet soon and we will not land in Sydney before 2 am. Apparently, this is to stop the Vietnam Moratorium protesters from clashing with us!"* With that announcement made, anyone could have heard a pin drop because there was now total silence among the returning soldiers. More time passed and then came the announcement, *"Returning Army Personnel from Vietnam, please reboard QF 712"* Soon, all returning men were again seated on QF 712 and the flight to Sydney began.

After a long time in the air, with Eastern Australian Standard Time approaching 01:50 hours, some lights appeared under the left wing. QF 712 banked and the men could plainly see that these were some of the lights of Sydney. A spontaneous cheer went through the aircraft. An announcement came the aircraft's public address system, *"This is your Captain speaking, Below are the lights of Sydney, gentlemen; please let me welcome you all home on behalf of Australia!"*

The QANTAS jet landed, did some taxiing, and then stopped. The Vietnam Veterans were mystified as to the reason for the aircraft's stopping. Soon after that, the QANTAS jet was boarded by men dressed in white coveralls gas masks and gloves. These men spayed something smalling a lot like disinfectant all over the interior of the plane and the soldiers. Next, every soldier had his footwear confiscated and replaced with a new issue oof army shoes.

Finally, the jet was again taxiing towards the international terminal of Mascot Airport and the soldiers were quick to notice that the entire building was darkened. There was only a single row of lights over the customs desk area and another small lighted area where soldier were given two months pay before being sent off for three months of leave.

It was now that the word of the Duty Officer of Larrakeyah Barracks in Darwin came back to Mick: *"You will arrive at a darkened airport, the airport will in fact be closed, and you will need all of the luck in the world to get a taxi"* All of the returning Vietnam Veterans now passed through customs. The Vietnam Veterans had heard stories of a Customs Officer serving at Mascot airport who liked to buy any pornographic photos the returning soldiers may have in their pockets.

As the line moved forward it was finally Mick's turn to go through customs. The attending Customs Officer said, *"Welcome home Digger! Do you by any chance have any pornographic photos on you?"* Mick replied, *"Yes,"* and produced the small number of photos from his pocket. The Customs Officer said, *"Very well, let me see them and if they are good enough, I shall buy them off you!"* Having seen the photos, the Customs Officer said, *"I am offering you Au$180.00 for all of them. Does that suit you?"* Mick said, *"Yes,"* so, the deal was concluded. The next act of the Customs Officer was to ask Mick, *"Do you have anything to declare?"*

Mick replied, *"No, but I do have 5 yards of high quality Thai silk as a gift for my mother."* That interested the Customs Officer and so, he opened Micks bags to check out the silk. Upon seeing it he said to Mick, *"I offer you Au$520.00 for that silk, which I will give you now. So, the* silk, I am buying off you for AuS520.00 and to that I am paying you the Au$180.00 for the photos. All up, that comes to Au$700.00, that is what I call a good coming home present!" He then counted out $700.00 in $50.00 notes and gave them to Mick.

Next came the pay desk. As the soldiers were approaching it, Mick noticed that it was manned by a Second Lieutenant and that he had an Australian Military Police sergeant of either side of him and that both of them were armed. As they moved towards the pay desk Mick could heard the conversations between the Paying Officer and the men. He would ask, Name and army number? Upon being told, he then gave the soldier two months pay. Now, it was Mick's turn to be paid.

The paying Officer asked, *"Name and Army Number?"* Mick answered, *"Kramer M. G. 7141, sir!"* The paying Officer paid Mick his three months' pay and then he said, *"Kramer, you are to immediately board the flight to Adelaide."* By now, Mick was fired up and he was not about to take bullshit from a 2nd Lt.! so Mick yelled at the paying Officer. *"Look over there you fucking half-wit! That is my missus standing there, and here you are, fucking telling me that I have to leave her and fly to Adelaide! If it is really so, then you have fucking rocks where your fucking brain should be, you bloody half-wit!"*

The officer now said, *"Kramer, if you do not immediately get on board the aircraft flying to Adelaide, you shall have to make your own way to Keswick Barracks at your own expense! Whatever happens, you are required to report to the personnel Depot of Keswick Barracks in Adelaide. There you shall be placed onto the Headquarters*

Company of Central Command un-allotted list. You must report for duty at 08:30 hours of the 8th of January 1970."

By now, Mick was disgusted with the army, and he had no intention of being bored while having to sit in a duty room doing nothing. So he said, *"Now look here sir, everything that you have told me is unsatisfactory and bullshit. I have a far better solution! Extend my leave to cover the Christmas and New year and I will report for duty at Keswick Barracks on the 18th of January 1970. That way, I and my wife can see my father in Melbourne and after that we can be with my mother and her new partner and their family over Christmas! The officer relented and Mick's leave was adjusted as he had suggested.*

Back in Australia

Carolyn and Mick tried to call a taxi. They found that they had to make many repeated calls to the taxi company, each time explaining that that they were in the International Terminal of Mascot Airport a this very early morning hour because Mick and the rest of the entire flight of returning Vietnam Veterans had landed in Sydney at 02:00 hours and that they had been waiting ever since for their taxi to arrive.

So far, this had already taken an hour and a half. The fiery Mick by now was extremely angry that as returning Australian soldiers they could be treated so shabbily. He now took off his 'dog tags' and found that the gold crucifix which had been a party gift from his mother was entwined among the 'Dog tags.'

He tried to separate them, but the more he tried to do that, the more entwined they became. Eventually, he threw these items as hard as he could. Twenty-five minutes later, which was two hours after the QANTAS jet had landed, a taxi finally appeared. The driver said, *"I am sorry Mate, I could have been here earlier, but I was under the impression that someone was pulling my leg! I mean that the airport is closed, yet here you and your wife are needing a taxi! The bloody Government of Australia should have been able to organise thigs better than this mess! So, Digger, where can I take you and your lady?"*

Carolyn and Mick were finally underway to her parents' home in Liverpool. After a taxi journey of twenty minutes, they arrived at the address in Northumberland Street of Liverpool, in the state of NSW in Australia and paid the taxi driver. They then walked into the home, and they were greeted by Carolyn's mother, Ella. She said, *"It is good to have you back alive and well, Mick! You and Carolyn now have a lot of work to do in preparing for your wedding!"*

As the time of their wedding was fast approaching, they decided to look at the price ranges of properties in and around the Sydney area in 1969. They saw a advertised in the window of a Liverpool real estate agent. The advertisement read, *"House on fourteen acres for sale at Minto. Price is $6,800.00.* Carolyn had $2,000.00 saved and Mick's account at the 'Commonwealth of Australia Bank' had $4,980.80 in it.

So, rightly or wrongly, they both assumed that the Commonwealth Bank would support them in purchasing the property at Minto. How wrong they were! When Carolyn and Mick went into the Liverpool branch of the Commonwealth Bank and asked about the possibility of getting a housing loan the manager said, *"No, you cannot have the money. That is too great an amount."* The manager said, *You are asking me for a loan of nine thousand and five hundred dollars! That is a lot of money! I shall not let you have it!"*

Mick and Caroyn were stunned by the words of the bank manager. With Mick not believing what his ears had heard, he said, *So, what is the problem? Carolyn has $2,000.00 in her account and I have savings of $4980.80 in my account here at this branch of the Commonwealth Bank! So, together we have $6,980.80 and here you are, telling me that you will not let me have the necessary housing loan!*

We need the money to purchase a home on 14 acres at Minto. We are only asking for $9,500.00 and we have almost $7,000.00 of our own money! On top of that, we are entitled to an Australian War Service Loan of $12,000.00. Mick was rather upset that the bank manager refused to let Carolyn and him have the necessary home loan.

As the wedding day for Carolyn and Mick was approaching, Mick simply said, *"Well then, we need $169.00 for immediate wedding expenses, so, I shall simply withdraw the money from my account here!"* The bank manager said, *Mr. Kramer, One hundred and Sixty Nine dollars is a lot of money! You cannot withdraw such a high amount without giving the bank at least two days' notice in writing that you are going to withdraw a high sum of money like that!"*

Mick could feel his temper rising and spoke to the bank manager. He said, *"Now let us get this straight; you are refusing to give us a housing loan even though we have almost that amount saved up and we both have secured and high incomes and now, even after I have explained that I need to withdraw some of my own money, you are fucking well refusing to let me have my own money! That is what I thought you have told me! Kindly confirm this!"*

The bank manager went on to confirm the statement he had made earlier, resulting in an angry Mick saying, *"You fucking arsehole, thanks to your bullshit against my wife and me, I am making an official complaint against you at the Head Office of the Commonwealth Bank! As well, your actions shall become known on the "John Laws Show" and I am taking all of the information to the Daily Mirror Newspaper. As well, I am closing the accounts here as well as complaining about your actions to your Head Office and the newspapers! I am informing the newspapers that a returning soldier from the war in Vietnam has been refused a housing loan by you and that you have even refused to let me withdraw my own money! I hope that the Head Office of the Commonwealth Bank sacks you over this debacle!"*

Transfer of Account to Bank of NSW

Carolyn and Mick left the Commonwealth Bank in Liverpool and transferred Mick's entire account to the nearby Bank of NSW, Liverpool Branch. The Bank of NSW, let Mick have the have the money. Now, armed with a bank for $6,800.00, Mick returned to the premises of the real estate agent, only to be told, *"The 14 acre property at Minto? Sorry, but it was sold some fifty minutes ago!"*

Mick returned to the Bank of NSW and redeposited the bank cheque into his savings account. After that, he withdrew enough money to help pay for the wedding and to go on a honeymoon. However, he had to take out a loan from the bank to cover the purchase a car. He was now far happier with the banking system than he had been while he was banking with the Commonwealth Bank of Australia!

The Marriage of Carolyn and Mick

On the 13th of September 1969, (the 2nd Saturday of September) Mick and Carolyn were married at Saint Luke's Church, in Liverpool, New South Wales. That was followed by a reception held at a Scout Hall. The caterers did a good job, and the guests all had a great time.

Eventually, Carolyn and Mick departed in their Holden car for their honeymoon accommodation, which was in the Barossa Valley, a wine growing area located bout fifty km to the north-west of Adelaide. They were delighted that their accommodation included their own toilet, lounge room, kitchen and sleeping areas. They explored various towns in the Barossa Valley, went fishing, had picnics attended art galleries and wineries. After a week a week of that, they drove to Adelaide, followed by driving to Millicent in the South East of South Australia.

Millicent is located 408 km (255 miles) from Adelaide. Their route took them along the Coorong. That is an area where the fresh water of the Murray River, mixes with the salt water trapped between a long line of sand hills and the open sea. Between the villages of Meningie and Kingston in the south East of the state, the dominant small is that of stagnant salt water.

Upon arriving at Meningie, the couple explored the small village. They found a fish and chips shop and purchased a meal of fish and chips, which they ate in the park overlooking Lake Alexandrina. Upon finishing their meal, they got into the car again and travelled to Policeman's Point. They refuelled the car and had a meal before continuing their drive to the village of Kinston in the South East of South Australia.

Arriving at Millicent in the south East of South Australia, the couple asked other people for directions to the Schmalfuss property on Rough Rock Road. As the properties all either had no markings at all, or else the address markings were indistinct, Carolyn and Mick had no choice but to drive right up to the home at the property concerned in order to find the home of his mother and her partner. As they were driving towards two homes situated near the back end of the small farm, a large German Shepard dog ran towards the car.

Neither Carolyn or Mick had any fear of dogs, and so, after stopping the car, Carolyn and Mick made a fuss over the dog who enjoyed the attention he was getting. Hildegard came out of the limestone house and greeted Carolyn and Mick. That was followed by her saying, *"Mick, your brothers and sisters are at school, except for Andy who is a baker's apprentice, and he is at work! Everyone should be here in about three hours from now!"*

Mick said, *"Great to see you, Mom! This is my wife, Carolyn! We were married a bit over a week ago, it is just too bad that the rest of you could not make it to our wedding in Sydney. Mom, why are there two houses here?"* His mother replied, *"The new Fibro home belongs to your brother Andy. He still in his latter years of completing his apprenticeship as a baker. I just hope that he will not have to serve in the army due to being drafted for National Service! It is bad enough that I already have a son on combat duties in Vietnam and I do not want your younger brother to be killed in that unjust and unwelcome war which is only Yankee business and nothing to do with Australia!"*

Hildegard was very opposed to the war in Vietnam, and she openly supported the Vietnamese leadership of Ho Chi Minh and General Giap! However, she was curious as to what was really happening in Indochina and so, she asked Mick about it all. For like most of the community, she had little idea of what war against insurgents was about.

Mick, on the other hand, did not want to speak about his war experiences at all, in case doing so, brought back unwelcomed memories which were still fresh and painful. Hildegard was determined to get answers to her questions about Vietnam, so she kept on pressing Mick to tell her, even though she could see that he was uncomfortable when speaking about it. Eventually she had her way and Mick told her of a typical action against an enemy bunker system.

Mick described the use of "Fire and Movement" which was used to close with and kill the enemy. As soon as Mick had finished the description of the action of assaulting and wiping out an enemy position, she was shocked. She said, *"My dear God! How awful and disgusting! What an immoral and disgusting thing to do to another human being!"*

Mick, during that outburst of disgust by his mother, was suffering from remorse at carrying out his duty to the Australian Army, because like many Australian combat soldiers he was questioning the moral and even the legality of the whole of the Allied actions in Vietnam! This proved to be the beginning of the symptoms of PTSD, which was very prevalent among Vietnam Veterans because of the guilt they were feeling about having been part of the Allied aggression and take-over of the southern part of Vietnam in direct contravention of the Geneva Conference on Indochina and the international agreements reached in 1954 after the French were forcibly removed from Vietnam after losing the fight for Bien Phu.

Hildegard still did not quite understand the concept of *"Fire and Movement."* She continued to press Mick for details, even though he did not want to say anything more about war. Finally, he said, *"Mum, a platoon is thirty-two men, counting the officer and sergeant. When the unit is at full strength! The sections are usually ten men when counting the commanding corporals! So, when attacking, two sections give covering fire, while the assaulting section moves forward by at least ten to fifteen metres before it takes cover and give covering fire for one of the rear sections to move forward. That is repeated until all three sections of the platoon are in the new position and a lot closer to the enemy. That continues to be done until we have closed with and killed the enemy!"*

It was now that Hildegard's partner, Edgar Schmalfuss returned from working at the same bakery as Andy. After meeting and greeting both Carolyn and Mick, he said, *"Carolyn and Mick, I would like to show both of you a project that Mick's sister, Angela has been working on! Please come with me!"*

And so, Hildegard, Edgar, Carolyn, and Mick followed Edgar to an area of the Schmalfuss property, and they saw a large hole measuring 12 metres long by 4 metre wide and at one point, it was two metres deep. Mick said, *"OK, so that is a large hole, but what has it got to do with my baby sister, Angela?"* Edgar answered, *"Angela did most of the work herself with a bit of help from the other kids! This is the beginning of her swimming pool!"*

What really amazed Mick about it was that it had been dug out of sand, sandstone, and limestone. He said, *"So, my little thirteen year old sister did all of that? I am very impressed! What a girl! so, what will happen now?"*

Edgar answered with, *"Your Mum and I agreed with Angela that if she could get the hole completed, then I would agree to complete the swimming pool by providing its water supply, and drainage as well as providing concrete and applying it to the walls and base of the swimming pool which must also be tiled for safety reasons. Your mother and I never thought that we would have to keep our end of the deal, but it now looks as if we have to do it. Your little sister is a tough negotiator, and she is a lot like you! She is thought of as being formidable by many others to say the least!*

In Australia & First Signs of PTSD

Mick thought that it could be in order for him to go to Nenke's Hotel in Millicent and enjoy a beer there. He walked to into thee saloon bar and he then slowly drank it. While he was doing so, a stranger walked into the bar and said to him, *"I am Dereck Crowe. Who are you and what do you do?"* Mick answered, *"My name is Mick Kramer, and I protect the citizens of this country!"* Dereck responded, *"Oh, bloody army, are you? I just hope that you are not one of those fucking Vietnam Veterans, who are just a pack of murdering, fucking child killers!"*

Meanwhile, the barman who was concerned about the situation that was developing between Mick and Dereck had contacted the Millicent Police Station and arranged for a police officer to attend the hotel. Now, yet again, Mick found that he was completely 'fired up.' Without saying anything more, he filled his left hand with coins and used his fist which he rotated as he hit forwards. That resulted in Dereck being hit right between his eyes and he suffered both of his eyes going black as a result of Mick's attack! With Mick now in full combat mode, he shaped up to Dereck and was about to give him a blow which would have felled him, when Mick felt a hand upon his shoulder.

A male voice from behind Mick said, *"Take it easy, Mate! I am Constable William Evans of the Milicent Police! The barman here has told me what has happened, and I am arresting Dereck Crowe for disturbing the peace! You have been identified as Michael Kramer, and we know that you have just returned from infantry combat duties in Vietnam. I urge you to from now on to keep a tight rein on your hair trigger temper, otherwise you will end up in lot of trouble!"*

With the confrontation over, Mick purchased two large bottles of 'Melbourne Bitter Beer and returned to his mother's home at Ruff Rock Road in Milicent. When he got there, he saw that Angela was there, as were his half-sister Rosemary and his half-brother Roland. Mick's other half-sister Sabine was not there because she had gone to her friend's home. All of Mick's siblings who were there, greeted him warmly. Angela and Mick began detailed conversation during which Angela brought Mick up to speed of what had happened while he was away in Vietnam.

Angela said, *"Bruv, my life at school is a misery due to my class teacher, a Mr. Humphries appearing to not like me and I am also getting a lot of shit from other kids at the school because they know that you are fighting in Vietnam, and they think that you and all other Vietnam Veterans are murdering baby killers and invaders doing Yankee bidding! No-one from our family has ever told anyone in Millicent that you are serving in Vietnam, because Mum is totally against the war there, yet everyone in the town knows about you service, and many resent you being there!*

Our mother thinks that the Vietnam War is just a case of Australia doing the bidding of the Yanks! I think that the people working at the Millicent Post Office have been doing a lot of talking whenever they saw letters from you to Mum and Dad arrive! Anyway, whatever their reasoning, most people in Millicent know that you are serving over there, and they do not like you for it!

The other school kids have been calling me the sister of a brutal baby killing prick, just because the newspapers and radio have reported that the American creep called Kelly did at the Vietnamese village of My Lai!

Mick answered, *"I am most sorry to hear that, sis! I sort of got that impression from the tone of the letters that you sent me while I was in Vietnam. With regards to your teacher Mr. Humphries, I do not know him as a teacher, but he did drive the school bus between Mount Burr and Millicent when I was going to school. At the time some of the other school children would taunt him! They would say, "What do you call two camels without humps? – Humphries!"*

Mick re-assured his sister that he would try to smooth things over for Angela by speaking to Mr. Humphries. Hildegard, who was becoming alarmed at the possibility of a looming confrontation between Mick and Angela's teacher, intervened and said, *"Look, you two, let Mr. Humphries do his job of teaching without interference from you! Mick, stay out of this because you may make things even worse!"*

Mick's mother, Hildegard, now got not her political high horse and said, *"Michael my son, do you not realise that by being a Vietnam Veteran, you are really just a tool of the*

American aggressors and invaders who are continuing to take things away from the people of Indochina without asking or paying for what they take? Please never wear your uniform here because I am so very ashamed of your involvement in that disgusting and immoral war of aggression and conquest of people who only ever wanted their own countries to be returned to them for themselves to govern without interference from Britain, France, and the immoral Yankee!"

The fiery Mick replied, *"Oh, fucking really Mum? I am an NCO and soldier of the Australian Infantry as well as being a British Subject and Australian Citizen! Are the rest of you Australian citizens yet? If you are, then good, and that means you are also British subjects! I told you before that I shall always serve Australia and it does not matter if my country is right or wrong, I will always do what is necessary for my country! There can be no other way!"*

Mick then spoke to his beloved sister, Angela. He said, *"Well, sis, it appears that I must get the fuck out of here! My own mother now appears to be in league with the Labour Party's ideals and the Vietnam Moratorium Movement which is responsible for giving many serving solders a tough time! Fuck, who needs this bullshit coming from even my own family! Carolyn and I are getting out of here right now! We will see all of you again at some other time!"*

That was happening on a Friday afternoon and so, Carolyn and Mick only drove as far as the Sommerset Hotel in Millicent and stayed there overnight. On the following morning they drove and returned to Sydney where they stayed with the parents of Carolyn. On the following Monday, Mick flew to Adelaide and reported to the

Personnel Depot HQ Company of Central Command. He walked into the orderly room and reported for duty. Sergeant O'Reilly said, *"Corporal Michael Kramer? It is good to finally meet you! I have been getting a mess of signals about you, direct from AHQ in Canberra! You are red hot! Here are your sealed orders which you are to open and read immediately."*

Mick did as he had been told and opened his orders and read them! The orders said, *"Corporal Kramer, you are to immediately board the next available flight to Sydney and travel to Victoria Barracks, Sydney where you will undergo a security assessment, Report to Lt. Colonel Richard Campbell when you arrive."* Mick showed Sgt O'Reilly the orders and he obtained the necessary tickets for travel from Adelaide Airport and the car to take Mick to the airport. So, Mick boarded TAA Flight TF 732 to Sydney. Soon after landing at Mascot Airport, Mick was taken by an Australian army duty car to Victoria Barracks in Sydney. He reported to Lt. Col. Campbell and passed a security assessment.

Diagnosis of PTSD

Mick had been very short tempered and he was required to report to physiatrist Doctor John Douglas. Mick entered the surgery of psychiatrist Doctor John Douglas, but without knowing what to expect, began to scan all around the surgery, looking for possible places that could be hiding aggressors and for possible escape routes. His behaviour was noticed by Doctor Douglas, who asked, *"Why are you scanning the aera? Do you not trust me?"* Mick replied, *"I do not know you and until I do know for sure that you are not a threat to my freedom or existence, I have to scan for possible threats and possible escape routes in case either fight or flight or even both become necessary!"*

With that introductory meeting over, the main interview between Mick and Doctor began. The doctor said, *"I have a sneaking suspicion that most if not all of your psychological problems cans be traced back to your war service and the attitudes of civilians in Australia towards you and other Vietnam Veterans when you returned from the war. Added to that is the fact that your wife was assaulted on multiple occasions while she was putting letters to you into the Australian Special Forces Mailbox at Sydney GPO! That must have affected you very badly as would have the treatment you received from the army and members of the public when you returned. So, let us start with some questions and answers which are mainly to ascertain if you have an adverse physiological condition!"*

The doctor then went through the list of symptoms of Post Traumatic Stress Disorder (PTSD) and asked, *"Firstly Michael let us establish if you have a severe stressor or other events that may have entered your mind and are just sitting there, just under the surface awaiting a trigger to bring it out. So, what do you see as a severe stressor or stressors that may have resulted in PTSD?"*

Mick answered, *"Fucking shit, Doctor, you want a severe stressor? There were bloody well heaps of them! I had to organise the recovery of two Australian KIA (Killed In Action) and the transport of their corpses back to the Australian Base Camp of Nui Dat! Also, I was often in action during more minor skirmishes which also resulted in either Australian or enemy dead or even both! As well, I ha to organise and take part in the burying of enemy dead, in a respectful way, without any interference with the enemies bodies, quite unlike what was done by other allied units!*

The simple fact is that I have never felt animosity towards the Vietnamese People; in fact, like many other Australian Vietnam Veterans, I think that we should have supported the Vietnamese freedom fighters instead of the God-damned Yankee bully! Also, consider that there was always the probability of enemy attack upon us by both day and night! After you have a year of this shit, your sleeping pattern becomes completely up to shit and you sleep very lightly, with the slightest sound awakening you! When out in the field, we would always sleep with our boots on, in order instantly ready for combat when the need to do so arose!"

Doctor Douglas asked, *"Did you find that the need actually arose?* Mick had managed to suppress his memories of the war found the memories now rushing back at him. He became agitated and said, *"What the fuck do you think? Holy Jesus, my unit had the distinction of being recognised as the most effective unit in the Australian Army during the years 1968 and 1969, and it had the highest ratio of enemy killed to the smallest number of Australian casualties, either Killed in Action, (KIA) or wounded in action (WIA) of any unit in the Australian Army. Do you get that? We were the bloody best! Yet here you are asking if I have had a fucking severe stressor? What do people want from me?"*

The Doctor replied, *"Thank you, and now let us move on to a series of questions related to the symptoms of PTSD! Do you have instances of re-experiencing traumatic war events?"* Mick replied, *"I just finished telling you that my company was, "Charlie Company of 1RAR and that it had the reputation of being the most effective unit in the Australian Army.*

The number of enemy killed by us was the absolute highest of any unit! So, fucking well yes, I have been re-experiencing the war events a lot of the time, in particular at fucking night! My sleeping pattern is up to shit, and I am constantly awake during the night; the slightest sound is enough to get me up to check what is happening! A lot of the time I cannot get to sleep before early morning and then it is usually only a few hours until it is time get up! The fucking result is that I am fatigued a lot of the time! Man, what I would give to be able to sleep like other people do!"

The doctor went on with, *"I see from your record that you are constantly avoiding functions at the mess. Is that because you are trying to avoid reminders of the traumas you have suffered?"* Mick answered, "Yes."

The doctor went on, *"These flashbacks you are experiencing, tell me about them."* Mick said, *"There are a number of them. There are two of them which bother me the most. The first is the face of a young man whom I killed in the line of duty. Whenever he appears, he says, "Uc da Loi, (Australian) you came to my country unannounced and uninvited, then you chose to lay in wait, while my comrades and me walked down the jungle path! Then you sprang the ambush which resulted in you killing me and my friends, even though none of us had ever seen any of you before!*

Yet there you were, with your Australian comrades, killing me and my people for the American aggressor! Why did you do that?" Mick paused and then continued, *"That Doctor, is the flashback/nightmare which I find most disturbing, because I agree with the people of Vietnam that no people from Australia, Britain, France, New Zealand, or the USA should ever have been in Cambodia, Laos, or Vietnam (those three countries are called Indochina). That* nightmare constantly returns and robs me of sleep, because I cannot answer the moral questions raised by the man whom I killed!"

Doctor Douglas said, *"I see, and I have the impression that you may be suffering from guilt associated with the killing of the man. Are there also other experiences which cause these nightmares and flashbacks?"* Mick said, *"One of the other memories that causes me pain is what happened during* "Operation Windsor." *We lost two men KIA on that, and I was part of the team sent in to recover the bodies of the two Australians!"*

Mick continued with his explanation. *Also, I had a meeting with a Buddhist Monk who asked me why I was in his country, doing the bidding of the Yankee aggressor. Apparently, he knew of my grandfather who had built the Tsingtao to Jinan Railway (384.2 km) in northern China. Apparently, his father met my grandfather, and they became friends. Upon his learning that I was an Australian soldier, he was dismayed at what that could do to my karma. So, in order to make up for what I have done for the bloody Yanks, I now must study engineering and return to Vietnam, this time to build, instead of destroying and killing!"*

Doctor Douglas said, *"I see, Do you get any intense physical reactions to reminders of your Vietnam Service?"* Mick replied, *"Often when these flashbacks are happening, I have a pounding heart, or nausea or heaving sweating or a tightening of my chest, and sometimes, I get all of those things at the same time for a few moments!"*

The doctor continued with, *"How is your recollection of the traumatic events?"* Mick replied, *"I remember things that I do not want to remember! However,*

The Full Circle for Mick

I cannot remember the dates when the actions occurred, and I cannot even remember the names of all of the operations without first consulting the records and looking things up!" The doctor continued with, *"Are you irritable and/or have outbursts of anger?"* Mick said, *"Yes, you had better believe it! It happens on a constant basis!"* The doctor then asked, *"Do you have difficulty in concentrating?"* Mick said, *"Yet again, you had better believe it! If I wish to learn something now, I have to study it and learn it by rote! All of that takes a long time, but I force myself to do it, because deep down, I could not be bothered at all!"*

The doctor said, *"Do you feel jumpy and are you easily startled?* Mick answered, *"Yes to both questions!* The doctor continued, *"Do you feel alone and/or alienated?"* Mick was becoming increasingly impatient and short tempered. He said, *"Fucking well yes on both counts! Anyway, what it the point of all of this fucking bullshit?"* Doctor Douglas replied, *"My boy, I detect a lot of seething emotions in you, boiling away just below the surface. Currently, you are like an explosive looking for a place to go off! If that happens, I would not like to see the result! You need to keep your mind focussed on the positive and I strongly urge you to enrol in a course of tertiary education! Earlier, you mentioned that you made a promise to the Buddhist Monk that one Day you would return to Vietnam as an engineer and then help to rebuild the country that you helped the Americans to destroy, so how about enrolling for an engineering degree?*

That would help to keep your mind focussed on the positive like you need to do! Otherwise the police may end up using you for target practice on account of the fact that you are not just a veteran, but a very capable one who has combat experience! I only point this out because if there is ever a situation involving you and a confrontation with police, the police will have access to your full records.

They will see that you are experienced and capable in combat, and so, they will simply kill you in order to minimise the danger of confronting you! I have prescribed a course of anti-depressants which you can have filled at any chemist in Australia. Your dosage will be reviewed on a six monthly basis. For now, you need to take of the anti-depressants per day. One must be taken at night and the other at midday! You must not consume alcohol during the time that you are on the anti-depressants!

You must stay off the grog! You shall attend this surgery for psychological treatment every fourteen days! During that time, I shall record your progress towards healing, and we shall see when your medication dosage can be varied or ended! So, Mick, I shall see you again next fortnight!"

Mick obtained his script from the doctor and had it completed at a local pharmacy. Later, he applied to the University of Southern Queensland, and he was enrolled into Bachelor Degree of Engineering Honours. The lessons were by computer link to the University of Southern Queensland and assignments were sent in by mail. There was also a portal on the computer which allowed direct contact with teaching staff at various times. This proved to be something that kept Mick very busy, but it was his saving grace because of his great interest in what he was learning.

Studying the Engineering Honours & Graduation

The next meeting with Doctor Duglas took place fourteen (14) days later. The doctor said, *"Well, my boy, did you enrol?"* Mick replied, *"Yes, in Bachelor of Engineering Honours, I shall be doing this initially by correspondence and that means that I must attend nine on-campus short courses which are the practical components of the Honours Degree! I am doing two major theory course per semester and two practical subjects per semester! The first of the practical subjects will be Geology and Survey practice which will for five days in June of this year, followed straight away by another short course, this being "Soil and Water Practice," which is the practical component of Hydraulics and Geomechanics courses. In all cases, the pass mark for all practical courses is 95%, and either students achieve that, or they have to do that course gain!"*

Five days later, a parcel was delivered to Mick's home in Culcairn. The parcel contained a rock sample kit which had samples of many different types of rock and that was to be used in conjunction with the theory course on Geology. Mick started his study and applied himself vigorously! It was noticed by others that he no longer appeared to be jumpy, but that he was both looking and feeling tired. Some people began to question if there was a change for the better in Mick or if he was just too tired to react.

Mick however, embraced the field of study with great enthusiasm and constantly had his nose in a text book. He joined the engineering classes on-line and enjoyed being part of the lectures. After the lecture on a given subject, study was required, and Mick also prepared his assignments then. Assignments had to be submitted by mail at first and later, Mick enjoyed submitting the entire assignment on-line.

The subject of Hydraulics was reputed to have a failure rate of sixty-eight percent (68%) of all students who attempted it. USQ mainly put that down to a lack of engineering knowledge. Mick vowed that he would pass the subject by making that he knew the fundamental concepts and units applying to engineering.

In the case of hydraulics, it became very apparent to Mick that the key to mastering the subject lay with the ability to manipulate algebraic formulae. He made sure that he knew the basics and he thought, *"OK, here I am doing hydraulics. By knowing how to manipulate formulae, and conduct transpositions, everything should fall into place! For example, when finding the water pressure on the wall of a dam, I should use $P = \rho g h$, where ρ is density, g = force of gravity and h = height of the fluid. P = pressure on the dam wall.*

His first practical subjects would take place at the campus of the university of Southern Queensland, Toowoomba. There are nine (9) of the practical courses that I have to pass. All of them have a pass mark of 95%, and only a pass or fail is given." As well, he learned the entire SI Meric System which had replaced the cumbersome British system of weights and measures in Australia.

As Mick applied himself to the study of Hydraulics One and Geomechanics One, he found that as soon as he got home from completing his duties, he had to immediately carry out his study, as he had to devote up to in excess of eight hours per week to each of the two subjects. Often, that resulted in him still studying or completing assignments at 00:30 hours.

That concerned Carolyn a bit and she would say, *"Darling, I think that you had better pack it in for tonight, remember that you have to be on duty from 08:00 hours and the army must come first!"* Her reasoning was unassailable, and Mick went to bed. After a great deal of study and work, he finally quailed as an engineer and returned to Vietnam to help out the people he had fought against during the war. After that, Mick completed several projects, but all of that is another story!

Ende

Bibliography

Chamberlain, E., 2013 *The Vietcong D440 Battalion: Their story.* Ernest Chamberlain, Point Lonsdale.

Giap, V.N., *The Military Art of People's War.* Monthly Review Press, New York.

Ham, P., 2007, *Vietnam – the Australian War.* Harper-Collins Publishers, Sydney.

Pelvin, R. 2006, *Vietnam – Australia's Ten-Year War 1962 – 1972.* Hardie Grant Books, Prahran.

McAulay, L., 1988. *The Battle Coral* Randon House, 20 Alfred Street, Milsons Point NSW 2061

Pemberton, G., 1990, *Vietnam Remembered.* Weldon + Associates Pty Ltd Sydney.

Vien, K. N., 2009, *Vietnam – A Long History.* The Gioi Publishers Hanoi.

www.ingramcontent.com/pod-product-compliance
Lightning Source LLC
Chambersburg PA
CBHW070959160426
43193CB00012B/1845